2019
3rd
EDITION

이번 시험에 나온 문제가
다음 시험의 적중률을 보장할까요?

파고다 어학원 토익 전문 연구진 108인은
다음 시험 적중률로 말합니다!

이번 시험에 나온 문제를 풀기만 하면,
내 토익 목표 점수를 달성할 수 있을까요?

파고다 토익 시리즈는
파고다 어학원 1타 강사들과 수십 만 수강생이
함께 만든 토익 목표 점수 달성 전략서입니다!

파고다 어학원 1타 토익 강사들의
토익 목표 점수 달성 전략 완전 정리

최신 경향 실전 모의고사 10회분
900~990점 목표

내 위치를
파악했다면
목표를 향해
나아갈 뿐!

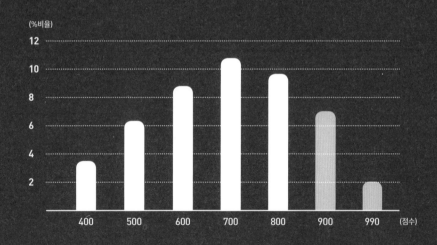

파고다 토익 프로그램

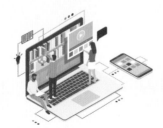

독학자를 위한 다양하고 품부한 학습 자료

세상 간편한 등업 신청으로 각종 학습 자료가 쏟아지는

파고다 토익 공식 온라인 카페
http://cafe.naver.com/pagodatoeicbooks

교재 Q&A
교재 학습 자료
나의 학습 코칭
정기 토익 분석 자료
기출 분석 자료
예상 적중 특강
논란 종결 총평

> 온라인 모의고사 2회분
> 받아쓰기 훈련 자료
> 단어 암기장
> 단어 시험지
> MP3 기본 버전
> MP3 추가 버전(1.2배속 등)
> 추가 연습 문제 등 각종 추가 자료

매회 업데이트! 토익 학습 센터

시험 전 적중 문제, 특강 제공

시험 직후 실시간 정답, 총평 특강, 분석 자료집 제공

토익에 풋! 빠져 풋TV

파고다 대표 강사진과 전문 연구원들의 다양한 무료 강의를 들으실 수 있습니다.

---

600 700 800

기본 완성 LC

토익 리스닝 기초 입문서

토익 초보 학습자들이 단기간에 쉽게 접근할 수 있도록 토익의 필수 개념을 집약한 입문서

실력 완성 LC

토익 개념&실전 종합서

토익의 기본 개념을 확실히 다질 수 있는 풍부한 문제 유형과 실전형 연습문제를 담은 훈련서

고득점 완성 LC

최상위권 토익 만점 전략서

기본기를 충분히 다진 토익 중고급자들의 고득점 완성을 위해 핵심 스킬만을 뽑아낸 토익 전략서

이제는 인강도 밀착 관리!

체계적인 학습 관리와 목표 달성까지 가능한

파고다 토익 인생 점수반
www.pagodastar.com

성적 달성만 해도 100% 환급
인생 점수 달성하면 최대 500% 환급

최단 기간 목표 달성 보장
X10배속 토익

현강으로 직접 듣는 1타 강사의 노하우

파고다 토익 점수 보장반
www.pagoda21.com

1개월 만에 2명 중 1명은 900점 달성!
파고다는 오직 결과로 증명합니다.

900

적중 실전 LC

최신 경향 실전 모의고사 10회분

끊임없이 변화하는 토익 트렌드에 대처하기 위해
적중률 높은 문제만을 엄선한 토익 실전서

VOCA

토익 VOCA

목표 점수대별 필수 어휘 30일 완성

600+/700+/800+/독해 완성 달성을 위한
필수 어휘 1200

초 판 1쇄 발행 2016년 4월 29일
개 정 판 1쇄 발행 2016년 12월 26일
개정2판 2쇄 발행 2019년 2월 1일

지 은 이 | 파고다교육그룹 언어교육연구소
펴 낸 이 | 고루다
펴 낸 곳 | Wit & Wisdom 도서출판 위트앤위즈덤
임프린트 | PAGODA Books
출판등록 | 2005년 5월 27일 제 300-2005-90호
주   소 | 06614 서울특별시 서초구 강남대로 419, 19층(서초동, 파고다타워)
전   화 | (02) 6940-4070
팩   스 | (02) 536-0660
홈페이지 | www.pagodabook.com

저작권자 | ⓒ 2019 파고다아카데미, 위트앤위즈덤

ISBN 978-89-6281-824-6 (13740)

도서출판 위트앤위즈덤   www.pagodabook.com
파고다 어학원   www.pagoda21.com
파고다 인강   www.pagodastar.com
테스트 클리닉   www.testclinic.com

3rd Edition

실전 모의고사 10회분

적중실전

LC

Vol. 1

목차

목차   2

이 책의 구성과 특징   4

토익이란?   6

파트별 토익 소개   8

학습 플랜   12

리스닝 기초 다지기   14

>> TEST

TEST 1   22

TEST 2   36

TEST 3   50

TEST 4   64

TEST 5   78

파고다토익 적중 실전 LC

TEST 6   92

TEST 7   106

TEST 8   120

TEST 9   134

TEST 10   148

Script   162

ANSWERS   238

토익 점수 환산표   244

ANSWER SHEET   245

▶ 해설서 유료 다운로드 (3,000원)   http://www.pagodabook.com
                                  http://www.pagodastar.com

▶ 교재 MP3 파일 다운로드 (무료)   http://www.pagodabook.com

이 책의 구성과 특징

>> **PART 1** 사진의 유형을 이해하고 유형별 사진 공략법과 시제와 태 표현을 정확하게 구분한다.

>> **PART 2** 의문사 의문문, 비의문사 의문문에 따른 다양한 응답 표현 및 빈출 오답 유형을 익힌다.

>> **PART 3** 빠르게 전개되는 지문을 정확하게 파악하는 직청·직해 능력과 더불어 문맥 파악 및 논리력 판단을 길러야 한다.

>> **PART 4** 출제되는 지문 유형을 익히고 해당 지문에 자주 나오는 빈출 어휘 및 표현을 학습한다.

실전 모의고사 10회분 VOL.1

토익 LC 유형에 대한 철저한 분석을 통해 예상 적중 문제 10회분 모의고사를 구성하였다. 개정판은 가장 최근 기출문제 경향을 정확하게 반영하여 정기 시험 전에 실제 문제와 가장 유사한 문제로 충분히 훈련, 준비할 수 있다.

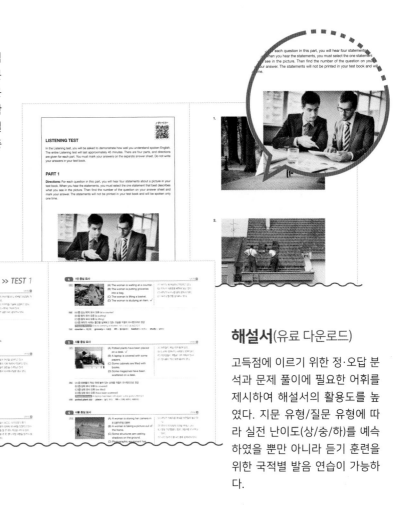

해설서(유료 다운로드)

고득점에 이르기 위한 정·오답 분석과 문제 풀이에 필요한 어휘를 제시하여 해설서의 활용도를 높였다. 지문 유형/질문 유형에 따라 실전 난이도(상/중/하)를 예측하였을 뿐만 아니라 듣기 훈련을 위한 국적별 발음 연습이 가능하다.

유료 해설서 온라인 구매방법

온라인 해설서
구매 바로 가기

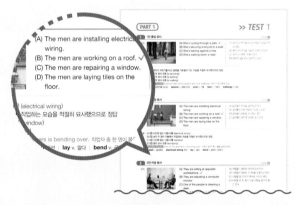

PART 1

선택지의 상태, 동작, 위치 묘사 오류 파악을 통해 정답·오답을 가려낼 수 있다.

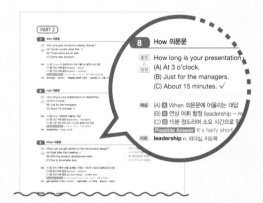

PART 2

동일어휘반복·파생어/유사의미 연상 함정을 포착하고, 이를 통해 정답·오답을 선별해 낼 수 있다.

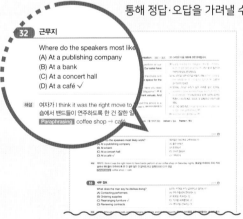

PART 3

문제의 키워드를 확인하고, 이어 지문 내 단서 찾기와 패러프레이징 학습을 통해 고득점을 공략한다.

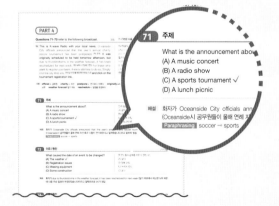

PART 4

문제의 키워드를 확인하고, 이어 지문 내 단서 찾기와 패러프레이징 학습을 통해 고득점을 공략한다.

토익이란?

TOEIC(Test Of English for International Communication)은 영어가 모국어가 아닌 사람들을 대상으로 일상생활 또는 국제 업무 등에 필요한 실용 영어 능력을 평가하는 시험입니다.

상대방과 '의사 소통할 수 있는 능력(Communication ability)'을 평가하는 데 중점을 두고 있으므로 영어에 대한 '지식'이 아니라 영어의 실용적이고 기능적인 '사용법'을 묻는 문항들이 출제됩니다.

TOEIC은 1979년 미국 ETS(Educational Testing Service)에 의해 개발된 이래 전 세계 150개 국가 14,000여 개의 기관에서 승진 또는 해외 파견 인원 선발 등의 목적으로 널리 활용하고 있으며 우리나라에는 1982년 도입되었습니다. 해마다 전 세계적으로 약 700만 명 이상이 응시하고 있습니다.

>> **토익 시험의 구성**

	파트	시험 형태		문항 수	시간	배점
듣기 (LC)	1	사진 문제		6	45분	495점
	2	질의응답		25		
	3	짧은 대화		39		
	4	짧은 담화		30		
읽기 (RC)	5	문장 빈칸 채우기		30	75분	495점
	6	지문 빈칸 채우기		16		
	7	독해	단일 지문	29		
			이중 지문	10		
			삼중 지문	15		
계				200	120분	990점

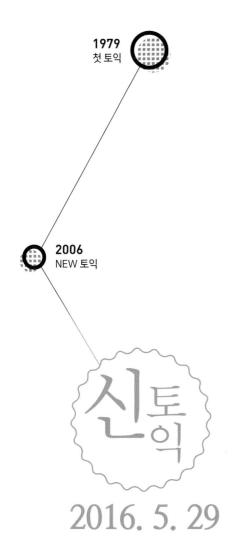

1979
첫 토익

2006
NEW 토익

2016. 5. 29

토익 시험 접수와 성적 확인

토익 시험은 TOEIC 위원회 웹사이트(www.toeic.co.kr)에서 접수할 수 있습니다. 본인이 원하는 날짜와 장소를 지정하고 필수 기재 항목을 기재한 후 본인 사진을 업로드하면 간단하게 끝납니다.

보통은 두 달 후에 있는 시험일까지 접수 가능합니다. 각 시험일의 정기 접수는 시험일로부터 2주 전까지 마감되지만, 시험일의 3일 전까지 추가 접수할 수 있는 특별 접수 기간이 있습니다. 그러나 특별 추가 접수 기간에는 응시료가 4,000원 더 비싸며, 희망하는 시험장을 선택할 수 없는 경우도 발생할 수 있습니다.

성적은 시험일로부터 16~18일 후에 인터넷이나 ARS(060-800-0515)를 통해 확인할 수 있습니다.

성적표는 우편이나 온라인으로 발급 받을 수 있습니다. 우편으로 발급 받을 경우는 성적 발표 후 대략 일주일이 소요되며, 온라인 발급을 선택하면 유효 기간 내에 홈페이지에서 본인이 직접 1회에 한해 무료 출력할 수 있습니다. 토익 성적은 시험일로부터 2년간 유효합니다.

시험 당일 준비물

시험 당일 준비물은 규정 신분증, 연필, 지우개입니다. 허용되는 규정 신분증은 토익 공식 웹사이트에서 확인하기 바랍니다. 필기구는 연필이나 샤프펜만 가능하고 볼펜이나 컴퓨터용 사인펜은 사용할 수 없습니다. 수험표는 출력해 가지 않아도 됩니다.

시험 진행 안내

시험 진행 일정은 시험 당일 고사장 사정에 따라 약간씩 다를 수 있지만 대부분 아래와 같이 진행됩니다.

≫ 시험 시간이 오전일 경우

AM 9:30 ~ 9:45	AM 9:45 ~ 9:50	AM 9:50 ~ 10:05	AM 10:05 ~ 10:10	AM 10:10 ~ 10:55	AM 10:55 ~ 12:10
15분	5분	15분	5분	45분	75분
답안지 작성에 관한 Orientation	수험자 휴식 시간	신분증 확인 (감독교사)	문제지 배부, 파본 확인	듣기 평가(LC)	읽기 평가(RC) 2차 신분증 확인

* 주의: 오전 9시 50분 입실통제

≫ 시험 시간이 오후일 경우

PM 2:30 ~ 2:45	PM 2:45 ~ 2:50	PM 2:50 ~ 3:05	PM 3:05 ~ 3:10	PM 3:10 ~ 3:55	PM 3:55 ~ 5:10
15분	5분	15분	5분	45분	75분
답안지 작성에 관한 Orientation	수험자 휴식 시간	신분증 확인 (감독교사)	문제지 배부, 파본 확인	듣기 평가(LC)	읽기 평가(RC) 2차 신분증 확인

* 주의: 오후 2시 50분 입실 통제

파트별 토익 소개

PART 1 PHOTOGRAPHS
사진 문제

Part 1은 제시한 사진을 올바르게 묘사한 문장을 찾는 문제로, 방송으로 사진에 대한 4개의 짧은 설명문을 한번 들려준다. 4개의 설명문은 문제지에 인쇄되어 있지 않으며 4개의 설명문을 잘 듣고 그 중에서 사진을 가장 정확하게 묘사하고 있는 문장을 답으로 선택한다.

문항 수	6문항 (1번 ~ 6번)
Direction 소요 시간	약 1분 30초
문제를 들려주는 시간	약 20초
다음 문제까지의 여유 시간	약 5초
문제 유형	1인 사진 2인 이상 사진 사물·풍경 사진

>> 시험지에 인쇄되어 있는 모양

>> 스피커에서 들리는 음성

Number 1. Look at the picture marked number 1 in your test book.

(A) They're writing on a board.
(B) They're taking a file from a shelf.
(C) They're working at a desk.
(D) They're listening to a presentation.

정답 (C)

PART 2

QUESTION-RESPONSE
질의응답

Part 2는 질문에 대한 올바른 답을 찾는 문제로, 방송을 통해 질문과 질문에 대한 3개의 응답문을 각 한 번씩 들려준다. 질문과 응답문은 문제지에 인쇄가 되어 있지 않으며 질문에 대한 가장 어울리는 응답문을 답으로 선택한다.

문항 수	25문항 (7번 ~ 31번)
Direction 소요 시간	약 25초
문제를 들려주는 시간	약 15초
다음 문제까지의 여유 시간	약 5초
문제 유형	의문사 의문문(Who/When/Where/What/Which/How/Why) 부정 의문문 / 부가 의문문 평서문 / 선택 의문문 제안 · 제공 · 요청문 / Be동사 조동사 의문문 / 간접 의문문

>> 시험지에 인쇄되어 있는 모양

Mark your answer on your answer sheet. (A) (B) (C)

>> 스피커에서 들리는 음성

Number 7. How was the English test you took today?

(A) I took the bus home.
(B) I thought it was too difficult.
(C) I have two classes today.

정답 (B)

PART 3 SHORT CONVERSATION
짧은 대화

Part 3은 짧은 대화문을 듣고 이에 대한 문제를 푸는 형식으로, 먼저 방송을 통해 짧은 대화를 들려준 뒤 이에 해당하는 질문을 들려 준다. 문제지에는 질문과 4개의 보기가 인쇄되어 있으며 문제를 들은 뒤 제시된 보기 중 가장 적절한 것을 답으로 선택한다.

문항 수	13개 대화문, 39문항 (32번 ~ 70번)
Direction 소요 시간	약 30초
문제를 들려주는 시간	약 30~40초
다음 문제까지의 여유 시간	약 8초
지문 유형	회사 생활, 일상생활, 공공 장소 및 서비스 기관 → 3인 대화문: 주고받는 대화 수 증가 → 실생활에서 사용하는 회화 표현(구어체)의 증가
질문 유형	- 전체 내용 관련 문제: 주제·목적, 인물, 장소 문제 - 세부사항 문제(문제점, 이유·방법, 핵심어 정보 찾기) - 제안·요청 문제 - 앞으로 할 일 문제 - 맥락상 화자의 의도 파악 문제 - 유추·추론 문제 - 시각 정보 연계 문제

▶▶ 시험지에 인쇄되어 있는 모양

32. What is the conversation mainly about?
    (A) Changes in business policies
    (B) Sales of a company's products
    (C) Expanding into a new market
    (D) Recruiting temporary employees

33. Why does the woman say, "There you go"?
    (A) She is happy to attend a meeting.
    (B) She is frustrated with a coworker.
    (C) She is offering encouragement.
    (D) She is handing over something.

34. What do the men imply about the company?
    (A) It has launched new merchandise.
    (B) It is planning to relocate soon.
    (C) It has clients in several countries.
    (D) It is having financial difficulties.

▶▶ 스피커에서 들리는 음성

Questions 32-34 refer to the following conversation with three speakers.

A: How have you two been doing with your sales lately?

B: Um, not too bad. My clients have been ordering about the same amount of promotional merchandise as before.

C: I haven't been doing so well. But I do have a meeting with a potential new client tomorrow.

B: There you go. I'm sure things will turn around for you.

A: Yeah, I hope it works out.

B: It's probably just temporary due to the recession.

C: Maybe, but I heard that the company may downsize to try to save money.

A: Actually, I heard that, too.

정답 32. (B) 33. (C) 34. (D)

PART 4

SHORT TALK
짧은 담화

Part 4는 짧은 담화를 듣고 이에 대한 문제를 푸는 형식으로, 먼저 방송을 통해 짧은 담화를 들려준 뒤 이에 해당하는 질문을 들려 준다. 문제지에는 질문과 4개의 보기가 인쇄되어 있으며 문제를 들은 뒤 제시된 보기 중 가장 적절한 것을 답으로 선택한다.

문항 수	10개 담화, 30문항 (71번 ~ 100번)
Direction 소요 시간	약 30초
문제를 들려주는 시간	약 30~40초
다음 문제까지의 여유 시간	약 8초
지문 유형	전화·녹음 메시지, 공지·안내, 인물 소개, 광고, 방송·보도 → 발음 생략, 군더더기 표현과 불완전한 문장이 포함된 지문의 실생활 영어(구어체)의 등장
질문 유형	- 전체 내용 관련 문제: 주제·목적, 인물, 장소 문제 - 세부사항 문제(문제점, 이유·방법, 핵심어 정보 찾기) - 제안·요청 문제 - 앞으로 할 일 문제 - 맥락상 화자의 의도 파악 문제 - 시각 정보 연계 문제

▶▶ 시험지에 인쇄되어 있는 모양

71. Where most likely is the speaker?
    (A) At a trade fair
    (B) At a corporate banquet
    (C) At a business seminar
    (D) At an anniversary celebration

72. What are the listeners asked to do?
    (A) Pick up programs for employees
    (B) Arrive early for a presentation
    (C) Turn off their mobile phones
    (D) Carry their personal belongings

73. Why does the schedule have to be changed?
    (A) A speaker has to leave early.
    (B) A piece of equipment is not working.
    (C) Lunch is not ready.
    (D) Some speakers have not yet arrived.

▶▶ 스피커에서 들리는 음성

Questions 71-73 refer to the following talk.

I'd like to welcome all of you to today's employee training and development seminar for business owners. I'll briefly go over a few details before we get started. There will be a 15 minute break for coffee and snacks halfway through the program. This will be a good opportunity for you to mingle. If you need to leave the room during a talk, make sure to keep your wallet, phone, and ...ah... any other valuable personal items with you. Also, please note that there will be a change in the order of the program. Um... Mr. Roland has to leave earlier than originally scheduled, so the last two speakers will be switched.

정답 71. (C) 72. (D) 73. (A)

학습 플랜

2주 플랜

DAY 1	DAY 2	DAY 3	DAY 4	DAY 5
TEST 01	TEST 02	TEST 03	TEST 04	TEST 05
시간 재고 풀기	시간 재고 풀기	시간 재고 풀기	시간 재고 풀기	시간 재고 풀기
채점하고 해설지로 복습	새점하고 해실지로 복습	채점하고 해설지로 복습	채점하고 해설지로 복습	채점하고 해설지로 복습
LC 1.2배속 버전으로 풀어보기	LC 1.2배속 버전으로 풀어보기	LC 1.2배속 버전으로 풀어보기	LC 1.2배속 버전으로 풀어보기	LC 1.2배속 버전으로 풀어보기
RC 어휘집 외우기	RC 어휘집 외우기	RC 어휘집 외우기	RC 어휘집 외우기	RC 어휘집 외우기

DAY 6	DAY 7	DAY 8	DAY 9	DAY 10
TEST 06	TEST 07	TEST 08	TEST 09	TEST 10
시간 재고 풀기	시간 재고 풀기	시간 재고 풀기	시간 재고 풀기	시간 재고 풀기
채점하고 해설지로 복습	채점하고 해설지로 복습	채점하고 해설지로 복습	채점하고 해설지로 복습	채점하고 해설지로 복습
LC 1.2배속 버전으로 풀어보기	LC 1.2배속 버전으로 풀어보기	LC 1.2배속 버전으로 풀어보기	LC 1.2배속 버전으로 풀어보기	LC 1.2배속 버전으로 풀어보기
RC 어휘집 외우기	RC 어휘집 외우기	RC 어휘집 외우기	RC 어휘집 외우기	RC 어휘집 외우기

* 어휘집 / 1.2배속 MP3 / 무료 모의고사 등 각종 부가자료 다운로드: https://cafe.naver.com/pagodatoeicbooks

4주 플랜

DAY 1	DAY 2	DAY 3	DAY 4	DAY 5
TEST 01 시간 재고 풀기 채점하고 해설지로 복습	TEST 01 복습 LC 1.2배속 버전으로 풀어보기 RC 어휘집 외우기	TEST 02 시간 재고 풀기 채점하고 해설지로 복습	TEST 02 복습 LC 1.2배속 버전으로 풀어보기 RC 어휘집 외우기	TEST 03 시간 재고 풀기 채점하고 해설지로 복습

DAY 6	DAY 7	DAY 8	DAY 9	DAY 10
TEST 03 복습 LC 1.2배속 버전으로 풀어보기 RC 어휘집 외우기	TEST 04 시간 재고 풀기 채점하고 해설지로 복습	TEST 04 복습 LC 1.2배속 버전으로 풀어보기 RC 어휘집 외우기	TEST 05 시간 재고 풀기 채점하고 해설지로 복습	TEST 05 복습 LC 1.2배속 버전으로 풀어보기 RC 어휘집 외우기

DAY 11	DAY 12	DAY 13	DAY 14	DAY 15
TEST 06 시간 재고 풀기 채점하고 해설지로 복습	TEST 06 복습 LC 1.2배속 버전으로 풀어보기 RC 어휘집 외우기	TEST 07 시간 재고 풀기 채점하고 해설지로 복습	TEST 07 복습 LC 1.2배속 버전으로 풀어보기 RC 어휘집 외우기	TEST 08 시간 재고 풀기 채점하고 해설지로 복습

DAY 16	DAY 17	DAY 18	DAY 19	DAY 20
TEST 08 복습 LC 1.2배속 버전으로 풀어보기 RC 어휘집 외우기	TEST 09 시간 재고 풀기 채점하고 해설지로 복습	TEST 09 복습 LC 1.2배속 버전으로 풀어보기 RC 어휘집 다운로드 하여 외우기	TEST 10 시간 재고 풀기 채점하고 해설지로 복습	TEST 10 복습 LC 1.2배속 버전으로 풀어보기 RC 어휘집 외우기

리스닝
기초 다지기

🇺🇸 미국식 발음 vs 영국식 발음 🇬🇧

토익 리스닝 시험에서는 미국식 발음뿐만 아니라, 영국, 호주, 뉴질랜드, 캐나다 등 미국 외의 다른 영어권 나라의 발음으로 문제가 출제되기도 한다. 한국의 토익 학습자들에게는 미국식 발음이 익숙하겠지만, 그 외 나라의 발음도 숙지해 두어야 발음 때문에 문제를 풀지 못하는 당황스러운 상황을 피할 수 있다.

캐나다 발음은 미국식 발음과, 호주와 뉴질랜드 발음은 영국식 발음과 유사하므로 이 책에서는 크게 미국식 발음과 영국식 발음으로 나누어 학습하도록 한다.

자음의 대표적인 차이

1. /r/ 발음의 차이

> 🇺🇸 **미국**: 항상 발음하며 부드럽게 굴려 발음한다.
> 🇬🇧 **영국**: 단어 첫소리에 나오는 경우만 발음하고 끝에 나오거나 다른 자음 앞에 나오면 발음하지 않는다.

≫ 단어 끝에 나오는 /r/

	🇺🇸미국식 발음	🇬🇧영국식 발음		🇺🇸미국식 발음	🇬🇧영국식 발음
car	[카r]	[카-]	wear	[웨어r]	[웨에-]
her	[허r]	[허-]	where	[웨어r]	[웨에-]
door	[도r]	[도-]	there	[데어r]	[데에-]
pour	[포우어r]	[포우어-]	here	[히어r]	[히어-]
mayor	[메이어r]	[메에-]	year	[이여r]	[이여-]
sure	[슈어r]	[슈어-]	repair	[뤼페어r]	[뤼페에-]
later	[레이러r]	[레이터-]	chair	[췌어r]	[췌에-]
author	[어떠r]	[오떠-]	fair	[f페어r]	[f페에-]
cashier	[캐쉬어r]	[캐쉬어]	hair	[헤어r]	[헤에-]

≫ 자음 앞에 나오는 /r+자음/

	🇺🇸미국식 발음	🇬🇧영국식 발음		🇺🇸미국식 발음	🇬🇧영국식 발음
airport	[에어r포rt]	[에-포-트]	short	[쇼rt]	[쇼-트]
award	[어워r드]	[어워드]	turn	[터r언]	[터-언]
board	[보r드]	[보-드]	alert	[얼러r트]	[얼러트]
cart	[카rt]	[카-트]	first	[퍼r스트]	[퍼스트]
circle	[써r클]	[써-클]	order	[오r더r]	[오-더]
concert	[컨써r트]	[컨써트]	purse	[퍼r스]	[퍼-스]

2. /t/ 발음의 차이

🇺🇸 **미국**: 모음 사이의 /t/를 부드럽게 굴려 [d]와 [r]의 중간으로 발음한다.
🇬🇧 **영국**: 모음 사이의 /t/를 철자 그대로 발음한다.

	🇺🇸 미국식 발음	🇬🇧 영국식 발음		🇺🇸 미국식 발음	🇬🇧 영국식 발음
bottom	[바름]	[버틈]	computer	[컴퓨러r]	[컴퓨터]
better	[베러r]	[베터]	item	[아이럼]	[아이틈]
chatting	[최링]	[최팅]	later	[레이러r]	[레이터]
getting	[게링]	[게팅]	meeting	[미링]	[미팅]
letter	[레러r]	[레터]	notice	[노리스]	[노티스]
little	[리를]	[리틀]	patio	[패리오]	[패티오]
matter	[매러r]	[매터]	water	[워러r]	[워타]
potted	[파리드]	[파티드]	waiter	[웨이러r]	[웨이터]
setting	[쎄링]	[쎄팅]	cater	[케이러r]	[케이터]
sitting	[씨링]	[씨팅]	competitor	[컴패리러r]	[컴패티터]
putting	[푸링]	[푸팅]	data	[데이러]	[데이터]

3. 모음 사이의 /nt/ 발음의 차이

🇺🇸 **미국**: /t/를 발음하지 않는다.
🇬🇧 **영국**: /t/를 철자 그대로 발음한다.

	🇺🇸 미국식 발음	🇬🇧 영국식 발음		🇺🇸 미국식 발음	🇬🇧 영국식 발음
Internet	[이너r넷]	[인터넷]	twenty	[트웨니]	[트웬티]
interview	[이너r뷰]	[인터뷰]	advantage	[어드배니쥐]	[어드반티쥐]
entertainment	[에너r테인먼트]	[엔터테인먼트]	identification	[아이데니피케이션]	[아이덴티피케이션]
international	[이너r내셔널]	[인터내셔널]	representative	[레프레제네리브]	[레프리젠터티브]

ST 1

기타 발음의 차이

	🇺🇸 미국식 발음	🇬🇧 영국식 발음		🇺🇸 미국식 발음	🇬🇧 영국식 발음
advertisement	[애드버r타이즈먼트]	[어드버티스먼트]	garage	[거라쥐]	[개라쥐]
fragile	[프래절]	[프리쟈일]	often	[어픈]	[오프튼]
however	[하우에버r]	[하우에바]	schedule	[스케쥴]	[쉐쥴]

연음의 차이

	🇺🇸 미국식 발음	🇬🇧 영국식 발음		🇺🇸 미국식 발음	🇬🇧 영국식 발음
a lot of	[얼라럽]	[얼로톱]	not at all	[나래롤]	[나태톨]
get in	[게린]	[게틴]	out of stock	[아우롭스탁]	[아우톱스톡]
in front of	[인프러넙]	[인프론톱]	pick it up	[피끼럽]	[피키텁]
it is	[이리즈]	[잍티즈]	put on	[푸론]	[푸톤]
look it up	[루끼럽]	[룩키텁]	talk about it	[터꺼바우릿]	[오커바우팉]

1. The _____ will be held next week. 취업 박람회가 다음주에 개최됩니다.

2. She's the _____ a best-selling book. 그녀는 베스트셀러 도서의 작가입니다.

3. The _____. 시장님은 출장 중입니다.

4. _____ network technicians? 네트워크 기술자들을 더 고용하면 안될까요?

5. We need to advertise _____. 스포츠 신발 신제품 라인의 광고를 해야 합니다.

6. She is _____ into glasses. 그녀는 잔에 물을 붓고 있다.

7. You _____ last fall.
   작년 가을에 당신 업체가 우리 회사 야유회에 음식을 공급했습니다.

8. _____ for me. 여섯 시 이후가 저에겐 편합니다.

9. Some _____ have been placed in a waiting area. 대기실에 몇 개의 화분이 놓여 있다.

10. _____ are the same. 많은 물건들이 똑같다.

11. Please sign on the _____. 마지막 페이지 하단에 서명해 주시기 바랍니다.

12. Do you know of a _____ in this area? 이 지역에 좋은 의사를 아시나요?

13. _____. 전혀요.

14. _____ posted on the Web site. 웹사이트에 게시된 구인광고를 봤습니다.

15. Why don't you _____ and speak to him? 의사에게 전화해서 말해 보세요.

16. What's _____ to the bank? 은행까지 가장 빠른 길은 무엇입니까?

17. _____ if she's available. 그녀가 시간이 괜찮은지 물어보겠습니다.

18. I'm so happy to see that _____ are here today.
    모든 무용수 여러분이 오늘 여기에 온 것을 보니 매우 기쁩니다.

19. _____ hold some flowers. 유리로 된 화병에 꽃이 있다.

20. _____ travel in the morning or in the evening? 오전, 오후 중 언제 이동하겠습니까?

21. The shipment is _____. 배송이 지연되고 있습니다.

22. _____ is fine with me. 둘 중 아무거나 상관없습니다.

23. _____. 저도 해본 적이 없습니다.

24. Why wasn't _____ printed in the magazine?
    왜 우리 광고가 잡지에 인쇄되지 않았나요?

25. Can you get me _____? 실험실 가는 길을 좀 알려주세요.

정답
1. job fair   2. author of   3. mayor is out of town   4. Can't we hire more   5. our new line of sports footwear
6. pouring water   7. catered our company outing   8. After six is better   9. potted plant   10. A lot of the items
11. bottom of the last page   12. good doctor   13. Not at all   14. I saw your job ad   15. call your doctor
16. the fastest way   17. I'll ask her   18. all you dancers   19. A glass vase   20. Would you rather
21. behind schedule   22. Either one   23. Neither have I   24. our advertisement   25. directions to the laboratory

4. /tn/ 발음의 차이

🇺🇸 미국: /t/로 발음하지 않고 한번 숨을 참았다가 /n/의 끝소리를 [응] 또는 [은]으로 콧소리를 내며 발음한다.
🇬🇧 영국: /t/를 그대로 살려 강하게 발음한다.

	🇺🇸 미국식 발음	🇬🇧 영국식 발음		🇺🇸 미국식 발음	🇬🇧 영국식 발음
button	[벋 · 은]	[버튼]	mountain	[마운 · 은]	[마운튼]
carton	[카r · 은]	[카튼]	written	[륃 · 은]	[뤼튼]
important	[임포r · 은트]	[임포턴트]	certainly	[써r · 은리]	[써튼리]

5. /rt/ 발음의 차이

🇺🇸 미국: /t/ 발음을 생략한다.
🇬🇧 영국: /r/ 발음을 생략하고 /t/ 발음은 그래도 살려서 발음한다.

	🇺🇸 미국식 발음	🇬🇧 영국식 발음		🇺🇸 미국식 발음	🇬🇧 영국식 발음
party	[파리]	[파-티]	reporter	[뤼포러r]	[뤼포-터]
quarter	[쿼러r]	[쿼-터]	property	[프라퍼리]	[프로퍼-티]

모음의 대표적인 차이

1. /a/ 발음의 차이

🇺🇸 미국: [애]로 발음한다.
🇬🇧 영국: [아]로 발음한다.

	🇺🇸 미국식 발음	🇬🇧 영국식 발음		🇺🇸 미국식 발음	🇬🇧 영국식 발음
can't	[캔트]	[칸트]	pass	[패쓰]	[파스]
grant	[그랜트]	[그란트]	path	[패쓰]	[파스]
plant	[플랜트]	[플란트]	vase	[베이스]	[바스]
chance	[챈스]	[찬스]	draft	[드래프트]	[드라프트]
advance	[어드밴쓰]	[어드반쓰]	after	[애프터]	[아프터]
answer	[앤써r]	[안써]	ask	[애스크]	[아스크]
sample	[쌤쁠]	[쌈플]	task	[태스크]	[타스크]
class	[클래스]	[클라스]	behalf	[비해프]	[비하프]
grass	[그래스]	[그라스]	rather	[래더r]	[라더]
glass	[글래스]	[글라스]	man	[맨]	[만]

2. /o/ 발음의 차이

🇺🇸 미국: [아]로 발음한다.
🇬🇧 영국: [오]로 발음한다.

	🇺🇸 미국식 발음	🇬🇧 영국식 발음		🇺🇸 미국식 발음	🇬🇧 영국식 발음
stop	[스탑]	[스톱]	bottle	[바를]	[보틀]
stock	[스탁]	[스톡]	model	[마를]	[모들]
shop	[샵]	[숍]	dollar	[달러r]	[돌라]
got	[갓]	[곳]	copy	[카피]	[코피]
hot	[핫]	[홋]	possible	[파써블]	[포쓰블]
not	[낫]	[놋]	shovel	[셔블]	[쇼블]
parking lot	[파r킹 랏]	[파킹 롣]	topic	[타픽]	[토픽]
knob	[납]	[놉]	doctor	[닥터]	[독타]
job	[잡]	[좝]	borrow	[바로우]	[보로우]
box	[박스]	[복스]	document	[다큐먼트]	[도큐먼트]

3. /i/ 발음의 차이

/i/가 영국식 발음에서 [아이]로 발음되는 경우가 있다.

	🇺🇸 미국식 발음	🇬🇧 영국식 발음		🇺🇸 미국식 발음	🇬🇧 영국식 발음
direct	[디렉트]	[다이렉트]	mobile	[모블]	[모바일]
either	[이더r]	[아이더]	organization	[오r거니제이션]	[오거나이제이션]

4. /ary/, /ory/ 발음의 차이

/ary/, /ory/ 가 영국식 발음에서 /a/, /o/를 빼고 [ry]만 발음되는 경우가 있다.

	🇺🇸 미국식 발음	🇬🇧 영국식 발음		🇺🇸 미국식 발음	🇬🇧 영국식 발음
laboratory	[래보러토리]	[러보러트리]	secretary	[쎄크러테뤼]	[쎄크러트리]

LISTENING TEST

In the Listening test, you will be asked to demonstrate how well you understand spoken English. The entire Listening test will last approximately 45 minutes. There are four parts, and directions are given for each part. You must mark your answers on the separate answer sheet. Do not write your answers in your test book.

PART 1

Directions: For each question in this part, you will hear four statements about a picture in your test book. When you hear the statements, you must select the one statement that best describes what you see in the picture. Then find the number of the question on your answer sheet and mark your answer. The statements will not be printed in your test book and will be spoken only one time.

Statement (B), "A man is pointing at a document," is the best description of the picture, so you should select answer (B) and mark it on your answer sheet.

1.

2.

GO ON TO THE NEXT PAGE →

3.

4.

5.

6.

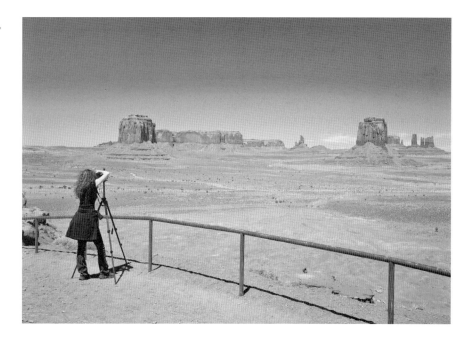

GO ON TO THE NEXT PAGE ➤

PART 2

Directions: You will hear a question or statement and three responses spoken in English. They will not be printed in your test book and will be spoken only one time. Select the best response to the question or statement and mark the letter (A), (B), or (C) on your answer sheet.

7. Mark your answer on your answer sheet.

8. Mark your answer on your answer sheet.

9. Mark your answer on your answer sheet.

10. Mark your answer on your answer sheet.

11. Mark your answer on your answer sheet.

12. Mark your answer on your answer sheet.

13. Mark your answer on your answer sheet.

14. Mark your answer on your answer sheet.

15. Mark your answer on your answer sheet.

16. Mark your answer on your answer sheet.

17. Mark your answer on your answer sheet.

18. Mark your answer on your answer sheet.

19. Mark your answer on your answer sheet.

20. Mark your answer on your answer sheet.

21. Mark your answer on your answer sheet.

22. Mark your answer on your answer sheet.

23. Mark your answer on your answer sheet.

24. Mark your answer on your answer sheet.

25. Mark your answer on your answer sheet.

26. Mark your answer on your answer sheet.

27. Mark your answer on your answer sheet.

28. Mark your answer on your answer sheet.

29. Mark your answer on your answer sheet.

30. Mark your answer on your answer sheet.

31. Mark your answer on your answer sheet.

PART 3

Directions: You will hear some conversations between two or more people. You will be asked to answer three questions about what the speakers say in each conversation. Select the best response to each question and mark the letter (A), (B), (C), or (D) on your answer sheet. The conversations will not be printed in your test book and will be spoken only one time.

32. Where do the speakers most likely work?

(A) At a publishing company
(B) At a bank
(C) At a concert hall
(D) At a café

33. What does the man say he dislikes doing?

(A) Contacting performers
(B) Ordering supplies
(C) Rearranging furniture
(D) Reviewing contracts

34. What does the woman say she will print out right now?

(A) A discount voucher
(B) A magazine article
(C) A sales report
(D) A guest list

35. What product is being discussed?

(A) A software program
(B) A piece of jewelry
(C) A laptop
(D) A bag

36. What does the man like about a product?

(A) It is attractive.
(B) It comes in many sizes.
(C) It is durable.
(D) It can be customized.

37. What does Valerie agree to do?

(A) Provide a Web address
(B) Track a delivery
(C) Contact a store
(D) Complete a form

38. Who most likely is the woman?

(A) A flight attendant
(B) A music teacher
(C) A tour operator
(D) A hotel clerk

39. What is the man concerned about?

(A) The safe transport of instruments
(B) The size of a room
(C) An additional luggage fee
(D) A travel connection

40. What does the woman suggest?

(A) Speaking with a security officer
(B) Calling the vendor directly
(C) Revising a travel itinerary
(D) Purchasing extra tickets

41. What does the woman say she needs?

(A) A ride to work
(B) Directions to a car repair shop
(C) An office floor plan
(D) A product serial number

42. What does the man imply when he says, "Actually, I just got to work a few minutes ago"?

(A) He had to deal with heavy traffic.
(B) He would like to reassure the woman.
(C) He will be late for a meeting.
(D) He is unable to assist the woman.

43. What does the woman decide to do?

(A) Talk to another coworker
(B) Request a vacation day
(C) Call a client
(D) Ask for a deadline extension

GO ON TO THE NEXT PAGE

44. Why is the woman at Mr. Winfield's office?

(A) To register for a seminar
(B) To interview for a job
(C) To sell a product
(D) To plan for a trip

45. Why is Mr. Winfield unable to meet with the woman?

(A) He is working from home.
(B) He is with a client.
(C) He is still out of town.
(D) He is training employees.

46. What will the man probably do next?

(A) Contact Mr. Winfield's assistant
(B) Postpone an appointment
(C) Give Mr. Winfield's number to the woman
(D) Make changes to an event schedule

---

47. Where does the woman work?

(A) At an electronics store
(B) At a medical clinic
(C) At a post office
(D) At a construction company

48. Why is the woman calling?

(A) To locate a shipment
(B) To refill a prescription
(C) To request details about a property
(D) To provide updated information about an order

49. Why is Mr. Alvez out of the office?

(A) He is feeling ill.
(B) He is working at a different location.
(C) He is on vacation.
(D) He is having lunch at a restaurant.

50. What career is the man interested in?

(A) Flight dispatcher
(B) Customs agent
(C) Aircraft mechanic
(D) Commercial pilot

51. What does the man say he will do?

(A) Obtain a loan
(B) Look at a handbook
(C) Compare different schools
(D) Submit some documents

52. According to the woman, what should the man ask about?

(A) Job placement
(B) Facility size
(C) Experience requirements
(D) Course length

---

53. What are the speakers talking about?

(A) An annual meal
(B) A movie premiere
(C) A product launch
(D) A play audition

54. How do the speakers know Ms. Romo?

(A) She gave a tour.
(B) She made a presentation.
(C) She provided some equipment.
(D) She planned a charity event.

55. What does the man say he will do?

(A) He will change some menu items.
(B) He will revise a guest list.
(C) He will book a room.
(D) He will arrange some transportation.

56. What are the speakers mainly discussing?

(A) A city election
(B) A town hall meeting
(C) A budget proposal
(D) A landscaping project

57. What does the man imply when he says, "Wow, I didn't expect that"?

(A) He is unhappy about a change.
(B) He is surprised by a request.
(C) He is pleased by some news.
(D) He is worried about some costs.

58. What will the man receive soon?

(A) An electronic bill
(B) A schedule update
(C) An agreement form
(D) A product catalog

59. What does the woman say is a problem?

(A) Several employees have been arriving late at work.
(B) There has been an increase in workload.
(C) A piece of equipment is not working properly.
(D) Some items have been damaged during transit.

60. How does the man propose solving the problem?

(A) By offering better incentives
(B) By purchasing additional machines
(C) By revising an inspection process
(D) By hiring more workers

61. What does the man request that the woman do?

(A) Put together some data
(B) Set up a meeting
(C) Update a Web site
(D) Reschedule some deliveries

Tour Schedule

Time	Spots Available
1:00 P.M.	2
2:00 P.M.	4
4:00 P.M.	3
6:00 P.M.	0

62. What do the speakers plan to tour?

(A) An old plant
(B) A historic library
(C) An art gallery
(D) A local restaurant

63. What does the man remind the woman about?

(A) Registering for a class
(B) Storing her personal belongings
(C) Participating in a demonstration
(D) Having dinner with colleagues

64. Look at the graphic. For what time will the speakers make reservations?

(A) 1:00 P.M.
(B) 2:00 P.M.
(C) 4:00 P.M.
(D) 6:00 P.M.

GO ON TO THE NEXT PAGE

| Name: Chris Walker | |
| Account: 510-11-1211 | |
Description	Amount
Bally Grocery (5/9)	$32.00
XD Gas (5/9)	$25.00
Rick's Hardware (5/9)	$7.25
Foreign transaction fee (5/9)	$3.50

65. Where does the woman probably work?

(A) At a credit card company
(B) At a supermarket
(C) At a job recruiting agency
(D) At a hardware store

66. Look at the graphic. What amount will be removed?

(A) $32.00
(B) $25.00
(C) $7.25
(D) $3.50

67. Why does the woman ask the man to wait?

(A) To explain a new process
(B) To have him talk to her manager
(C) To verify some contact information
(D) To receive some feedback

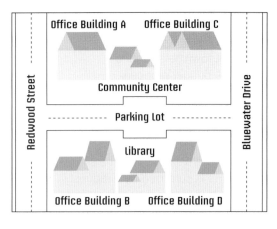

68. What are the speakers mainly discussing?

(A) A business opening
(B) A job interview
(C) A renovation project
(D) A moving plan

69. Look at the graphic. In which office building is Nertech, Inc. located?

(A) Office Building A
(B) Office Building B
(C) Office Building C
(D) Office Building D

70. What does the man tell the woman about parking?

(A) A parking space has been reserved for her.
(B) A parking permit must be displayed.
(C) She will need to pay cash for a parking space.
(D) She should park in a guest spot.

PART 4

Directions: You will hear some talks given by a single speaker. You will be asked to answer three questions about what the speaker says in each talk. Select the best response to each question and mark the letter (A), (B), (C), or (D) on your answer sheet. The talks will not be printed in your test book and will be spoken only one time.

71. What is the announcement about?

(A) A music concert
(B) A radio show
(C) A sports tournament
(D) A lunch picnic

72. What caused the date of an event to be changed?

(A) The weather
(B) Registration issues
(C) Missing equipment
(D) Some construction

73. Why are listeners told to visit a Web site?

(A) To obtain directions
(B) To view a calendar
(C) To buy tickets
(D) To register a team

74. What is the destination of the flight?

(A) New York
(B) Miami
(C) Rio de Janeiro
(D) Barcelona

75. What have some people inquired about?

(A) Storing their luggage
(B) Moving to another seat
(C) Ordering duty-free items
(D) Using mobile phone devices

76. Why are passengers instructed to notify a flight attendant?

(A) To get a magazine
(B) To request a special meal
(C) To obtain a headset
(D) To fill out a customs form

77. What is the purpose of the talk?

(A) To request feedback from residents
(B) To introduce a new procedure
(C) To announce a training session
(D) To discuss staff changes

78. What will the coordinator do?

(A) Reschedule work hours
(B) Invite more guests
(C) Set up another meeting
(D) Review residents' records

79. What advantage does the speaker mention?

(A) Improved work environment
(B) Faster delivery
(C) Reduced food waste
(D) Lower prices

80. What is the speaker calling about?

(A) Reassigning a project
(B) Changing a schedule
(C) Preparing a presentation
(D) Moving into a new office

81. Why does the speaker say, "you're right next to the staff lounge"?

(A) To refuse a coworker's request
(B) To ask for extra supplies
(C) To suggest renovating a lounge
(D) To point out that an area is undesirable

82. What does the speaker say will take place on Friday?

(A) The opening of a new store
(B) The installation of some equipment
(C) A training workshop
(D) A management meeting

GO ON TO THE NEXT PAGE

83. What is the purpose of the speech?

(A) To describe a new project
(B) To introduce an award recipient
(C) To demonstrate a process
(D) To honor a retiring employee

84. What industry does Maggie Olmstead most likely work in?

(A) Construction
(B) Software
(C) Medical
(D) Travel

85. According to the speaker, what does Ms. Olmstead plan to do?

(A) Hire additional employees
(B) Update a logo
(C) Launch an advertising campaign
(D) Relocate her business

86. What business is being advertised?

(A) An electronics store
(B) An equipment rental shop
(C) A conference center
(D) A shipping company

87. What new service is available this year?

(A) 24-hour photocopying
(B) Online reservation
(C) Wireless internet
(D) Express delivery

88. How can listeners get a discount?

(A) By mentioning an advertisement
(B) By referring a friend
(C) By printing out a voucher
(D) By booking one month in advance

89. What does the speaker mean when he says, "You're all aware of last quarter's sales performance"?

(A) The listeners will not review a report.
(B) Some data should not have been released.
(C) The listeners know that a product has not sold well.
(D) Some sales figures are incorrect.

90. What does Raymond's report indicate?

(A) A competitor's product is more affordable.
(B) A competitor's advertising campaign is better.
(C) Consumers cannot tell the difference between some products.
(D) Consumers have complained about the features of an item.

91. What are listeners asked to do next?

(A) Submit an invoice
(B) Contact some clients
(C) Test some devices
(D) Look over a document

92. Who most likely is the speaker?

(A) A manager
(B) A researcher
(C) A chef
(D) A waiter

93. According to the speaker, what is the business known for?

(A) High-quality food
(B) Cheap prices
(C) Helpful staff
(D) Fast service

94. What does the speaker mean when she says, "I know you can do it"?

(A) She wishes employees will stay later.
(B) She hopes customers will give feedback.
(C) She thinks new dishes can be created.
(D) She believes staff can work faster.

Health Inspection	
Name of Store: The Boxton	**Officer:** Marcus Graham
Health Checklist: ☑ Sanitation ☑ Waste Disposal ☑ Employee Hygiene	**Notes:** Failure of inspection: Freezer

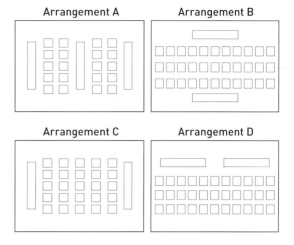

Arrangement A Arrangement B Arrangement C Arrangement D

95. Where does the speaker work?

(A) At a flower shop
(B) At an appliance store
(C) At a catering business
(D) At a delivery company

96. Look at the graphic. Which section of the report does the speaker ask about?

(A) Name of Store
(B) Officer
(C) Health Checklist
(D) Notes

97. What does the speaker say she is concerned about?

(A) Fulfilling an order
(B) Losing merchandise
(C) Hiring more workers
(D) Paying a penalty

98. What kind of event is being discussed?

(A) A medical conference
(B) A movie premiere
(C) An anniversary celebration
(D) An investors' meeting

99. Why is the speaker anticipating attendance to be high?

(A) Many volunteers were recruited.
(B) The venue is in a convenient location.
(C) Some experts will be giving talks.
(D) Some prizes will be distributed.

100. Look at the graphic. Which arrangement will be used in the Malone Auditorium?

(A) Arrangement A
(B) Arrangement B
(C) Arrangement C
(D) Arrangement D

This is the end of the Listening test.

음원 바로 듣기

LISTENING TEST

In the Listening test, you will be asked to demonstrate how well you understand spoken English. The entire Listening test will last approximately 45 minutes. There are four parts, and directions are given for each part. You must mark your answers on the separate answer sheet. Do not write your answers in your test book.

PART 1

Directions: For each question in this part, you will hear four statements about a picture in your test book. When you hear the statements, you must select the one statement that best describes what you see in the picture. Then find the number of the question on your answer sheet and mark your answer. The statements will not be printed in your test book and will be spoken only one time.

Statement (B), "A man is pointing at a document," is the best description of the picture, so you should select answer (B) and mark it on your answer sheet.

1.

2.

GO ON TO THE NEXT PAGE ➡

3.

4.

5.

6.

GO ON TO THE NEXT PAGE

PART 2

Directions: You will hear a question or statement and three responses spoken in English. They will not be printed in your test book and will be spoken only one time. Select the best response to the question or statement and mark the letter (A), (B), or (C) on your answer sheet.

7. Mark your answer on your answer sheet.

8. Mark your answer on your answer sheet.

9. Mark your answer on your answer sheet.

10. Mark your answer on your answer sheet.

11. Mark your answer on your answer sheet.

12. Mark your answer on your answer sheet.

13. Mark your answer on your answer sheet.

14. Mark your answer on your answer sheet.

15. Mark your answer on your answer sheet.

16. Mark your answer on your answer sheet.

17. Mark your answer on your answer sheet.

18. Mark your answer on your answer sheet.

19. Mark your answer on your answer sheet.

20. Mark your answer on your answer sheet.

21. Mark your answer on your answer sheet.

22. Mark your answer on your answer sheet.

23. Mark your answer on your answer sheet.

24. Mark your answer on your answer sheet.

25. Mark your answer on your answer sheet.

26. Mark your answer on your answer sheet.

27. Mark your answer on your answer sheet.

28. Mark your answer on your answer sheet.

29. Mark your answer on your answer sheet.

30. Mark your answer on your answer sheet.

31. Mark your answer on your answer sheet.

PART 3

Directions: You will hear some conversations between two or more people. You will be asked to answer three questions about what the speakers say in each conversation. Select the best response to each question and mark the letter (A), (B), (C), or (D) on your answer sheet. The conversations will not be printed in your test book and will be spoken only one time.

32. What has been written about the company?

(A) It received an award.
(B) It is growing quickly.
(C) It will relocate soon.
(D) It has launched a new product.

33. According to the speakers, what will the article help to do?

(A) Increase job applications
(B) Lower operating costs
(C) Improve staff training
(D) Attract international customers

34. What will the man do next?

(A) Revise a schedule
(B) Post a job opening
(C) Send an email
(D) Update a Web site

35. What problem has the woman identified?

(A) Some documents are out of date.
(B) Some files have been misplaced.
(C) A software program is not working properly.
(D) Two seminars have been double-booked.

36. What does the woman say about employees who were certified last year?

(A) They must contact their managers.
(B) They may work at another plant.
(C) They will train new staff members.
(D) They need to attend a review session.

37. What does the man ask the woman to do?

(A) Lead a training workshop
(B) Complete a registration form
(C) Provide names of employees
(D) Send out invitations

38. What is the conversation mainly about?

(A) Visiting a friend
(B) Reporting on an event
(C) Attending university
(D) Shopping for clothes

39. What does the man say he wants to do before he travels?

(A) Take some courses
(B) Call a hotel
(C) Book a tour
(D) Research some designers

40. What does the woman offer to do?

(A) Show some product catalogs
(B) Check a schedule
(C) Find some contact information
(D) Make a reservation

41. Why is the man calling?

(A) To purchase a train ticket
(B) To request a ride
(C) To discuss a car repair service
(D) To inquire about a charge

42. According to the woman, what has recently changed?

(A) Hiring requirements
(B) A company policy
(C) Business hours
(D) An office location

43. What does the woman agree to do?

(A) Revise an agreement
(B) Contact a manager
(C) Cancel an appointment
(D) Remove a fee

GO ON TO THE NEXT PAGE

44. What does the woman offer to do?

(A) Reschedule an appointment
(B) Transport some boxes
(C) Track a delivery
(D) Call another department

45. According to the woman, what happened last week?

(A) A shipment was damaged.
(B) A storage room was cleaned.
(C) A door would not open.
(D) An elevator broke down.

46. Why does the man say, "the control system had to be reconfigured"?

(A) To give a reason for a delay
(B) To request new equipment
(C) To point out an inefficient process
(D) To apologize for a costly service

47. What product are the speakers discussing?

(A) Stationery
(B) Cosmetics
(C) Computers
(D) Beverages

48. What does Chris recommend?

(A) Offering discounts
(B) Recruiting more workers
(C) Updating a Website
(D) Adjusting a budget

49. What does the woman propose?

(A) Expanding store space
(B) Delaying a decision
(C) Extending business hours
(D) Distributing a questionnaire

50. Who most likely is the woman?

(A) An HR manager
(B) A corporate intern
(C) A financial analyst
(D) A marketing director

51. What does the man ask the woman for?

(A) Some samples of a design
(B) Some details about a company
(C) Some feedback on an experience
(D) Some funding for a project

52. What will the woman receive?

(A) An increased budget
(B) A compensation package
(C) A pay raise
(D) A work schedule

53. What kind of product is being discussed?

(A) A laptop computer
(B) A mobile phone
(C) A home appliance
(D) A digital camera

54. What feature of the product is the woman particularly proud about?

(A) Its speed
(B) Its durability
(C) Its color
(D) Its weight

55. Why does the woman say, "I'm watching a play that evening"?

(A) To praise a performance
(B) To turn down an invitation
(C) To reschedule a meeting
(D) To ask for a recommendation

56. What kind of event is being organized?

(A) A business convention
(B) A product launch
(C) A graduation ceremony
(D) An anniversary celebration

57. What does the woman inquire about?

(A) Food preferences
(B) Accommodations
(C) Parking
(D) Fitness facilities

58. What does the resort provide for free?

(A) Transportation
(B) Breakfast
(C) Wireless internet
(D) Travel guides

---

59. According to the woman, what caused some shipments to be late?

(A) Some workers were not available.
(B) Some documents could not be located.
(C) There was an issue with an online system.
(D) A delivery van experienced engine trouble.

60. What step does the woman suggest adding to a procedure?

(A) Distributing a survey
(B) Making phone calls
(C) Reviewing an inventory list
(D) Performing daily inspections

61. What do the speakers agree to do tomorrow morning?

(A) Contact some job candidates
(B) Visit a new facility
(C) Provide an update
(D) Book some plane tickets

Dental Work Type	Code #
Teeth whitening	T30
Gum surgery	G55
Root canal surgery	R01
Tooth extraction	T86

62. What is the woman having a problem with?

(A) Making an invoice
(B) Locating a package
(C) Performing a surgery
(D) Calling a patient

63. Look at the graphic. Which code should the woman use?

(A) T30
(B) G55
(C) R01
(D) T86

64. What does the man say will happen next week?

(A) A doctor will go on vacation.
(B) Some important clients will visit.
(C) Some staff members will attend a workshop.
(D) A chart will be accessible electronically.

TEST 2

GO ON TO THE NEXT PAGE

STANDARD SHIPPING RATES
(For orders under 5kg)

Domestic Zone	U.S., Canada	$3
Overseas Zone A	Central and South America	$5
Overseas Zone B	Europe, Asia, Africa	$7
Overseas Zone C	Australia, South Pacific	$9

Product Name	LluviaWear
Country of Origin	Dominican Republic
Color	Black
Material	Nylon
Cleaning Instructions	Dry clean only

65. Who most likely is the man?

(A) A customer service associate
(B) A delivery driver
(C) A fashion designer
(D) A Web site developer

66. Look at the graphic. What rate will the woman pay for shipping?

(A) $3
(B) $5
(C) $7
(D) $9

67. What will the woman most likely do next?

(A) Update a contact number
(B) Choose some product features
(C) Confirm a delivery address
(D) Provide some payment information

68. What does the man say they will have to do?

(A) Increase inventory
(B) Find a new storage facility
(C) Create an ad campaign
(D) Print a clothing catalog

69. What does the woman recommend?

(A) Taking pictures of a product
(B) Updating a Web site
(C) Calling some clients
(D) Talking to another department

70. Look at the graphic. Which part of the tag will need to be changed?

(A) Country of Origin
(B) Color
(C) Material
(D) Cleaning Instructions

PART 4

Directions: You will hear some talks given by a single speaker. You will be asked to answer three questions about what the speaker says in each talk. Select the best response to each question and mark the letter (A), (B), (C), or (D) on your answer sheet. The talks will not be printed in your test book and will be spoken only one time.

71. Where does the speaker most likely work?

(A) At a newspaper company
(B) At a furniture store
(C) At a conference center
(D) At a real estate office

72. What is the purpose of the call?

(A) To address a delivery error
(B) To review a defective product
(C) To resolve a scheduling conflict
(D) To acknowledge an incorrect change

73. What will the speaker email the listener?

(A) A discount coupon
(B) A sample item
(C) A new invoice
(D) A refund form

74. Which is mentioned about the restaurant?

(A) It received positive reviews.
(B) Its head chef received an award.
(C) Its menu will change.
(D) It has been open for over 10 years.

75. What does the restaurant specialize in?

(A) Seafood
(B) Pizza
(C) Vegetable dishes
(D) Pastries

76. What will customers receive if they mention the advertisement?

(A) A T-shirt
(B) A discount coupon
(C) A cook book
(D) A free dessert

77. What event is being held?

(A) A job fair
(B) A sales conference
(C) A fundraising dinner
(D) A retirement party

78. Which is Travis Kim's most outstanding achievement?

(A) He developed a training program.
(B) He created a best-selling product.
(C) He expanded a client base.
(D) He founded a charity organization.

79. What does the speaker ask Travis Kim to do?

(A) Make a donation
(B) Accept a gift
(C) Give a speech
(D) Watch a presentation

80. What is the broadcast mainly about?

(A) A traffic report
(B) City council nominees
(C) A new shopping center
(D) Upcoming local events

81. What are the listeners encouraged to do by Friday morning?

(A) Donate some items
(B) Fill out a survey
(C) Enter an art contest
(D) Sign up for volunteer work

82. What does the speaker suggest when she says, "we may be looking at some heavy rain on those days"?

(A) Listeners should avoid going outside.
(B) Listeners should not use a certain road.
(C) The weather can affect a schedule.
(D) A weather report was wrong.

GO ON TO THE NEXT PAGE

83. According to the speaker, what is special about the café?

(A) It operates a farm.
(B) It has a remodeled kitchen.
(C) It provides a cooking course.
(D) It employs an Indian chef.

84. Who is Marco?

(A) A food critic
(B) A university professor
(C) An interior designer
(D) A business owner

85. Why does the speaker say, "All my friends come here to eat this"?

(A) He recommends a menu item.
(B) He knows that a restaurant is popular.
(C) He would like to try a new dish.
(D) He knows how to prepare a dish.

86. What is the main topic of the talk?

(A) Changes to a production schedule
(B) Instructions for repairing machines
(C) Software for teaching work skills
(D) Consequences of a recent merger

87. What does the speaker recommend doing?

(A) Comparing service costs
(B) Extending staff contracts
(C) Talking to a manager after a meeting
(D) Beginning a program with new recruits

88. According to the speaker, what can the company expect to see?

(A) Increased productivity
(B) Higher employee morale
(C) Improved sales
(D) Better customer relations

89. Where does the speaker most likely work?

(A) At an advertising agency
(B) At a publishing company
(C) At a bookstore
(D) At a library

90. What does the speaker mean when she says, "we were very surprised"?

(A) Some documents are missing.
(B) A positive review was given.
(C) Some complaints were made.
(D) An employee is resigning.

91. What will employees be required to do in the future?

(A) Meet monthly sales goals
(B) Request days off in advance
(C) Submit original receipts
(D) Fill out an authorization form

92. What does the speaker mention about himself?

(A) He is a scientist.
(B) He grew up in the region.
(C) He started a new job recently.
(D) He has received an award.

93. According to the speaker, why will the group make several stops?

(A) To take some breaks
(B) To study animal behavior
(C) To learn about different plants
(D) To perform some experiments

94. According to the speaker, what can the listeners do on a Web site?

(A) Read some articles
(B) Download pictures
(C) Sign up for a membership
(D) Complete a questionnaire

Arca Department Store Directory

4F	Clothing & Accessories
3F	Electronics & Appliances
2F	Office Supplies & Furniture
1F	Sporting Goods & Customer Support

95. Look at the graphic. Where is the sale being held at?

(A) The 1st Floor
(B) The 2nd Floor
(C) The 3rd Floor
(D) The 4th Floor

96. According to the speaker, how can shoppers locate sale items?

(A) By checking for a special label
(B) By looking at a product catalog
(C) By speaking to a worker
(D) By going on a store Web site

97. Why are listeners encouraged to visit the customer support center?

(A) To sign up for a membership card
(B) To exchange an item
(C) To schedule a delivery
(D) To purchase a gift certificate

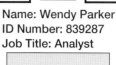

Name: Wendy Parker
ID Number: 839287
Job Title: Analyst

Department: Finance
Office Building: Miller
Contact Information: 555-3824

98. Which department is the speaker calling?

(A) Technology
(B) Personnel
(C) Finance
(D) Security

99. Look at the graphic. What information does the speaker say is incorrect?

(A) 839287
(B) Analyst
(C) Miller
(D) 555-3824

100. What does the speaker request the listener to do?

(A) Return a call
(B) Check a database
(C) Make a reservation
(D) Submit a document

This is the end of the Listening test.

LISTENING TEST

In the Listening test, you will be asked to demonstrate how well you understand spoken English. The entire Listening test will last approximately 45 minutes. There are four parts, and directions are given for each part. You must mark your answers on the separate answer sheet. Do not write your answers in your test book.

PART 1

Directions: For each question in this part, you will hear four statements about a picture in your test book. When you hear the statements, you must select the one statement that best describes what you see in the picture. Then find the number of the question on your answer sheet and mark your answer. The statements will not be printed in your test book and will be spoken only one time.

Statement (B), "A man is pointing at a document," is the best description of the picture, so you should select answer (B) and mark it on your answer sheet.

1.

2.

GO ON TO THE NEXT PAGE ➡

3.

4.

5.

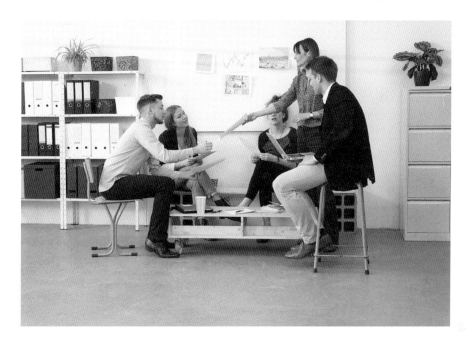

6.

GO ON TO THE NEXT PAGE ➡

PART 2

Directions: You will hear a question or statement and three responses spoken in English. They will not be printed in your test book and will be spoken only one time. Select the best response to the question or statement and mark the letter (A), (B), or (C) on your answer sheet.

7. Mark your answer on your answer sheet.

8. Mark your answer on your answer sheet.

9. Mark your answer on your answer sheet.

10. Mark your answer on your answer sheet.

11. Mark your answer on your answer sheet.

12. Mark your answer on your answer sheet.

13. Mark your answer on your answer sheet.

14. Mark your answer on your answer sheet.

15. Mark your answer on your answer sheet.

16. Mark your answer on your answer sheet.

17. Mark your answer on your answer sheet.

18. Mark your answer on your answer sheet.

19. Mark your answer on your answer sheet.

20. Mark your answer on your answer sheet.

21. Mark your answer on your answer sheet.

22. Mark your answer on your answer sheet.

23. Mark your answer on your answer sheet.

24. Mark your answer on your answer sheet.

25. Mark your answer on your answer sheet.

26. Mark your answer on your answer sheet.

27. Mark your answer on your answer sheet.

28. Mark your answer on your answer sheet.

29. Mark your answer on your answer sheet.

30. Mark your answer on your answer sheet.

31. Mark your answer on your answer sheet.

PART 3

Directions: You will hear some conversations between two or more people. You will be asked to answer three questions about what the speakers say in each conversation. Select the best response to each question and mark the letter (A), (B), (C), or (D) on your answer sheet. The conversations will not be printed in your test book and will be spoken only one time.

32. What are the speakers mainly discussing?
  (A) Local grocery stores
  (B) Public libraries
  (C) Auto repair shops
  (D) Neighborhood restaurants

33. Why does the woman say she likes the man's suggestion?
  (A) The workers are friendly.
  (B) The location is convenient.
  (C) The business closes late.
  (D) The food is healthy.

34. What does the man say is available this week?
  (A) A price discount
  (B) Free parking
  (C) A sample product
  (D) Cooking courses

35. What would the woman like to do?
  (A) Reserve a tour
  (B) Check a city map
  (C) Book a flight
  (D) Review an event calendar

36. What is the woman asked to select?
  (A) Menu items
  (B) A payment method
  (C) A departure time
  (D) Entertainment options

37. What does the man recommend doing?
  (A) Bringing some cash
  (B) Printing out a voucher
  (C) Checking a Web site
  (D) Wearing warm clothing

38. What are the women trying to do?
  (A) Post some signs
  (B) Reserve a meeting room
  (C) Order a new computer
  (D) Get ready for a training session

39. Who is the man?
  (A) A delivery driver
  (B) A store owner
  (C) A facility manager
  (D) A software developer

40. What does the man advise the women to do?
  (A) Relocate to another room
  (B) Update a system
  (C) Provide some feedback
  (D) Read a user guide

41. What are the speakers discussing?
  (A) Repairing some furniture
  (B) Renovating some bathrooms
  (C) Recycling some clothes
  (D) Replacing some flooring

42. What is the man concerned about?
  (A) A price
  (B) Some noise
  (C) An odor
  (D) Some designs

43. What does the woman say she will do?
  (A) Change a date
  (B) Provide an estimate
  (C) Inspect an apartment
  (D) Employ a contractor

GO ON TO THE NEXT PAGE

44. Where do the speakers most likely work?

(A) At a library
(B) At an electronics store
(C) At a hospital
(D) At a financial firm

45. What did Ms. Shah recommend?

(A) Purchasing a magazine subscription
(B) Watching a video demonstration
(C) Holding personal meetings with staff
(D) Enrolling in some online courses

46. What does the man say he will do?

(A) Review a presentation
(B) Try out a product
(C) Research some pricing information
(D) Print out an article

47. Where are the speakers?

(A) At a training workshop
(B) At a fashion show
(C) At a department meeting
(D) At a company luncheon

48. What project are the women working on?

(A) A budget proposal
(B) A catalog redesign
(C) A marketing campaign
(D) An instructional video

49. What does the man say he was responsible for?

(A) Looking over customer feedback
(B) Hiring new staff members
(C) Organizing a volunteer program
(D) Revising some news articles

50. According to the man, what will happen on Friday?

(A) A business will reopen.
(B) A newspaper will be published.
(C) A workshop will begin.
(D) A staff member will be interviewed.

51. What does the woman request?

(A) Directions to an office
(B) Permission to bring a colleague
(C) A sample of a product
(D) A tour of a facility

52. What does the man say he will prepare?

(A) Some badges
(B) Some pictures
(C) Some snacks
(D) Some documents

53. What does the man request the woman do?

(A) Mail some invitations
(B) Review some charts
(C) Reserve a booth
(D) Postpone an event

54. What does the man plan to do today?

(A) Register for a workshop
(B) Meet with a client
(C) Purchase a ticket
(D) Contact a catering company

55. Why does the man say, "I haven't been here long, and it's a big presentation"?

(A) He wants to get feedback from the woman on a proposal.
(B) He is providing an excuse for why he has postponed an event.
(C) He would like to thank the woman for helping him with a project.
(D) He is concerned about performing a task by himself.

56. Who most likely is the woman?

    (A) A receptionist
    (B) A reporter
    (C) A salesperson
    (D) An actress

57. According to the man, what change is expected?

    (A) More colors will be used in clothing designs.
    (B) Production costs will significantly increase.
    (C) Consumers will spend less money in the future.
    (D) Merchandise will only be sold online.

58. What does the woman want to do?

    (A) Visit a store
    (B) Take photographs
    (C) Meet the company CEO
    (D) Take a tour

59. What did a client dislike about the stairway lights?

    (A) Their shape
    (B) Their cost
    (C) Their brightness
    (D) Their color

60. Why does the woman say, "according to the contract, we need to finish everything by this week"?

    (A) She believes some contract terms should be changed.
    (B) She is concerned about meeting a deadline.
    (C) She is surprised at the progress of a landscaping project.
    (D) She will repair some broken equipment this week.

61. What does the man say he will do?

    (A) Go to a work site
    (B) Revise a document
    (C) Place an order
    (D) Contact a customer

Possible Event Locations	
Venue	Guest Capacity
Ocean Grill	200 guests
Bistro 324	150 guests
The Vine	125 guests
Olive Grove	100 guests

62. What information about the party did the man receive this morning?

    (A) The finalized date
    (B) The amount of budgeted funds
    (C) The number of attendees
    (D) The directions to the event

63. Look at the graphic. Which venue will the speakers most likely choose?

    (A) Ocean Grill
    (B) Bistro 324
    (C) The Vine
    (D) Olive Grove

64. What does the woman say she will take care of?

    (A) A security deposit
    (B) Entertainment
    (C) Menu items
    (D) Transportation

GO ON TO THE NEXT PAGE

Invoice (#483740)	
Customer Name: Raymond Posner	
Description	**Price**
9"x12" Oil Painting	$380
12"x16" Watercolor Painting	$560
20"x24" Acrylic Painting	$720
30"x40" Landscape Painting	$910

Boston to Chicago		
Train	**Departure**	**Arrival**
Train 1024	12:50 P.M.	9:50 A.M.
Train 116	3:15 P.M.	12:10 P.M.
Train 894	5:30 P.M.	3:40 P.M.
Train 3479	7:25 P.M.	5:45 P.M.

65. What does the man say he will do with the restored paintings?

(A) Sell them at an auction
(B) Use them as office decorations
(C) Display them at a museum
(D) Give them as gifts to coworkers

66. Look at the graphic. Which amount will be taken off of the invoice?

(A) $380
(B) $560
(C) $720
(D) $910

67. What does the woman say her assistant will do?

(A) Print out some forms
(B) Give the man a tour of a store
(C) Carry some items to a vehicle
(D) Process a payment

68. Why does the woman apologize?

(A) A payment was not processed.
(B) A ticket is not available online.
(C) A train has been overbooked.
(D) A schedule is incorrect.

69. Look at the graphic. What train will the man most likely take?

(A) Train 1024
(B) Train 116
(C) Train 894
(D) Train 3479

70. What does the man say he will do in Chicago?

(A) Attend a seminar
(B) Tour a factory
(C) Watch a performance
(D) Meet a client

PART 4

Directions: You will hear some talks given by a single speaker. You will be asked to answer three questions about what the speaker says in each talk. Select the best response to each question and mark the letter (A), (B), (C), or (D) on your answer sheet. The talks will not be printed in your test book and will be spoken only one time.

71. Who most likely are the listeners?

(A) Sales associates
(B) Product designers
(C) Computer specialists
(D) Human Resources employees

72. According to the speaker, what is the next step of the project?

(A) To develop training materials
(B) To create a prototype
(C) To determine a cost
(D) To obtain some feedback

73. What does the speaker ask for help with?

(A) Reviewing some documents
(B) Interviewing job candidates
(C) Contacting other departments
(D) Selecting some instruments

74. Where does the speaker work?

(A) At a uniform retailer
(B) At a taxi company
(C) At a car dealership
(D) At a post office

75. What does the speaker mean when he says, "some of our drivers are out sick at the moment"?

(A) A shipment will not arrive on time.
(B) A company will hire more employees.
(C) Some staff will be working extra shifts.
(D) Some automobiles are available for use.

76. What does the speaker offer?

(A) A future discount
(B) A product catalog
(C) A complimentary item
(D) A full refund

77. What does the business produce?

(A) Car tires
(B) Mobile phones
(C) Airplane engines
(D) Laptop computers

78. According to the speaker, what will the business do in August?

(A) Raise its workers' wages
(B) Launch a new product line
(C) Create additional parking spaces
(D) Open a new manufacturing plant

79. What does the mayor expect will happen in Willington?

(A) A recycling program will begin.
(B) New traffic laws will be enforced.
(C) More public transportation will be provided.
(D) Employment opportunities will increase.

80. What is being advertised?

(A) Residential real estate
(B) Heating maintenance
(C) Appliance recycling
(D) A technology institute

81. Why are listeners asked to call?

(A) To sign up for a class
(B) To set up an inspection
(C) To arrange transportation
(D) To receive a brochure

82. What will happen at the end of the month?

(A) A special offer will expire.
(B) A report will be published.
(C) Payments will be due.
(D) Construction will begin.

GO ON TO THE NEXT PAGE

83. Where is the talk taking place?

(A) In a factory
(B) In a laboratory
(C) In a supermarket
(D) In a bakery

84. What are listeners given?

(A) A location map
(B) A discount coupon
(C) Product samples
(D) Some ingredients

85. What does the speaker remind the listeners to do?

(A) Wear safety equipment
(B) Use a back entrance
(C) Return their passes
(D) Fill out a security form

86. What does the speaker remind listeners to do by the end of the day?

(A) Submit a task report
(B) Make a reservation
(C) Pick up a visitor's pass
(D) Nominate an employee

87. What good news does the speaker mention?

(A) Workers will receive cash incentives.
(B) Production has gone up.
(C) A product launch was successful.
(D) A shipment arrived on time.

88. Why does the speaker say, "we've been hosting visitors from Japan for several days"?

(A) To introduce a guest speaker
(B) To begin a tour of a facility
(C) To review details of a business trip
(D) To give a reason for a delay

89. What is the purpose of the talk?

(A) To ask for financial contributions
(B) To share information about a program
(C) To explain a job application process
(D) To announce a new exhibit

90. What requirement does the speaker mention?

(A) Holding local events
(B) Providing weekly feedback
(C) Submitting work samples
(D) Visiting different cities

91. Who is invited to speak next?

(A) School teachers
(B) Museum directors
(C) Famous artists
(D) Professional athletes

92. Why is the speaker postponing today's meeting?

(A) A manager was busy.
(B) A room was not available.
(C) Some designs were not completed.
(D) His travel arrangements were changed.

93. According to the speaker, what was the listener's report about?

(A) Suggestions for being more environmentally friendly
(B) Results of a recent customer survey
(C) Plans to cut back on operating costs
(D) Strategies to attract new customers

94. What does the speaker imply when he says, "Let's discuss this in more detail"?

(A) He is planning to research some new suppliers.
(B) He believes a proposal may cause problems.
(C) He would like review a contract more carefully.
(D) He wants to extend a project deadline.

Service	Fee
Late payment	$20
Line reconnection	$40
In-home service	$60
Early cancelation	$80

95. Where does the speaker most likely work?

(A) At a book publisher
(B) At a fitness center
(C) At a telephone provider
(D) At a landscaping company

96. Look at the graphic. How much will Ms. Preston pay?

(A) $20
(B) $40
(C) $60
(D) $80

97. What is Ms. Preston encouraged to do on the Web site?

(A) Provide feedback
(B) Renew her membership
(C) Download a contract
(D) Register for a mailing list

Innomax Convention Schedule		
Time	Event	Speaker
13:00	Best Sport Cars	Jeremy Fong
14:00	Latest Navigation Systems	Kelly Brown
15:00	Improving Fuel Efficiency	Sherman Bernstein
16:00	Designing Your Vehicle	Emily Lithmore
17:00	Reception	Innomax President

98. What is the purpose of the call?

(A) To offer a job
(B) To check on an order
(C) To request product samples
(D) To make a reservation

99. Look at the graphic. Who is the speaker calling?

(A) Jeremy Fong
(B) Kelly Brown
(C) Sherman Bernstein
(D) Emily Lithmore

100. What does the speaker ask the listener to do?

(A) Provide pricing information
(B) Visit a Web site
(C) Review a convention schedule
(D) Send a registration payment

This is the end of the Listening test.

ST 4

LISTENING TEST

In the Listening test, you will be asked to demonstrate how well you understand spoken English. The entire Listening test will last approximately 45 minutes. There are four parts, and directions are given for each part. You must mark your answers on the separate answer sheet. Do not write your answers in your test book.

PART 1

Directions: For each question in this part, you will hear four statements about a picture in your test book. When you hear the statements, you must select the one statement that best describes what you see in the picture. Then find the number of the question on your answer sheet and mark your answer. The statements will not be printed in your test book and will be spoken only one time.

Statement (B), "A man is pointing at a document," is the best description of the picture, so you should select answer (B) and mark it on your answer sheet.

1.

2.

GO ON TO THE NEXT PAGE

3.

4.

5.

6.

GO ON TO THE NEXT PAGE →

PART 2

Directions: You will hear a question or statement and three responses spoken in English. They will not be printed in your test book and will be spoken only one time. Select the best response to the question or statement and mark the letter (A), (B), or (C) on your answer sheet.

7. Mark your answer on your answer sheet.

8. Mark your answer on your answer sheet.

9. Mark your answer on your answer sheet.

10. Mark your answer on your answer sheet.

11. Mark your answer on your answer sheet.

12. Mark your answer on your answer sheet.

13. Mark your answer on your answer sheet.

14. Mark your answer on your answer sheet.

15. Mark your answer on your answer sheet.

16. Mark your answer on your answer sheet.

17. Mark your answer on your answer sheet.

18. Mark your answer on your answer sheet.

19. Mark your answer on your answer sheet.

20. Mark your answer on your answer sheet.

21. Mark your answer on your answer sheet.

22. Mark your answer on your answer sheet.

23. Mark your answer on your answer sheet.

24. Mark your answer on your answer sheet.

25. Mark your answer on your answer sheet.

26. Mark your answer on your answer sheet.

27. Mark your answer on your answer sheet.

28. Mark your answer on your answer sheet.

29. Mark your answer on your answer sheet.

30. Mark your answer on your answer sheet.

31. Mark your answer on your answer sheet.

PART 3

Directions: You will hear some conversations between two or more people. You will be asked to answer three questions about what the speakers say in each conversation. Select the best response to each question and mark the letter (A), (B), (C), or (D) on your answer sheet. The conversations will not be printed in your test book and will be spoken only one time.

32. Where does the conversation most likely take place?

(A) In a shopping mall
(B) In a train station
(C) In a fitness center
(D) In a coffee shop

33. What does the woman ask the man to do?

(A) Respond to a survey
(B) Try out a product
(C) Provide contact information
(D) Come back later

34. What does the man suggest?

(A) Extending business hours
(B) Improving exercise facilities
(C) Offering more discounts
(D) Increasing dining options

35. What is the woman's occupation?

(A) Floral designer
(B) Car repairperson
(C) Landscape professional
(D) Construction worker

36. What is the woman's problem?

(A) Her vehicle is not starting.
(B) She cannot make it to her next appointment.
(C) Her coworker is not available.
(D) She doesn't have enough supplies.

37. What does the man recommend doing?

(A) Reading a manual
(B) Extending a project deadline
(C) Taking a detour
(D) Checking a traffic report

38. What type of product is being discussed?

(A) Office furniture
(B) Clothing
(C) Electronics
(D) Home appliances

39. What does the woman imply when she says, "It looks like only three boxes are left"?

(A) She is too busy to check inventory.
(B) She wants a worker to organize some shelves.
(C) Some boxes need to be moved.
(D) An item is very popular.

40. What will the woman do next?

(A) Contact a Sales Department
(B) Hang up some signs
(C) Clean some shelves
(D) Place a new order

41. Where most likely are the speakers?

(A) At a manufacturing plant
(B) At a post office
(C) At a hotel
(D) At a retailer

42. What does the man say will happen tomorrow?

(A) A shipment will be delivered.
(B) A seminar will be held.
(C) An inspection will be conducted.
(D) An advertisement will be posted.

43. What will the woman probably do next?

(A) Organize a storage room
(B) Order some food
(C) Send out some invitations
(D) Show a customer some merchandise

GO ON TO THE NEXT PAGE

44. What is the main topic of the conversation?

(A) Chocolate
(B) Pastries
(C) Vegetables
(D) Fruit

45. What is the man's problem?

(A) A computer is malfunctioning.
(B) A credit card payment was not approved.
(C) A box is too heavy to carry.
(D) A shipment is missing some items.

46. What does the woman say she will give the man?

(A) A discount voucher
(B) A postage stamp
(C) Complimentary merchandise
(D) Cash reimbursement

47. Who most likely is the man?

(A) A professional photographer
(B) A corporate event organizer
(C) A customer service associate
(D) A computer technician

48. What does the woman inquire about?

(A) Repairing a camera
(B) Arranging a photo session
(C) Purchasing a warranty
(D) Applying an internet discount

49. According to the man, what should the woman do?

(A) Visit a store
(B) Send a photograph
(C) Download a manual
(D) Contact a manufacturer

50. What is the conversation mainly about?

(A) Relocating a business
(B) Hiring better workers
(C) Reviewing features of a new product
(D) Expanding a section of a store

51. What is the woman asked to do?

(A) Place an online ad
(B) Contact a supplier
(C) Submit a sales report
(D) Download a catalog

52. What will the man probably do next?

(A) Take inventory
(B) Compare some costs
(C) Visit another branch
(D) Put up some posters

53. What is the man working on?

(A) A user guide
(B) A software program
(C) A market survey
(D) An event schedule

54. What does the man mean when he says, "You'll need to ask someone in the IT Department about that"?

(A) He is unable to give an answer.
(B) A project requires additional team members.
(C) The department made a specific request.
(D) He has to attend a meeting soon.

55. What is the woman worried about?

(A) Training new employees
(B) Attracting many customers
(C) Exceeding a budget
(D) Meeting a deadline

56. What is the woman inquiring about?

(A) Flight arrival times
(B) Payment methods
(C) Extra baggage allowances
(D) Seat upgrades

57. What does the woman say she needs to do in Rome?

(A) Visit a local bank
(B) Rent a car
(C) Catch a connecting flight
(D) Prepare for a talk

58. What does the man recommend?

(A) Using a credit card
(B) Taking an alternate route
(C) Rescheduling a meeting
(D) Speaking to a supervisor

59. Why will the man meet with Ms. Gomez?

(A) To receive marketing advice
(B) To interview her
(C) To sign a contract
(D) To show her some products

60. What does the man agree to do?

(A) Reschedule an appointment
(B) Make a donation
(C) Complete a visitor form
(D) Purchase a magazine subscription

61. Why does Ms. Gomez apologize?

(A) A meeting will not start on time.
(B) She does not know the man's phone number.
(C) She lost some documents.
(D) An article contains inaccurate information.

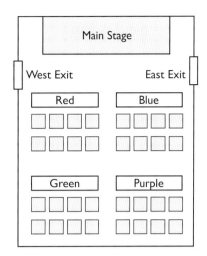

62. What kind of event are the speakers planning to attend?

(A) A product demonstration
(B) A dance show
(C) A movie premiere
(D) A business conference

63. Look at the graphic. Where will the speakers most likely sit?

(A) The red section
(B) The blue section
(C) The green section
(D) The purple section

64. What does the woman recommend?

(A) Calling different vendors
(B) Inviting more coworkers
(C) Using a public transit service
(D) Viewing an online map

GO ON TO THE NEXT PAGE

Daily Specials
1. Mini burgers.......................................$9.75
2. Steak nachos...................................$10.50
3. Sausage platter $11.25
4. Cobb salad $7.50

65. What most likely is the woman's job?

(A) Delivery driver
(B) Chef
(C) Server
(D) Restaurant manager

66. According to the man, why will a list be updated?

(A) Some ingredients are not available.
(B) A package will not come in today.
(C) A chef prepared the wrong item.
(D) Many complaints were filed.

67. Look at the graphic. How much will the new special cost?

(A) $9.75
(B) $10.50
(C) $11.25
(D) $7.50

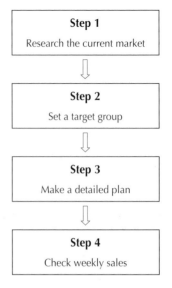

Step 1
Research the current market

⇩

Step 2
Set a target group

⇩

Step 3
Make a detailed plan

⇩

Step 4
Check weekly sales

68. What type of business does the woman operate?

(A) An online clothing store
(B) A travel agency
(C) A digital marketing firm
(D) A computer shop

69. What does the woman hope to do in the future?

(A) Become a fashion designer
(B) Earn an advanced degree
(C) Increase her customer base
(D) Move to another country

70. Look at the graphic. What step would the woman like to discuss?

(A) Step 1
(B) Step 2
(C) Step 3
(D) Step 4

PART 4

Directions: You will hear some talks given by a single speaker. You will be asked to answer three questions about what the speaker says in each talk. Select the best response to each question and mark the letter (A), (B), (C), or (D) on your answer sheet. The talks will not be printed in your test book and will be spoken only one time.

71. What type of business is being advertised?
    (A) An art studio
    (B) A grocery store
    (C) An exercise club
    (D) A software company

72. What will the listeners be able to do beginning in October?
    (A) Participate in a competition
    (B) Receive a consultation
    (C) Access a database
    (D) Purchase a new product

73. Why does the speaker invite the listeners to visit a Web site?
    (A) To download a program
    (B) To view some testimonials
    (C) To read a manual
    (D) To get some directions

74. Why does the speaker thank the listeners?
    (A) For organizing a seminar
    (B) For working overtime
    (C) For conducting an interview
    (D) For teaching a course

75. What will happen later this month?
    (A) An athletic competition will take place.
    (B) Some remodeling will be finished.
    (C) A book fair will be held.
    (D) Some rooms will be booked.

76. What does the speaker mean when he says, "there's plenty of room"?
    (A) Everybody will be able to attend an event.
    (B) Accommodations are available at a hotel.
    (C) A number of staff could be hired.
    (D) Space is available to add a product to an exhibit.

77. For whom is Mr. Greenwald's advice intended?
    (A) Web designers
    (B) Event organizers
    (C) Film producers
    (D) Department heads

78. According to Mr. Greenwald, what is a good way to improve productivity?
    (A) Offering better incentives
    (B) Setting reasonable deadlines
    (C) Taking regular breaks
    (D) Reducing meeting times

79. What are the listeners encouraged to do?
    (A) Watch some videos
    (B) Read an article
    (C) Download an application
    (D) Call a radio station

80. Why is the speaker calling?
    (A) To apologize for a mistake
    (B) To explain a policy
    (C) To reschedule a meeting
    (D) To set up a delivery

81. What does the speaker say happened last week?
    (A) A facility was closed for repairs.
    (B) New products were launched.
    (C) Some data were recorded incorrectly.
    (D) Some employees were not available.

82. What will the company provide to the listener?
    (A) Express shipping
    (B) Complimentary shuttle service
    (C) A seat upgrade
    (D) A free meal

GO ON TO THE NEXT PAGE

83. Who is the speaker?

(A) A delivery person
(B) A product designer
(C) A store receptionist
(D) A plant manager

84. What does the company sell?

(A) Consumer electronics
(B) Automotive parts
(C) Office furniture
(D) Garden equipment

85. What does the speaker imply when he says, "I've only seen houses"?

(A) He believes an error was made.
(B) He is worried about a new housing rule.
(C) A construction permit cannot be provided.
(D) Some funds cannot be acquired.

86. What department does the speaker work in?

(A) Marketing
(B) Finance
(C) Administration
(D) Sales

87. What is the topic of the workshop?

(A) Creating detailed financial plans
(B) Presenting business proposals
(C) Reducing work-related stress
(D) Setting up client meetings

88. What will the listeners do next?

(A) Find a partner
(B) Complete a questionnaire
(C) Watch a video
(D) Discuss a contract

89. What is the message mainly about?

(A) Signing up for a cooking contest
(B) Updating some files
(C) Revising an itinerary
(D) Organizing a celebration

90. What does the speaker imply when she says, "I still can't believe what happened"?

(A) She is unhappy with the results of a competition.
(B) She misunderstood some instructions.
(C) She is surprised by a decision.
(D) She wants to avoid making a mistake again.

91. What is the speaker going to do after work?

(A) Visit a dining establishment
(B) Attend a performance
(C) Shop at a store
(D) Depart for a conference

92. Why is the speaker qualified to host the program?

(A) He has received many broadcasting awards.
(B) He has extensive work experience.
(C) He has studied business at a famous university.
(D) He has published many financial books.

93. Why does the speaker say, "having a booth at an expo isn't cheap"?

(A) To suggest paying in installments
(B) To agree with a professional's advice
(C) To refuse a request
(D) To acknowledge a common concern

94. What will the speaker most likely do next?

(A) Call some listeners
(B) Announce contest winners
(C) Sign up for a conference
(D) Give some detailed advice

Thursday	Friday	Saturday	Sunday
Rain	Cloudy	Sunny	Partly Cloudy

95. What event is being described?

(A) A charity function
(B) An art contest
(C) A sports competition
(D) A book fair

96. According to the speaker, what can the listeners find on a Web site?

(A) A weather report
(B) A list of participants
(C) A schedule of events
(D) A park map

97. Look at the graphic. On which day will the event be held?

(A) Thursday
(B) Friday
(C) Saturday
(D) Sunday

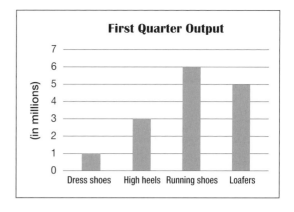

First Quarter Output

98. Who most likely are the listeners?

(A) Factory workers
(B) Sales associates
(C) Fashion designers
(D) Financial planners

99. Look at the graphic. Which category is the speaker concerned about?

(A) Dress shoes
(B) High heels
(C) Running shoes
(D) Loafers

100. What has the company decided to do?

(A) Purchase some equipment
(B) Delay a schedule
(C) Revise a safety policy
(D) Recruit more employees

This is the end of the Listening test.

TES

ST 5

LISTENING TEST

In the Listening test, you will be asked to demonstrate how well you understand spoken English. The entire Listening test will last approximately 45 minutes. There are four parts, and directions are given for each part. You must mark your answers on the separate answer sheet. Do not write your answers in your test book.

PART 1

Directions: For each question in this part, you will hear four statements about a picture in your test book. When you hear the statements, you must select the one statement that best describes what you see in the picture. Then find the number of the question on your answer sheet and mark your answer. The statements will not be printed in your test book and will be spoken only one time.

Statement (B), "A man is pointing at a document," is the best description of the picture, so you should select answer (B) and mark it on your answer sheet.

1.

2.

GO ON TO THE NEXT PAGE

TEST 5

3.

4.

5.

6.

GO ON TO THE NEXT PAGE

PART 2

Directions: You will hear a question or statement and three responses spoken in English. They will not be printed in your test book and will be spoken only one time. Select the best response to the question or statement and mark the letter (A), (B), or (C) on your answer sheet.

7. Mark your answer on your answer sheet.

8. Mark your answer on your answer sheet.

9. Mark your answer on your answer sheet.

10. Mark your answer on your answer sheet.

11. Mark your answer on your answer sheet.

12. Mark your answer on your answer sheet.

13. Mark your answer on your answer sheet.

14. Mark your answer on your answer sheet.

15. Mark your answer on your answer sheet.

16. Mark your answer on your answer sheet.

17. Mark your answer on your answer sheet.

18. Mark your answer on your answer sheet.

19. Mark your answer on your answer sheet.

20. Mark your answer on your answer sheet.

21. Mark your answer on your answer sheet.

22. Mark your answer on your answer sheet.

23. Mark your answer on your answer sheet.

24. Mark your answer on your answer sheet.

25. Mark your answer on your answer sheet.

26. Mark your answer on your answer sheet.

27. Mark your answer on your answer sheet.

28. Mark your answer on your answer sheet.

29. Mark your answer on your answer sheet.

30. Mark your answer on your answer sheet.

31. Mark your answer on your answer sheet.

PART 3

Directions: You will hear some conversations between two or more people. You will be asked to answer three questions about what the speakers say in each conversation. Select the best response to each question and mark the letter (A), (B), (C), or (D) on your answer sheet. The conversations will not be printed in your test book and will be spoken only one time.

32. What is the main topic of the conversation?

(A) Renovating a cafeteria
(B) Reviewing research findings
(C) Designing some furniture
(D) Finding an event venue

33. What will happen during the first week of February?

(A) A budget proposal will be presented.
(B) A business will extend its office hours.
(C) A new CEO will be appointed.
(D) A company gathering will take place.

34. What will the woman most likely send in the afternoon?

(A) A blueprint
(B) Some pictures
(C) An invoice
(D) Some equipment

35. What is the main topic of the conversation?

(A) The recipes of a renowned chef
(B) Extending a store's business hours
(C) The availability of a special dish
(D) How to best advertise a restaurant

36. What does the man say will happen soon?

(A) A delivery will be made.
(B) A group of customers will arrive.
(C) Some new employees will be hired.
(D) Some products will become available.

37. What does the woman ask the man?

(A) How many customers are waiting
(B) Where a chef learned to cook
(C) What time he will be leaving
(D) If she should update the menu offerings

38. Who most likely are the women?

(A) Corporate lawyers
(B) New workers
(C) Fitness trainers
(D) Construction managers

39. What does the man say about the leisure facilities?

(A) The sauna is being renovated.
(B) They close early on the weekends.
(C) The membership fee has recently increased.
(D) They require a company ID to enter.

40. What will the women do after lunch?

(A) Participate in another building tour
(B) Meet some department members
(C) Listen to a speech
(D) Complete a questionnaire

41. Why is the man calling?

(A) To recommend a new office
(B) To request assistance with a computer
(C) To report a leak
(D) To reserve a meeting room

42. What does the woman say she will do?

(A) Revise a client list
(B) Send an employee to help
(C) Install an accounting program
(D) Call a utility company

43. What does the man say he will be doing at 3 o'clock?

(A) Meeting with a client
(B) Examining some documents
(C) Interviewing job applicants
(D) Leaving for a business trip

GO ON TO THE NEXT PAGE

44. What industry do the speakers most likely work in?

(A) Food service
(B) Architecture
(C) Fine arts
(D) Packaging

45. What does the man mean when he says, "It's supposed to be delivered around 6 P.M."?

(A) He may not be available for a task.
(B) He will have to place a new order.
(C) He plans to request a refund.
(D) He is not satisfied with a service.

46. What does the man say about Corinna?

(A) She will enroll in a training workshop.
(B) She drives her car to the office.
(C) She is more experienced than him.
(D) She is interested in working more hours.

47. What is the woman preparing for?

(A) A business trip to Seoul
(B) An engineering seminar
(C) A corporate merger
(D) A meeting with investors

48. What is the woman calling about?

(A) A travel itinerary
(B) Translation services
(C) A conference room
(D) Contract details

49. What does the man offer to do?

(A) Make a reservation
(B) Send an email
(C) Refer a colleague
(D) Explain a schedule

50. What are the speakers discussing?

(A) An inventory check
(B) A finance presentation
(C) A business merger
(D) A television advertisement

51. What does the man say he is missing?

(A) A video file
(B) A signature
(C) A desk key
(D) An account password

52. What does the man ask the woman to do after lunch?

(A) Attend a committee meeting
(B) Submit an investment proposal
(C) Check a computer
(D) Review a contract

53. What will the woman do next week?

(A) Submit a research paper
(B) Give a guest lecture
(C) Publish a book
(D) Take an exam

54. What did Drew do in the morning?

(A) He edited a document.
(B) He met with a professor.
(C) He purchased office supplies.
(D) He delivered a package.

55. What does Drew ask the woman to do?

(A) Complete a form
(B) Come back later
(C) Present identification
(D) Visit another office

56. Who most likely are the speakers?

(A) Hotel workers
(B) Broadcasting executives
(C) Travel agents
(D) Restaurant employees

57. What does the man imply when he says, "but winter's nearly over"?

(A) The woman needs to finish an assignment quickly.
(B) A marketing campaign will be released too late.
(C) Some data in a sales report must be revised.
(D) He would like to take his vacation at a later time.

58. What will the woman do next?

(A) Speak with a supervisor
(B) Distribute a questionnaire
(C) Contact some businesses
(D) Print out additional flyers

---

59. Who most likely is the woman?

(A) A corporate accountant
(B) A delivery driver
(C) A sales representative
(D) A plant manager

60. What feature of the Pro-X Gauge does the man mention?

(A) It tracks packages.
(B) It monitors pressure levels.
(C) It records daily finances.
(D) It calculates shipping rates.

61. Why does the woman say she will call back tomorrow?

(A) She has to review a financial plan.
(B) She is late for a meeting.
(C) She requires her supervisor's authorization.
(D) She would like to check out other models.

Monthly Report	
Equipment Expenses	$9,000
Packaging Materials	$8,000
Property Rent	$6,000
Utilities (gas and electricity)	$1,000

62. What kind of product does the company most likely make?

(A) Office furniture
(B) Cleaning supplies
(C) Clothing
(D) Electronics

63. What does the woman point out about the report?

(A) Some monthly objectives were achieved.
(B) Some figures were incorrect.
(C) Some expenditures have gone up.
(D) Some sections are blank.

64. Look at the graphic. Which amount does the woman say might change?

(A) $9,000
(B) $8,000
(C) $6,000
(D) $1,000

GO ON TO THE NEXT PAGE

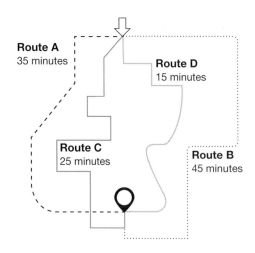

Route A
35 minutes

Route D
15 minutes

Route C
25 minutes

Route B
45 minutes

To	Raya Shah
From	Brian McFadder

Plant Location	Completion Date
Newcrest	July 31
Westmark	September 26
Callington	October 27
Plateforth	November 30

65. Why is the man driving the woman to work?

(A) Her public transit pass expired.
(B) She does not own a car.
(C) She recently moved to a new city.
(D) Her vehicle is being repaired.

66. What event does the man say is being held today?

(A) A retirement banquet
(B) A cycling competition
(C) An art exhibition
(D) A film festival

67. Look at the graphic. What route will the man probably take?

(A) Route A
(B) Route B
(C) Route C
(D) Route D

68. What did the speakers just attend?

(A) An employee meeting
(B) A factory tour
(C) A career fair
(D) A product demonstration

69. Look at the graphic. What date has to be changed?

(A) July 31
(B) September 26
(C) October 27
(D) November 30

70. What is causing a delay in construction?

(A) Some equipment is not working.
(B) Some materials have not been delivered.
(C) A building permit has been denied.
(D) An area has had inclement weather.

PART 4

Directions: You will hear some talks given by a single speaker. You will be asked to answer three questions about what the speaker says in each talk. Select the best response to each question and mark the letter (A), (B), (C), or (D) on your answer sheet. The talks will not be printed in your test book and will be spoken only one time.

71. According to the speaker, what event was postponed?

(A) A film festival
(B) A bicycle race
(C) A dance performance
(D) A cooking competition

72. Why was the event postponed?

(A) An application was rejected.
(B) A guest could not make it.
(C) Some funds were not secured.
(D) Some repair work needs to be done.

73. What will the listeners hear next?

(A) A new song
(B) A celebrity interview
(C) A traffic report
(D) A business advertisement

74. What happened in the afternoon?

(A) An old structure was sold.
(B) A movie premiere was held.
(C) A new product was released.
(D) An anniversary party took place.

75. According to the speaker, why was Wight and Company chosen?

(A) It knows how to do challenging renovations.
(B) It owns multiple shopping complexes.
(C) It will offer jobs to local residents.
(D) It has previously worked on government projects.

76. What do city council members hope to do?

(A) Increase revenue
(B) Hire better building designers
(C) Expand public transportation
(D) Construct more parks

77. What is the subject of the convention?

(A) Finance
(B) Agriculture
(C) Healthcare
(D) Travel

78. What does the speaker mean when she says, "I hope everyone brought plenty of business cards"?

(A) Identification cards are required for registration.
(B) Event organizers will be holding a raffle.
(C) There will be many networking opportunities.
(D) Some guests do not have name tags.

79. What does the speaker say is difficult?

(A) Preparing a presentation
(B) Managing a facility
(C) Securing a venue
(D) Quitting a role

80. What is the purpose of the message?

(A) To make changes to an order
(B) To request additional workers
(C) To inquire about office vacancies
(D) To explain details about a delivery

81. What does the speaker want the listener to do?

(A) Contact a factory supervisor
(B) Send a package to an office
(C) Review a company policy
(D) Allow access to a building

82. What does the speaker say he will be doing this morning?

(A) Training an employee
(B) Cleaning his apartment
(C) Working in his office
(D) Visiting a client

GO ON TO THE NEXT PAGE

83. What problem is being addressed?

(A) Inclement weather
(B) Passenger delays
(C) Technical difficulties
(D) Missing bags

84. What are listeners asked to do?

(A) Prepare to present documents
(B) Go to a different gate of the airport
(C) Complete a special request form
(D) Request a refund for a ticket

85. According to the speaker, what will attendants be doing?

(A) Checking departure times
(B) Issuing new tickets
(C) Offering shuttle service
(D) Distributing luggage tags

86. Why does the speaker say, "There was an unexpected turn of events"?

(A) Some equipment is not working.
(B) Some instruments are missing.
(C) A musician is arriving late.
(D) The venue is being renovated.

87. According to the speaker, what can be purchased in the lobby?

(A) Snacks and drinks
(B) Performance tickets
(C) An orchestra's recordings
(D) Signed posters of musicians

88. What is being advertised at the auditorium?

(A) Music lessons
(B) Upcoming performances
(C) Guided tours
(D) Famous restaurants

89. Where do the listeners most likely work?

(A) At an electronics manufacturer
(B) At a courier company
(C) At a security firm
(D) At a grocery store

90. Why does the speaker say, "All of this information is coming from our customers"?

(A) To emphasize the importance of a process
(B) To express her disagreement with an opinion
(C) To recognize the listeners' efforts
(D) To ensure listeners report to their supervisors

91. According to the speaker, what will a new manager start doing?

(A) Working on the weekends
(B) Visiting different branches
(C) Conducting inspections
(D) Purchasing replacement parts

92. What is the announcement mainly about?

(A) A revised safety policy
(B) A new office manager
(C) A conversion to an electronic database
(D) A directory of local health clinics

93. What is mentioned as an advantage of the change?

(A) There will be more free space.
(B) Information will be protected.
(C) There will be fewer accidents.
(D) Productivity will be increased.

94. What has the office manager been asked to do?

(A) Arrange for medical checkups
(B) Send patient records
(C) Contact a document-disposal company
(D) Create an employee evaluation form

Informational Sessions	
Monday	Advanced Computer Skills Course
Tuesday	Best Accounting Software Programs
Wednesday	Popular Social Networking Sites
Thursday	Effective Employee Motivation Techniques

95. Which department does the speaker most likely work in?

(A) Information Technology
(B) Marketing
(C) Accounting
(D) Human Resources

96. Look at the graphic. When are the listeners encouraged to attend a session?

(A) Monday
(B) Tuesday
(C) Wednesday
(D) Thursday

97. What will participants receive at every session?

(A) A free meal
(B) A certificate
(C) A bonus
(D) A survey form

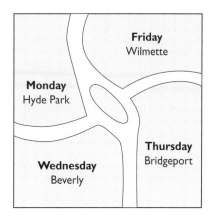

98. Where does the speaker most likely work?

(A) At a vehicle rental agency
(B) At a dental clinic
(C) At a recycling company
(D) At a public transportation service

99. Look at the graphic. Which neighborhood will be affected by a schedule change?

(A) Hyde Park
(B) Beverly
(C) Bridgeport
(D) Wilmette

100. What does the speaker hope to purchase?

(A) New machinery
(B) Packaging boxes
(C) A larger warehouse
(D) More advertising space

This is the end of the Listening test.

LISTENING TEST

In the Listening test, you will be asked to demonstrate how well you understand spoken English. The entire Listening test will last approximately 45 minutes. There are four parts, and directions are given for each part. You must mark your answers on the separate answer sheet. Do not write your answers in your test book.

PART 1

Directions: For each question in this part, you will hear four statements about a picture in your test book. When you hear the statements, you must select the one statement that best describes what you see in the picture. Then find the number of the question on your answer sheet and mark your answer. The statements will not be printed in your test book and will be spoken only one time.

Statement (B), "A man is pointing at a document," is the best description of the picture, so you should select answer (B) and mark it on your answer sheet.

1.

2.

GO ON TO THE NEXT PAGE

3.

4.

5.

6.

GO ON TO THE NEXT PAGE ➡

PART 2

Directions: You will hear a question or statement and three responses spoken in English. They will not be printed in your test book and will be spoken only one time. Select the best response to the question or statement and mark the letter (A), (B), or (C) on your answer sheet.

7. Mark your answer on your answer sheet.

8. Mark your answer on your answer sheet.

9. Mark your answer on your answer sheet.

10. Mark your answer on your answer sheet.

11. Mark your answer on your answer sheet.

12. Mark your answer on your answer sheet.

13. Mark your answer on your answer sheet.

14. Mark your answer on your answer sheet.

15. Mark your answer on your answer sheet.

16. Mark your answer on your answer sheet.

17. Mark your answer on your answer sheet.

18. Mark your answer on your answer sheet.

19. Mark your answer on your answer sheet.

20. Mark your answer on your answer sheet.

21. Mark your answer on your answer sheet.

22. Mark your answer on your answer sheet.

23. Mark your answer on your answer sheet.

24. Mark your answer on your answer sheet.

25. Mark your answer on your answer sheet.

26. Mark your answer on your answer sheet.

27. Mark your answer on your answer sheet.

28. Mark your answer on your answer sheet.

29. Mark your answer on your answer sheet.

30. Mark your answer on your answer sheet.

31. Mark your answer on your answer sheet.

PART 3

Directions: You will hear some conversations between two or more people. You will be asked to answer three questions about what the speakers say in each conversation. Select the best response to each question and mark the letter (A), (B), (C), or (D) on your answer sheet. The conversations will not be printed in your test book and will be spoken only one time.

32. Where does the conversation probably take place?

(A) At a health clinic
(B) At a hotel
(C) At a restaurant
(D) At a law firm

33. Why does the man apologize?

(A) An invoice is incorrect.
(B) Some data was not saved.
(C) There are no more parking spaces.
(D) A product is defective.

34. What does the man encourage the woman to pick up?

(A) A parking permit
(B) A magazine
(C) Some forms
(D) Some refreshments

35. What does the man mention about the Telco Complex?

(A) It offers cheap rental rates.
(B) It is in a quiet neighborhood.
(C) It offers a free parking space.
(D) It is conveniently located.

36. What does the woman say she has done?

(A) She has purchased a vehicle.
(B) She has scheduled a meeting.
(C) She has quit her current job.
(D) She has contacted a relocation firm.

37. What does the man invite the woman to?

(A) A store opening
(B) A cooking contest
(C) A building tour
(D) A lunch gathering

38. Why did the man call the meeting?

(A) To discuss a budget report
(B) To give a new employee orientation
(C) To come up with some solutions
(D) To go over a revised policy

39. What will probably change at the business?

(A) A brochure
(B) A Web site
(C) Some operating hours
(D) Some devices

40. What will the man do next?

(A) Submit a payment
(B) Make an appointment
(C) Review some applications
(D) Install some equipment

41. What most likely is the woman's profession?

(A) Journalist
(B) Interior designer
(C) Software technician
(D) Realtor

42. Why does the woman say, "The work here will take me all day"?

(A) To turn down a request
(B) To approve a plan
(C) To volunteer for an assignment
(D) To ask for an extension

43. What does the man say he will do?

(A) Go to an office
(B) Purchase more supplies
(C) Check a colleague's schedule
(D) Contact a client

GO ON TO THE NEXT PAGE

44. What did the woman recently do?

(A) Registered at a fitness center
(B) Exchanged a defective product
(C) Taught a business course
(D) Canceled enrollment in a class

45. What has caused a delay?

(A) A name was missing.
(B) A system malfunctioned.
(C) A form was incomplete.
(D) A payment was not made.

46. What does the man suggest?

(A) Signing up for another class
(B) Reading a manual
(C) Checking a Web site
(D) Coming back at a later time

47. What was the topic of the woman's lecture?

(A) Web site designs
(B) Vacation spots
(C) Self-publishing
(D) Popular books

48. What problem did the man have during the lecture?

(A) He had trouble finding a seat.
(B) He did not understand some material.
(C) He could not ask any questions.
(D) He was not able to write down some information.

49. What does the woman say she will send to attendees?

(A) Links to some Web sites
(B) A survey form
(C) A list of future events
(D) A copy of some slides

50. What kind of business does the woman work at?

(A) A utility company
(B) An appliance manufacturer
(C) An auto shop
(D) A catering business

51. What does the woman say the business is known for?

(A) Its affordable pricing
(B) Its helpful employees
(C) Its wide collection
(D) Its durable products

52. What problem does the man mention?

(A) Some merchandise is damaged.
(B) An item is missing.
(C) An extra fee has been charged.
(D) Some boxes are too heavy to transport.

53. Where does the woman probably work?

(A) At a party decoration shop
(B) At a packaging plant
(C) At a café
(D) At a hotel

54. Why does the man say, "Gallagher's Tavern's cheapest bottle is $25"?

(A) To correct a mistake
(B) To compliment a service
(C) To recommend an item
(D) To request a discount

55. How does the woman offer to assist the man?

(A) By refunding his purchase
(B) By letting him sample a product
(C) By reserving some merchandise
(D) By talking to a supervisor

56. What is the man asking for?

(A) Some job descriptions
(B) An increase in his salary
(C) More funds for a project
(D) Some time off from work

57. What is the woman concerned about?

(A) Achieving a sales target
(B) Impressing an important client
(C) Meeting a project deadline
(D) Recruiting skilled employees

58. What does the man say he can do?

(A) Accept additional assignments
(B) Train more staff members
(C) Post a vacation schedule
(D) Contact the human resources manager

59. What industry do the speakers most likely work in?

(A) Jewelry
(B) Healthcare
(C) Journalism
(D) Marketing

60. What is the problem?

(A) Some descriptions are inaccurate.
(B) An image is missing.
(C) A design is not good.
(D) Some materials were damaged.

61. What does the woman promise to do by the end of today?

(A) Install a program
(B) Create a new draft
(C) Send an invoice
(D) Call a business

Winter Suits		
Manufacturer: Groenlandia Ltd.	p. 3	
Sweater Vests		
Manufacturer: La Lluvia	p. 6	
Padded Jackets		
Manufacturer: Allons Co.	p. 9	
Long Coats		
Manufacturer: Cara Norte	p. 11	

62. What most likely is the man's job?

(A) Computer programmer
(B) Fashion designer
(C) Sales representative
(D) Personal trainer

63. Look at the graphic. Which manufacturer does the woman say she likes?

(A) Groenlandia Ltd.
(B) La Lluvia
(C) Allons Co.
(D) Cara Norte

64. What does the man offer to do?

(A) Provide a coupon
(B) Print a catalog
(C) Call a different branch
(D) Search a system

GO ON TO THE NEXT PAGE

Custom USB Flash Drives	
1 GB Memory	$5.25
2 GB Memory	$5.75
4 GB Memory	$6.00
8 GB Memory	$6.50

Arriving From	Time	Status
Dalian	2:30 P.M.	Arrived
Tianjin	2:55 P.M.	Arrived
Fukuoka	3:25 P.M.	On schedule
Vladivostok	3:40 P.M.	Delayed

65. What does the woman plan to do with the flash drives?

(A) Display them at a shop
(B) Send them to her friends
(C) Sell them to some clients
(D) Give them to event guests

66. Look at the graphic. Which memory capacity does the woman decide to choose?

(A) 1 GB
(B) 2 GB
(C) 4 GB
(D) 8 GB

67. What does the man suggest?

(A) Calling another store
(B) Selecting a different product
(C) Adjusting the quantity of an order
(D) Revising a budget

68. Look at the graphic. Which city is Michelle Funakoshi traveling from?

(A) Dalian
(B) Tianjin
(C) Fukuoka
(D) Vladivostok

69. According to the woman, why should the speakers leave soon?

(A) A highway is inaccessible.
(B) Tickets must be bought in advance.
(C) A store will be closing within the hour.
(D) The port is undergoing construction.

70. What does the man suggest doing while they wait?

(A) Going over a presentation
(B) Touring a facility
(C) Checking a map
(D) Getting a beverage

PART 4

Directions: You will hear some talks given by a single speaker. You will be asked to answer three questions about what the speaker says in each talk. Select the best response to each question and mark the letter (A), (B), (C), or (D) on your answer sheet. The talks will not be printed in your test book and will be spoken only one time.

71. Why is the speaker contacting the listener?

(A) To arrange a transportation service
(B) To check a client's schedule
(C) To postpone an appointment
(D) To discuss a job advertisement

72. What is the speaker doing tomorrow afternoon?

(A) Filming a commercial
(B) Going on a business trip
(C) Holding a training session for new employees
(D) Sharing information about some projects

73. What does the speaker recommend that the listener do?

(A) Contact a business
(B) Book a larger conference room
(C) Speak to another coworker
(D) Register for a marketing class

74. What industry does Mr. Sawada work in?

(A) Information Technology
(B) Healthcare
(C) Engineering
(D) Finance

75. What main accomplishment is Mr. Sawada recognized for?

(A) Making financial donations
(B) Improving work conditions
(C) Revising a national curriculum
(D) Developing a computer program

76. According to the speaker, what will Mr. Sawada do next?

(A) Provide a demonstration
(B) Tour a building
(C) Present an award
(D) Attend a book signing

77. What does the speaker imply when he says, "there seems to be a lot of construction on the highway"?

(A) He is going to take public transportation.
(B) He wants to change a project location.
(C) He will arrive late to a meeting.
(D) He is unable to hear the listener's message.

78. What will the speaker send to the listener?

(A) A list of participants
(B) A proposal
(C) An invoice
(D) Directions to an office

79. What does the speaker want Jeanell to do?

(A) Prepare a report
(B) Contact a client
(C) Conduct some training
(D) Transfer some money

80. What product is being advertised?

(A) A software program
(B) A video recorder
(C) A mobile phone
(D) A laptop computer

81. What does the speaker say is special about the product?

(A) It has an extended warranty.
(B) It supports any language.
(C) It includes instructional material.
(D) It can be custom-made.

82. Why should listeners visit a Web site?

(A) To order a product
(B) To sign up for a lesson
(C) To download a user guide
(D) To read customer testimonials

GO ON TO THE NEXT PAGE

83. Who most likely are the listeners?

(A) Job recruiters
(B) Event coordinators
(C) Financial advisors
(D) Local reporters

84. What does the speaker imply when she says, "the application deadline is at the end of the month"?

(A) She is planning to extend a deadline.
(B) She does not want the listeners to worry.
(C) Some guidelines need to be revised.
(D) Some fees have not been received.

85. Why should the listeners talk to the speaker after the meeting?

(A) To borrow some materials
(B) To submit a payment
(C) To join a project group
(D) To decide on some menu items

86. Where most likely is the talk being given?

(A) At a training session
(B) At a company dinner
(C) At a job fair
(D) At a sales meeting

87. What does the speaker say is broken?

(A) A phone
(B) A speaker
(C) A camera
(D) A projector

88. What will the listeners do next?

(A) Give a presentation
(B) Obtain identification badges
(C) Report to their managers
(D) Enter some data

89. What does the man imply when he says, "Who can say how long that will take"?

(A) He wants the exact completion date of a project.
(B) He is requesting suggestions from the listeners.
(C) He would like staff members to work more hours.
(D) He does not know when a merger will be finalized.

90. What is the subject of the meeting?

(A) Expanding a product line
(B) Opening a new store
(C) Increasing profits
(D) Finding a different supplier

91. What does the man say he will make some time to do?

(A) Visit various branches
(B) Conduct individual meetings
(C) Revise some legal documents
(D) Contact a Dos Mundos employee

92. What was recently authorized?

(A) The construction of some residential buildings
(B) The opening of a community library
(C) The extension of some subway lines
(D) The restoration of a historic museum

93. According to the speaker, what is an advantage of a location?

(A) The area is quiet.
(B) A fitness facility is nearby.
(C) There are many parking spaces.
(D) The scenery is beautiful.

94. Why are listeners encouraged to visit a Web site?

(A) To sign up for a membership
(B) To watch a video
(C) To fill out a survey
(D) To download some files

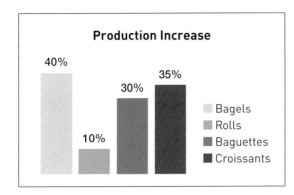

Production Increase

Bagels 40%
Rolls 10%
Baguettes 30%
Croissants 35%

Nutrition Facts

Serving size - 1 Bar	
Calories 180	

Sodium - 210mg	
Fiber - 8g	
Sugar - 25g	
Potassium - 150mg	

95. Who is the message for?

    (A) A bakery manager
    (B) A warehouse supervisor
    (C) A machinery salesperson
    (D) A food importer

96. Look at the graphic. Which product's production does the speaker mention?

    (A) Bagels
    (B) Rolls
    (C) Baguettes
    (D) Croissants

97. What will happen at the end of the month?

    (A) Building renovation will start.
    (B) New products will be offered.
    (C) A special offer will expire.
    (D) A demonstration will be given.

98. What is the main purpose of the meeting?

    (A) To introduce a new employee
    (B) To discuss the sales of a product
    (C) To announce the building of a new plant
    (D) To describe a manufacturing process

99. What type of business is Fresh and Good?

    (A) A grocery store
    (B) A restaurant
    (C) A local farm
    (D) A food manufacturer

100. Look at the graphic. Which of the ingredients does the speaker say needs to be reduced?

    (A) Sodium
    (B) Fiber
    (C) Sugar
    (D) Potassium

TEST 6

This is the end of the Listening test.

ST 7

LISTENING TEST

In the Listening test, you will be asked to demonstrate how well you understand spoken English. The entire Listening test will last approximately 45 minutes. There are four parts, and directions are given for each part. You must mark your answers on the separate answer sheet. Do not write your answers in your test book.

PART 1

Directions: For each question in this part, you will hear four statements about a picture in your test book. When you hear the statements, you must select the one statement that best describes what you see in the picture. Then find the number of the question on your answer sheet and mark your answer. The statements will not be printed in your test book and will be spoken only one time.

Statement (B), "A man is pointing at a document," is the best description of the picture, so you should select answer (B) and mark it on your answer sheet.

1.

2.

GO ON TO THE NEXT PAGE

TEST 7

3.

4.

5.

6.

GO ON TO THE NEXT PAGE ➡

PART 2

Directions: You will hear a question or statement and three responses spoken in English. They will not be printed in your test book and will be spoken only one time. Select the best response to the question or statement and mark the letter (A), (B), or (C) on your answer sheet.

7. Mark your answer on your answer sheet.

8. Mark your answer on your answer sheet.

9. Mark your answer on your answer sheet.

10. Mark your answer on your answer sheet.

11. Mark your answer on your answer sheet.

12. Mark your answer on your answer sheet.

13. Mark your answer on your answer sheet.

14. Mark your answer on your answer sheet.

15. Mark your answer on your answer sheet.

16. Mark your answer on your answer sheet.

17. Mark your answer on your answer sheet.

18. Mark your answer on your answer sheet.

19. Mark your answer on your answer sheet.

20. Mark your answer on your answer sheet.

21. Mark your answer on your answer sheet.

22. Mark your answer on your answer sheet.

23. Mark your answer on your answer sheet.

24. Mark your answer on your answer sheet.

25. Mark your answer on your answer sheet.

26. Mark your answer on your answer sheet.

27. Mark your answer on your answer sheet.

28. Mark your answer on your answer sheet.

29. Mark your answer on your answer sheet.

30. Mark your answer on your answer sheet.

31. Mark your answer on your answer sheet.

PART 3

Directions: You will hear some conversations between two or more people. You will be asked to answer three questions about what the speakers say in each conversation. Select the best response to each question and mark the letter (A), (B), (C), or (D) on your answer sheet. The conversations will not be printed in your test book and will be spoken only one time.

32. What would the man like to do tomorrow?
    (A) Leave the office early
    (B) Speak to a client
    (C) Work from home
    (D) Make a presentation

33. What is the woman concerned about?
    (A) Losing customers
    (B) Submitting work late
    (C) Holding a conference
    (D) Finding some paperwork

34. What does the woman say will happen next week?
    (A) A business will open.
    (B) A proposal will be given.
    (C) A machine will be installed.
    (D) A new employee will be hired.

35. What most likely is the woman's job?
    (A) Travel agent
    (B) Bus driver
    (C) Telephone operator
    (D) Hotel clerk

36. What does the man ask the woman to do?
    (A) Direct him to a tour company
    (B) Make a lunch reservation for him
    (C) Take a message for him
    (D) Move him to a larger room

37. What does the woman offer to do?
    (A) Arrange transportation
    (B) Ask for directions
    (C) Purchase a ticket
    (D) Inquire about a schedule

38. What would the woman like the man to do?
    (A) Give a demonstration
    (B) Revise some designs
    (C) Fix some machines
    (D) Visit an office

39. Why is the woman unavailable on Friday?
    (A) She will be meeting her parents.
    (B) She will be on a business trip.
    (C) She will be getting a medical check-up.
    (D) She will be leaving on vacation.

40. What does the man remind the woman to do?
    (A) Print out a map
    (B) Review an invoice
    (C) Arrive before a certain time
    (D) Talk to a store manager

41. What does the woman say will happen today?
    (A) Kitchen appliances will be installed.
    (B) A corporate event will take place.
    (C) Repair work will begin.
    (D) A plant inspection will be performed.

42. What is the woman worried about?
    (A) Losing customers
    (B) Spending more money
    (C) Delayed shipments
    (D) Power outages

43. What does the man offer to do?
    (A) Contact some customers
    (B) Work additional hours
    (C) Order some supplies
    (D) Display a sign

GO ON TO THE NEXT PAGE

44. What is the main topic of the conversation?

(A) Arranging travel accommodations
(B) Changing an event coordinator
(C) Planning a musical performance
(D) Selecting a better venue

45. What does Donna instruct the man to do?

(A) Meet with some clients
(B) Conduct some research
(C) Monitor a budget
(D) Review a floor plan

46. What does Donna say she looks forward to?

(A) Going on international business trips
(B) Managing a new team
(C) Working on a promotional campaign
(D) Receiving an award

47. Who most likely is the man?

(A) An insurance agent
(B) A receptionist
(C) A cleaning worker
(D) A technician

48. Why did the woman visit the office?

(A) To make a delivery
(B) To complete an application
(C) To submit a payment
(D) To visit a colleague

49. What does the man mean when he says, "Ms. Dorsett has just stepped out for lunch"?

(A) He will order some lunch.
(B) Ms. Dorsett is unavailable.
(C) Ms. Dorsett forgot about an appointment.
(D) A meeting must be postponed.

50. Why does the man apologize to the woman?

(A) He did not respond to a telephone message.
(B) He is not able to complete a project on time.
(C) He will be late for a meeting.
(D) He submitted the wrong document.

51. What must be ready by Tuesday?

(A) An employee questionnaire
(B) An expense report
(C) A client presentation
(D) A flight itinerary

52. What does the woman request that the man do?

(A) Pick up a customer
(B) Collaborate with a colleague
(C) Reserve a meeting room
(D) Hire a consultant

53. What did the man recently do?

(A) He returned from his vacation.
(B) He moved to a new city.
(C) He purchased swimming gear.
(D) He started working at a new company.

54. What does the woman mean when she says, "I think that should be OK"?

(A) A membership fee will be discounted.
(B) A schedule can be adjusted.
(C) The man can pay by credit card.
(D) The man will be able to upgrade his service.

55. What will the man probably do next?

(A) Email the woman a file
(B) Sign up for some classes
(C) Provide some information
(D) Look around a facility

56. What upcoming event are the speakers talking about?

(A) A business trip
(B) A retirement celebration
(C) A holiday party
(D) A board meeting

57. What problem occurred last year?

(A) Some documents were lost.
(B) Some equipment was damaged.
(C) A reservation was lost.
(D) A budget was exceeded.

58. What does Michael say he will do?

(A) Make a deposit
(B) Conduct some research
(C) Contact a manager
(D) Review some itineraries

---

59. What change does the woman suggest?

(A) Renovating a Web site
(B) Ordering from another company
(C) Hiring additional workers
(D) Lowering some prices

60. What does the man mean when he says, "that doesn't really apply to us"?

(A) A service fee cannot be waived.
(B) An item cannot be shipped.
(C) A coupon cannot be used.
(D) A policy cannot be changed.

61. What might staff be asked to do?

(A) Fill out forms in advance
(B) Purchase less than usual
(C) Make deliveries
(D) Train employees

Train Timetable

	Hemsforth	Bertiz	Faverton	Poly
XB10 Train	2:20 P.M.	2:50 P.M.		3:40 P.M.
XB20 Train	2:50 P.M.	3:05 P.M.	3:20 P.M.	

62. What is the woman's problem?

(A) An express train has just departed.
(B) A train is experiencing mechanical issues.
(C) She brought an expired train ticket.
(D) She boarded the wrong train.

63. Look at the graphic. At which station should the woman transfer?

(A) Hemsforth
(B) Bertiz
(C) Faverton
(D) Poly

64. Why is the woman in a hurry?

(A) She will be speaking at a conference.
(B) She is going to watch a performance.
(C) She needs to get on a train.
(D) She is interviewing for a job.

GO ON TO THE NEXT PAGE

Name	Award
1 **Stacey Roberts**	Investment Management
2 **Brian Lee**	Global Pension
3 **Richard Kim**	Corporate Finance
4 **Jamie Brown**	Real Estate

Discount Coupon

Order for 100 business cards → $5 OFF
Order for 200 business cards → $10 OFF
Order for 300 business cards → $15 OFF
Order for 400 business cards → $20 OFF

65. Who is the man?

(A) An event planner
(B) An executive officer
(C) An awards presenter
(D) A job applicant

66. What is mentioned about the Reinheim Consulting Group?

(A) It is located overseas.
(B) It offers group sessions.
(C) It has a position open.
(D) It specializes in advertising.

67. Look at the graphic. Who most likely will the man talk to next?

(A) Stacey Roberts
(B) Brian Lee
(C) Richard Kim
(D) Jamie Brown

68. Why is the man calling?

(A) To reschedule a delivery
(B) To increase an order
(C) To apply for a membership card
(D) To inquire about an invoice

69. Where does the woman probably work?

(A) At a printing company
(B) At a flower shop
(C) At a bookstore
(D) At a bank

70. Look at the graphic. What discount will the man most likely receive?

(A) $5
(B) $10
(C) $15
(D) $20

PART 4

Directions: You will hear some talks given by a single speaker. You will be asked to answer three questions about what the speaker says in each talk. Select the best response to each question and mark the letter (A), (B), (C), or (D) on your answer sheet. The talks will not be printed in your test book and will be spoken only one time.

71. According to the speaker, what is scheduled for the afternoon?

(A) A store opening
(B) A road closure
(C) A sports event
(D) A musical performance

72. What does the speaker suggest for the people traveling to the city center?

(A) Sharing cars
(B) Allowing extra time
(C) Taking a detour
(D) Bringing an umbrella

73. Who is Michael Robinson?

(A) A news reporter
(B) A rock musician
(C) A financial expert
(D) A city official

74. Why does the speaker thank the listener?

(A) For attending a convention
(B) For opening up a business
(C) For submitting a payment
(D) For preparing a presentation

75. What does the speaker imply when he says, "I'm driving to the convention center now"?

(A) He does not know where to park.
(B) He cannot make it to a meeting on time.
(C) He is unable to take care of an issue.
(D) He needs to take an alternate route.

76. According to the speaker, what will happen in the afternoon?

(A) An order will be placed.
(B) A sale will start.
(C) Some devices will be installed.
(D) Some documents will be mailed.

77. What is the speaker discussing?

(A) Hiring a head chef
(B) Relocating a corporate office
(C) Changing a menu
(D) Renovating a diner

78. What does the speaker say Harold will help do?

(A) Train some kitchen workers
(B) Create some healthy recipes
(C) Manage a new restaurant location
(D) Find a different food supplier

79. According to the speaker, what is the purpose of the change?

(A) To retain current personnel
(B) To lower business expenses
(C) To improve employee morale
(D) To bring in more customers

80. What problem is the speaker addressing?

(A) Some project deadlines will not be met.
(B) A contract has not been finalized.
(C) Some time-recording information is out of date.
(D) A client account has been terminated.

81. What are listeners instructed to do?

(A) Correct their timesheets
(B) Meet their clients
(C) Remove current software
(D) Use new passwords

82. Why should listeners contact Perry Kay?

(A) To resolve customer complaints
(B) To update contact information
(C) To request a code
(D) To submit a proposal

GO ON TO THE NEXT PAGE

83. Where is the introduction taking place?

(A) At a fundraising banquet
(B) At a professional conference
(C) At a training seminar
(D) At an awards ceremony

84. Who is Charlene Young?

(A) A human resources manager
(B) A chief executive officer
(C) An environmental engineer
(D) An event organizer

85. What does the speaker mean when she says, "compliments of Barry's Corner"?

(A) Beverages were supplied by a business.
(B) A company has received positive feedback.
(C) Food was catered by a restaurant.
(D) A demonstration was given by an organization.

86. What has the company recently done?

(A) Bought new equipment
(B) Received customer feedback
(C) Recruited more employees
(D) Updated a computer system

87. What does the speaker say was surprising?

(A) Complaints about a product
(B) Costs of delivery
(C) Forecasts of sales
(D) Advancements in technology

88. What does the speaker ask Brian to do?

(A) Complete a questionnaire
(B) Lead a group
(C) Try out a product
(D) Visit a store

89. What is being advertised?

(A) A digital camera
(B) A fitness watch
(C) A computer
(D) A television

90. What does the speaker emphasize about the product?

(A) It is colorful.
(B) It is affordable.
(C) It is lightweight.
(D) It is durable.

91. Why should the listeners visit a Web site?

(A) To check out user reviews
(B) To reserve an item
(C) To find a store location
(D) To obtain a discount voucher

92. What industry is the speaker reporting on?

(A) Hospitality
(B) Construction
(C) Finance
(D) Agriculture

93. According to the speaker, what benefit will the project provide to the public?

(A) Access to cheaper products
(B) Better financing options
(C) More job openings
(D) Improvement of public health

94. What does the speaker imply when she says, "this is an enormous task"?

(A) A budget should be adjusted.
(B) More workers should be hired.
(C) Extra time may be needed.
(D) A larger venue may be required.

Sushi Heaven

Private parties welcome!
Book a banquet hall for 5 hours!

20% discount for groups of 20 or more!

Offer valid at all Sushi Heaven locations
until October 21.

Bus 909 Timetable	
Union Drive	12:10 P.M.
Market Lane	12:25 P.M.
Oakwood Avenue	12:40 P.M.
Orchard Road	12:55 P.M.

95. Why is the event being held?

(A) To reward some employees
(B) To mark a company's anniversary
(C) To welcome new staff
(D) To celebrate an office relocation

96. Look at the graphic. Why is the speaker unable to use the coupon for the event?

(A) The coupon does not apply to large groups.
(B) The coupon will expire before the event takes place.
(C) The event will run longer than anticipated.
(D) The event will be held on the weekend.

97. What does the speaker want the listener to do?

(A) Decide on a venue
(B) Provide a meal preference
(C) Make a deposit
(D) Create a list

98. Who most likely is the speaker?

(A) A career advisor
(B) A construction manager
(C) A public transportation official
(D) A real estate agent

99. What does the speaker remind the listener to do?

(A) Sign a document
(B) Retrieve an item
(C) Review a reservation
(D) Make a deposit

100. Look at the graphic. When would the listener board the bus?

(A) 12:10 P.M.
(B) 12:25 P.M.
(C) 12:40 P.M.
(D) 12:55 P.M.

LISTENING TEST

In the Listening test, you will be asked to demonstrate how well you understand spoken English. The entire Listening test will last approximately 45 minutes. There are four parts, and directions are given for each part. You must mark your answers on the separate answer sheet. Do not write your answers in your test book.

PART 1

Directions: For each question in this part, you will hear four statements about a picture in your test book. When you hear the statements, you must select the one statement that best describes what you see in the picture. Then find the number of the question on your answer sheet and mark your answer. The statements will not be printed in your test book and will be spoken only one time.

Statement (B), "A man is pointing at a document," is the best description of the picture, so you should select answer (B) and mark it on your answer sheet.

1.

2.

GO ON TO THE NEXT PAGE ➡

TEST 8

3.

4.

5.

6.

GO ON TO THE NEXT PAGE

TEST 8

PART 2

Directions: You will hear a question or statement and three responses spoken in English. They will not be printed in your test book and will be spoken only one time. Select the best response to the question or statement and mark the letter (A), (B), or (C) on your answer sheet.

7. Mark your answer on your answer sheet.

8. Mark your answer on your answer sheet.

9. Mark your answer on your answer sheet.

10. Mark your answer on your answer sheet.

11. Mark your answer on your answer sheet.

12. Mark your answer on your answer sheet.

13. Mark your answer on your answer sheet.

14. Mark your answer on your answer sheet.

15. Mark your answer on your answer sheet.

16. Mark your answer on your answer sheet.

17. Mark your answer on your answer sheet.

18. Mark your answer on your answer sheet.

19. Mark your answer on your answer sheet.

20. Mark your answer on your answer sheet.

21. Mark your answer on your answer sheet.

22. Mark your answer on your answer sheet.

23. Mark your answer on your answer sheet.

24. Mark your answer on your answer sheet.

25. Mark your answer on your answer sheet.

26. Mark your answer on your answer sheet.

27. Mark your answer on your answer sheet.

28. Mark your answer on your answer sheet.

29. Mark your answer on your answer sheet.

30. Mark your answer on your answer sheet.

31. Mark your answer on your answer sheet.

PART 3

Directions: You will hear some conversations between two or more people. You will be asked to answer three questions about what the speakers say in each conversation. Select the best response to each question and mark the letter (A), (B), (C), or (D) on your answer sheet. The conversations will not be printed in your test book and will be spoken only one time.

32. What kind of business do the speakers most likely work for?

(A) A public library
(B) An architecture firm
(C) A printing shop
(D) A history museum

33. What problem is being discussed?

(A) Some supplies are running low.
(B) Some paperwork is missing.
(C) Some glass is dirty.
(D) Some expenses are too high.

34. What will the woman probably do next?

(A) Install some equipment
(B) Contact some businesses
(C) Review a budget
(D) Make a deposit

35. Why is the man calling?

(A) To inquire about a bill
(B) To report a gas leak
(C) To open an account
(D) To cancel a service

36. Why is the woman unable to help the man?

(A) He lost his password.
(B) He called the wrong department.
(C) The company's office is not open.
(D) A Web site is down.

37. What will the man probably do next?

(A) Visit a Web site
(B) Provide a confirmation number
(C) Call another company
(D) Complete an application

38. What does the man say has caused a problem?

(A) Some damaged machines
(B) Inclement weather
(C) Heavy traffic
(D) An old booking system

39. What is the woman planning to do tomorrow?

(A) Get a medical check-up
(B) Attend a seminar
(C) Fix a computer
(D) Visit a factory

40. Why does the man say, "there's a train that leaves at 8 o'clock"?

(A) To recommend an alternative choice
(B) To provide a seat upgrade
(C) To offer an explanation for a delay
(D) To point out an error

41. Where is the man calling from?

(A) An apartment management office
(B) A hotel front desk
(C) A furniture store
(D) A construction company

42. What problem are the speakers discussing?

(A) A water leak
(B) A reservation error
(C) Some missing orders
(D) Some defective cables

43. What does the woman request?

(A) An exchange for a product
(B) A discount on a service
(C) A list of replacement parts
(D) An inspection for damage

GO ON TO THE NEXT PAGE

44. What does the man want to purchase?

(A) Gym equipment
(B) Office supplies
(C) Advertising space
(D) Promotional clothing

45. How can the man receive a discount?

(A) By subscribing to a magazine
(B) By placing a large order
(C) By signing up for a membership
(D) By paying in cash

46. What does the woman tell the man to do?

(A) Visit another location
(B) Speak to a supervisor
(C) Go to a Web site
(D) Check out a sample

47. What is the company's plan?

(A) To increase energy efficiency
(B) To reduce travel expenses
(C) To open an overseas branch
(D) To elect new board members

48. What is the woman considering?

(A) Submitting a proposal
(B) Contacting an organizer
(C) Joining a committee
(D) Performing a survey

49. Why is the man unable to attend the meeting?

(A) He is picking up a client.
(B) He is giving a presentation.
(C) He is training an employee.
(D) He is going on a vacation.

50. What type of event are the speakers discussing?

(A) A music festival
(B) A gallery opening
(C) A business seminar
(D) A company party

51. What does the woman ask the man to do?

(A) Transport some equipment
(B) Reserve a reception hall
(C) Set up some tables
(D) Contact a band

52. What does the man say he has to do Sunday morning?

(A) Practice a musical instrument
(B) Attend a sporting event
(C) Work extra hours
(D) Get his car repaired

53. Who most likely are Mr. Anderson and Ms. Walsh?

(A) Real estate agents
(B) Business owners
(C) Construction workers
(D) City officials

54. What are Mr. Anderson and Ms. Walsh concerned about?

(A) Paying for major renovations
(B) Attracting more clients
(C) The size of an office space
(D) The date of a move

55. What is mentioned about the landlord?

(A) He will meet the speakers tomorrow.
(B) He will negotiate a price.
(C) He is currently on a business trip.
(D) He is relocating overseas.

56. What industry do the speakers most likely work in?

(A) Clothing manufacturing
(B) Event organizing
(C) Equipment sales
(D) Food production

57. What problem are the speakers discussing?

(A) A customer complaint was received.
(B) The quality of a product is poor.
(C) Some tools have not been cleaned.
(D) More workers are needed.

58. What does the man suggest?

(A) Lowering prices
(B) Informing a manager
(C) Discarding some materials
(D) Replacing a machine

59. Who is visiting the company?

(A) A property manager
(B) A local journalist
(C) A government employee
(D) An overseas client

60. Why does the man say, "I'm leading a workshop all day on Friday"?

(A) He is unable to take on a task.
(B) He would like some help with an event.
(C) He would like an updated guest list.
(D) He is concerned about giving a presentation.

61. According to the woman, what does the company hope to do by the end of the year?

(A) Transfer some workers
(B) Launch a product line
(C) Build another facility
(D) Appoint a new CEO

Mallie's Place

Dessert Deals for May

Strawberry Pie – 10% OFF

Vanilla Ice Cream – 20% OFF

Chocolate Cake – 30% OFF

Banana Pudding – 40% OFF

62. What information does the woman share with the man?

(A) A product will be launched early.
(B) A managers' meeting will be held.
(C) A contract will be awarded soon.
(D) A colleague will be transferred.

63. Look at the graphic. Which discount will the speakers most likely receive?

(A) 10%
(B) 20%
(C) 30%
(D) 40%

64. What does the man offer to do?

(A) Update a calendar
(B) Contact a different café
(C) Make a reservation
(D) Rent a vehicle

GO ON TO THE NEXT PAGE

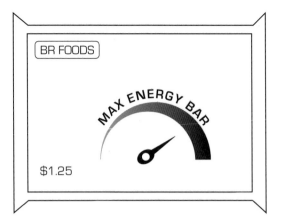

BR FOODS

MAX ENERGY BAR

$1.25

HEALTH AWARENESS WEEK

Only open to LCO Employees
Free Admission!

Mon	Tue	Wed	Thu	Fri
Medical Consultations	Nutrition Seminar	Cooking Class	Farm Visit	Well-being Lunch

65. What does the woman say is the target market for Max Energy Bar?

(A) Food experts
(B) Traveling workers
(C) Fitness enthusiasts
(D) Senior citizens

66. Look at the graphic. What will be displayed at the top of the bar wrapper after a change?

(A) The firm's logo
(B) The product's name
(C) The energy meter
(D) The price

67. What is scheduled for next week?

(A) An industry convention
(B) A store opening
(C) A client visit
(D) A sales event

68. What does the woman say is new about the Health Awareness Week this year?

(A) A contest will be held.
(B) A movie will be shown to staff.
(C) Presents will be provided to staff.
(D) Celebrities will be signing autographs.

69. Look at the graphic. Which event will the woman probably attend?

(A) The medical consultations
(B) The nutrition seminar
(C) The cooking class
(D) The farm visit

70. What does the man ask the woman to do?

(A) Contact some department managers
(B) Review an order form
(C) Complete a questionnaire
(D) Distribute some materials

PART 4

Directions: You will hear some talks given by a single speaker. You will be asked to answer three questions about what the speaker says in each talk. Select the best response to each question and mark the letter (A), (B), (C), or (D) on your answer sheet. The talks will not be printed in your test book and will be spoken only one time.

71. Who is the intended audience for the talk?

(A) Sales staff members
(B) Delivery drivers
(C) Factory employees
(D) Security guards

72. What is mentioned as an advantage of the new machines?

(A) They work faster.
(B) They seldom malfunction.
(C) They are reasonably priced.
(D) They are energy-efficient.

73. What is the speaker about to do?

(A) Give a demonstration
(B) Place an order
(C) Attend a meeting
(D) Call a supplier

74. Which department in Culliver Hills recorded the message?

(A) Health
(B) Transportation
(C) Parks and Recreation
(D) Planning and Development

75. According to the message, why is a procedure taking longer to complete?

(A) More applications are being received.
(B) A community center is being renovated.
(C) There has been a shortage of workers.
(D) There has been inclement weather.

76. What does the speaker ask the listeners to do?

(A) Meet with a city official
(B) Submit a payment
(C) Present a photo ID
(D) Include a detailed description

77. What does the speaker imply when she says, "you won't be late for any of your appointments"?

(A) Appointments must be canceled in advance.
(B) Some members have complained.
(C) Workers should come to work on time.
(D) A meeting will be short.

78. What does the speaker say happened on Monday?

(A) An expert examined a business.
(B) A fitness center closed early.
(C) A promotional event was held.
(D) A new policy was announced.

79. According to the speaker, what will the listeners practice?

(A) Building customer relationships
(B) Selling some products
(C) Cooking healthy meals
(D) Installing exercise machines

80. What type of business do the listeners work for?

(A) A post office
(B) A stationery store
(C) A printing center
(D) A health clinic

81. According to the speaker, what is being changed?

(A) How work schedules are created
(B) How payments are processed
(C) How information is recorded
(D) How facilities are inspected

82. What will the listeners do next?

(A) Fill out some forms
(B) Use some devices
(C) Watch a demonstration
(D) Read a user guide

GO ON TO THE NEXT PAGE

TEST 8

TEST 8   131

83. What type of event is taking place?

(A) A business opening
(B) A product launch
(C) A marketing presentation
(D) A retirement party

84. Why was the event delayed?

(A) Some devices were not working.
(B) A speaker arrived late.
(C) A facility was being cleaned.
(D) Some bad weather was approaching.

85. What does the speaker imply when she says, "I have extras here in the front"?

(A) Some listeners should pick up a document.
(B) Complimentary beverages are available.
(C) Tickets will be given away.
(D) Attendees should return some merchandise.

86. What is the purpose of the announcement?

(A) To describe a new printer
(B) To outline safety regulations
(C) To announce an upcoming inspection
(D) To share some sales figures

87. What benefit does the speaker mention?

(A) Less maintenance work
(B) Increased sales
(C) Reduced damage to the environment
(D) Greater morale among employees

88. According to the speaker, why have two training sessions been scheduled?

(A) To ensure sufficient practice time
(B) To accommodate all employees
(C) To meet a project deadline
(D) To comply with company policy

89. Why does the speaker apologize?

(A) A machine is not working.
(B) A presentation was canceled.
(C) A program was inaccurate.
(D) A registration procedure was confusing.

90. Who most likely is Mr. Griffin?

(A) An event organizer
(B) A financial advisor
(C) A building manager
(D) A newspaper journalist

91. What will Mr. Griffin discuss?

(A) Team management tips
(B) Public speaking skills
(C) Marketing trends
(D) Careful planning

92. Where do the listeners work?

(A) At a software company
(B) At a graphic design studio
(C) At a construction firm
(D) At a travel agency

93. According to the speaker, how can the listeners save money?

(A) By selecting an affordable distributor
(B) By hiring a foreign business partner
(C) By using fuel-efficient vehicles
(D) By holding online meetings

94. What does the speaker imply when she says, "Did everybody turn on their laptops"?

(A) She will update a system.
(B) She will demonstrate a product.
(C) Her laptop is not working.
(D) Her password is incorrect.

<table>
<tr><td colspan="2" align="center">Dress Shirt Styling</td></tr>
<tr><td align="center">Color: 6 choices</td><td align="center">Fabric: 3 choices</td></tr>
<tr><td>Blue   Indigo
Red   Yellow
Green   Purple</td><td align="center">Polyester
Cotton
Flannel</td></tr>
<tr><td align="center">Collar: 4 choices</td><td align="center">Sleeves: 2 choices</td></tr>
<tr><td>Classic   Mandarin
Spread   Pinned</td><td align="center">Long
Short</td></tr>
</table>

95. What is the speaker mainly discussing?

(A) Customer comments
(B) A delivery method
(C) A marketing strategy
(D) Sales figures

96. Look at the graphic. Which option quantity will increase in February?

(A) 6
(B) 3
(C) 4
(D) 2

97. What is the speaker concerned about?

(A) A Web site needs to be updated.
(B) Some employees have wrong information.
(C) Some items are getting damaged.
(D) A rival has launched a similar product.

<table>
<tr><td colspan="2" align="center">Customer order: BSA</td></tr>
<tr><td align="center">Order Item</td><td align="center">Total number</td></tr>
<tr><td>Hamburgers</td><td align="center">20</td></tr>
<tr><td>Chicken soup</td><td align="center">24</td></tr>
<tr><td>Bottled water</td><td align="center">20</td></tr>
<tr><td>Forks and spoons</td><td align="center">24</td></tr>
</table>

98. What kind of event is being held?

(A) A business conference
(B) An awards ceremony
(C) A graduation party
(D) A cooking demonstration

99. Look at the graphic. Which item on the order form will be removed?

(A) Hamburgers
(B) Chicken soup
(C) Bottled water
(D) Forks and spoons

100. What does the speaker ask the listener to do?

(A) Pick up a package
(B) Make a payment
(C) Update an invoice
(D) Give a speech

This is the end of the Listening test.

LISTENING TEST

In the Listening test, you will be asked to demonstrate how well you understand spoken English. The entire Listening test will last approximately 45 minutes. There are four parts, and directions are given for each part. You must mark your answers on the separate answer sheet. Do not write your answers in your test book.

PART 1

Directions: For each question in this part, you will hear four statements about a picture in your test book. When you hear the statements, you must select the one statement that best describes what you see in the picture. Then find the number of the question on your answer sheet and mark your answer. The statements will not be printed in your test book and will be spoken only one time.

Statement (B), "A man is pointing at a document," is the best description of the picture, so you should select answer (B) and mark it on your answer sheet.

1.

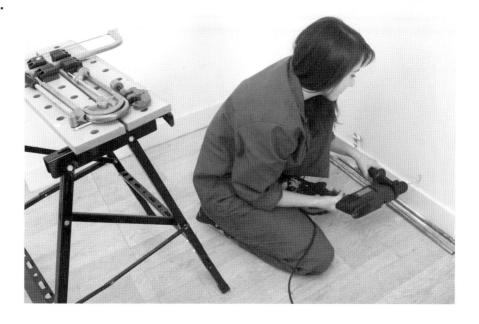

2.

GO ON TO THE NEXT PAGE ➡

3.

4.

5.

6.

GO ON TO THE NEXT PAGE ➡

PART 2

Directions: You will hear a question or statement and three responses spoken in English. They will not be printed in your test book and will be spoken only one time. Select the best response to the question or statement and mark the letter (A), (B), or (C) on your answer sheet.

7. Mark your answer on your answer sheet.

8. Mark your answer on your answer sheet.

9. Mark your answer on your answer sheet.

10. Mark your answer on your answer sheet.

11. Mark your answer on your answer sheet.

12. Mark your answer on your answer sheet.

13. Mark your answer on your answer sheet.

14. Mark your answer on your answer sheet.

15. Mark your answer on your answer sheet.

16. Mark your answer on your answer sheet.

17. Mark your answer on your answer sheet.

18. Mark your answer on your answer sheet.

19. Mark your answer on your answer sheet.

20. Mark your answer on your answer sheet.

21. Mark your answer on your answer sheet.

22. Mark your answer on your answer sheet.

23. Mark your answer on your answer sheet.

24. Mark your answer on your answer sheet.

25. Mark your answer on your answer sheet.

26. Mark your answer on your answer sheet.

27. Mark your answer on your answer sheet.

28. Mark your answer on your answer sheet.

29. Mark your answer on your answer sheet.

30. Mark your answer on your answer sheet.

31. Mark your answer on your answer sheet.

PART 3

Directions: You will hear some conversations between two or more people. You will be asked to answer three questions about what the speakers say in each conversation. Select the best response to each question and mark the letter (A), (B), (C), or (D) on your answer sheet. The conversations will not be printed in your test book and will be spoken only one time.

32. What does the man want to do at the art gallery?

(A) Register for a class
(B) Display a painting
(C) Meet an artist
(D) Volunteer for an event

33. What problem does the woman mention?

(A) A board is broken.
(B) A document is missing.
(C) A curator is not available.
(D) A room is not big enough.

34. What does the woman offer to do for the man?

(A) Refund a payment
(B) Order materials from a store
(C) Post a schedule
(D) Add his name to a list

35. What does the woman want to do?

(A) Use a computer
(B) Claim a package
(C) Book a room
(D) See a friend

36. Why most likely is the woman's name missing from the list?

(A) Her name was spelled incorrectly.
(B) Her subscription was canceled.
(C) She is a past employee.
(D) She is a new resident.

37. What does the man ask for?

(A) A contract
(B) An account number
(C) A photo identification
(D) A mailing address

38. What would the man like to purchase?

(A) Bathroom supplies
(B) Patio furniture
(C) A carpet
(D) A beverage machine

39. What does the woman suggest the man do?

(A) Select a different model
(B) Come back later
(C) Check some measurements
(D) Sign up for a payment plan

40. What does the man ask the woman about?

(A) The operation hours of a business
(B) The location of a store
(C) The length of an application process
(D) The details of a warranty

41. Where are the speakers?

(A) At an athletic competition
(B) At a technology convention
(C) At a music festival
(D) At a gallery opening

42. What is the man's problem?

(A) He missed an important event.
(B) He brought an expired credit card.
(C) He is unable to reach a manager.
(D) He misplaced a badge.

43. What does the manager ask the man to do?

(A) Submit an extra fee
(B) Refer to a map
(C) Sign some paperwork
(D) Return at another time

GO ON TO THE NEXT PAGE

44. What does the man require assistance with?

(A) Finding a language course
(B) Scheduling a business trip
(C) Preparing for a presentation
(D) Submitting a job application

45. Why is Yuriko Sugimoto unable to help immediately?

(A) She is working on another project.
(B) She is away on vacation.
(C) She has not received training.
(D) She is meeting a client.

46. What does the man want to know about Yuriko Sugimoto?

(A) The contact information of her references
(B) The arrival time of her flight
(C) Her hourly fee
(D) Details about her work experience

47. What does the woman say she is unsure about?

(A) Whether a message was received
(B) Whether a facility is available
(C) The arrangements for a meeting
(D) The length of a project

48. Why does the man apologize?

(A) He sent the woman incorrect information.
(B) He missed an important meeting.
(C) He did not contact the woman yesterday.
(D) He will not be able to meet a deadline.

49. What does the woman want to have for a meeting?

(A) A list of attendees
(B) A budget estimate
(C) A blueprint of a building
(D) An updated agenda

50. Why did Mr. Collins miss his consultation?

(A) He forgot to check a schedule.
(B) He woke up too late.
(C) He experienced some traffic.
(D) He had to finish an assignment.

51. What is mentioned about Ms. Feinstein?

(A) She went on vacation.
(B) She is a well-known lawyer.
(C) She will retire soon.
(D) She received a prize.

52. What will Mr. Workman do next?

(A) Review an agreement
(B) Fax some papers
(C) Give a tour
(D) Call some clients

53. Why is Mr. Hemsley calling?

(A) To arrange a recording session
(B) To ask for a document
(C) To reschedule an appointment
(D) To report an issue

54. What does Mr. Hemsley mean when he says, "someone is coming here for an interview in 10 minutes"?

(A) He will be temporarily unavailable.
(B) He requires assistance immediately.
(C) He is going to leave the office soon.
(D) He wants to reserve a conference room.

55. What does Mr. Hemsley say is unique about the interview?

(A) It will include a meeting with the CEO.
(B) It will be a group interview.
(C) It will include a luncheon.
(D) It will be done remotely.

56. What most likely is the man's job?

(A) Instructor
(B) Lawyer
(C) Architect
(D) Realtor

57. Why does the man want an office on the top floor?

(A) It is reasonably priced.
(B) It is quiet.
(C) It has the most space.
(D) It has a good view.

58. What benefit is mentioned?

(A) An office has been expanded recently.
(B) A complex has its own dining area.
(C) An office is fully furnished.
(D) A complex is in a convenient location.

59. Where is the conversation most likely taking place?

(A) At a factory
(B) At a restaurant
(C) At a clothing store
(D) At an advertising agency

60. What does Giselle imply when she says, "I'm meeting with them in our office in 20 minutes"?

(A) She has to print some documents.
(B) She is unable to participate in an event.
(C) She needs a larger meeting room.
(D) She will have an answer soon.

61. What may happen due to a delay?

(A) Some overtime could be required.
(B) Some training sessions could be held.
(C) A deadline could be extended.
(D) A new supplier could be hired.

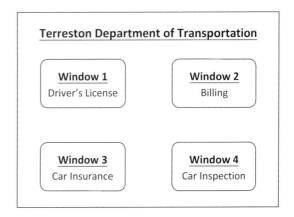

62. What is the woman surprised about?

(A) A wait time
(B) A sign-up fee
(C) Results of a car inspection
(D) The speed of a service

63. According to the woman, what will she do during the last week of May?

(A) Order some parts
(B) Enroll in a class
(C) Rent a vehicle
(D) Go on a business trip

64. Look at the graphic. Which window will the woman most likely go to next?

(A) Window 1
(B) Window 2
(C) Window 3
(D) Window 4

TEST 9

GO ON TO THE NEXT PAGE

AVAILABLE APARTMENT

3-Bedroom	3-Bedroom
(A)	(B)
$950/month	$900/month

2-Bedroom	2-Bedroom
(C)	(D)
$825/month	$750/month

www.employnet.com

Open positions

• **Brand Manager**	Some in-state travel
• **Marketing Manager**	Overseas business trips
• **Advertising Director**	Work at headquarters
• **Publicity Director**	Visit local regions

65. Why does the man say he is moving to Cerksville?

(A) He is opening his own store.
(B) He is being transferred to another office.
(C) He would like a more convenient commute.
(D) He wants to live closer to his family.

66. Look at the graphic. Which apartment is the man most interested in?

(A) Apartment A
(B) Apartment B
(C) Apartment C
(D) Apartment D

67. What will the speakers probably do next?

(A) Look over a rental contract
(B) Discuss parking options
(C) Set up an appointment
(D) Edit some blueprints

68. What does the woman like about her current job?

(A) The hours are flexible.
(B) Her boss is kind.
(C) It offers a good salary.
(D) It is in a convenient location.

69. Look at the graphic. Which position will the woman probably apply for?

(A) Brand Manager
(B) Marketing Manager
(C) Advertising Director
(D) Publicity Director

70. What does the man say he will do soon?

(A) Go on a trip
(B) Relocate to another team
(C) Accept a promotion
(D) Start his own company

PART 4

Directions: You will hear some talks given by a single speaker. You will be asked to answer three questions about what the speaker says in each talk. Select the best response to each question and mark the letter (A), (B), (C), or (D) on your answer sheet. The talks will not be printed in your test book and will be spoken only one time.

71. What does the speaker say is available to staff?
    (A) A fitness program
    (B) A company loan
    (C) A volunteer opportunity
    (D) A medical checkup

72. According to the speaker, what will employees receive for their participation?
    (A) Complimentary parking
    (B) Extra vacation days
    (C) A cash bonus
    (D) Free refreshments

73. What must employees do to register?
    (A) Submit a form
    (B) Contact a business
    (C) Attend a workshop
    (D) Pay a fee

74. What kind of team does the speaker coach?
    (A) Soccer
    (B) Baseball
    (C) Hockey
    (D) Golf

75. What does the speaker mention about her players?
    (A) Many of them live far away.
    (B) Most of them work late.
    (C) They are going to participate in a tournament.
    (D) They need to practice more often.

76. Why does the speaker say, "Your team has the field from 6 to 7"?
    (A) To request a switch
    (B) To extend a game time
    (C) To praise a team member
    (D) To verify an appointment

77. What is the purpose of the announcement?
    (A) To describe a new menu
    (B) To explain a parking policy
    (C) To promote a volunteer opportunity
    (D) To introduce a keynote speaker

78. What will happen on May 12?
    (A) Some equipment will be installed.
    (B) Some gardening work will be done.
    (C) An art exhibition will be held.
    (D) A parking area will be closed.

79. What does the speaker say will be distributed?
    (A) A book
    (B) A tool
    (C) Some food
    (D) Some plants

80. What is the report mainly about?
    (A) A town festival
    (B) A community fundraiser
    (C) An art exhibition
    (D) A renovation project

81. What does the speaker say is available on a Web site?
    (A) Job descriptions
    (B) A price chart
    (C) A list of events
    (D) Traffic updates

82. Why does the speaker say, "there are a few subway lines"?
    (A) The subway system is complex.
    (B) He takes the subway to the office daily.
    (C) Visitors should ride the subway to an event.
    (D) Additional subway lines must be built.

GO ON TO THE NEXT PAGE

TEST 9

83. What industry does the speaker most likely work in?

(A) Automobile
(B) Publishing
(C) Sports
(D) Advertising

84. What would the speaker like the listeners to do at today's meeting?

(A) Watch a video
(B) Test some products
(C) Discuss some ideas
(D) Sign a document

85. What will the speaker do next?

(A) Take a group picture
(B) Provide details about some vehicles
(C) Meet some new staff members
(D) Print out a catalog

86. What is the purpose of the speech?

(A) To announce an award recipient
(B) To honor a retiring employee
(C) To explain organizational changes
(D) To promote a marketing campaign

87. What does the speaker say he appreciates about Randy Milton?

(A) His leadership ability
(B) His technical knowledge
(C) His design skills
(D) His financial expertise

88. What does the speaker say about the company?

(A) It will have a new headquarters.
(B) It was featured in a magazine.
(C) It is well-known throughout the country.
(D) It plans on hiring more workers.

89. Who are the listeners?

(A) Property managers
(B) Interior designers
(C) Company executives
(D) Mechanical engineers

90. Why is the speaker discussing a change?

(A) A budget is being reduced.
(B) A work area is too noisy.
(C) A department is understaffed.
(D) A manager is retiring.

91. Why does the speaker say, "We can't afford for Engineering to lose focus"?

(A) To approve a revised process
(B) To criticize another team
(C) To justify the reason for a proposal
(D) To complain about a new product

92. What is the speaker mainly discussing?

(A) A corporate policy
(B) A visiting client
(C) An annual budget
(D) An evaluation process

93. What are the listeners encouraged to do?

(A) Participate in a survey
(B) Join a social gathering
(C) Take some time off
(D) Visit some clients

94. What will the speaker do after the meeting?

(A) Distribute a brochure
(B) Order some tickets
(C) Interview some candidates
(D) Send out a survey

Suggested Items to Repair	
1	Damaged passenger seat
2	Worn out tires
3	Broken glove compartment
4	Loose rearview mirror

95. What does the speaker mention about Mecho Auto?

(A) It offers a pick-up service.
(B) It has extended its operating hours.
(C) It will undergo renovations.
(D) It is moving to another location.

96. According to the speaker, what did Ms. Menks do yesterday?

(A) Provided an email address
(B) Approved a request
(C) Made a payment
(D) Ordered additional supplies

97. Look at the graphic. Which item number can Ms. Menks receive a discount on?

(A) 1
(B) 2
(C) 3
(D) 4

Hooper's Supermarket	Memorial Park	Police Station
Central Road		
Jorgensen's Donuts	Lionel's Coffee	Moon's Gym

98. What most likely is the speaker's job?

(A) Hair stylist
(B) Supermarket manager
(C) Coffee shop owner
(D) Real estate agent

99. Look at the graphic. Which location is the speaker describing?

(A) Hooper's Supermarket
(B) Lionel's Coffee
(C) Jorgensen's Donuts
(D) Moon's Gym

100. What plan does the speaker recommend changing?

(A) A building design
(B) A budget
(C) An advertisement
(D) A project timetable

This is the end of the Listening test.

LISTENING TEST

In the Listening test, you will be asked to demonstrate how well you understand spoken English. The entire Listening test will last approximately 45 minutes. There are four parts, and directions are given for each part. You must mark your answers on the separate answer sheet. Do not write your answers in your test book.

PART 1

Directions: For each question in this part, you will hear four statements about a picture in your test book. When you hear the statements, you must select the one statement that best describes what you see in the picture. Then find the number of the question on your answer sheet and mark your answer. The statements will not be printed in your test book and will be spoken only one time.

Statement (B), "A man is pointing at a document," is the best description of the picture, so you should select answer (B) and mark it on your answer sheet.

1.

2.

GO ON TO THE NEXT PAGE

TEST 10

3.

4.

5.

6.

GO ON TO THE NEXT PAGE ➡

PART 2

Directions: You will hear a question or statement and three responses spoken in English. They will not be printed in your test book and will be spoken only one time. Select the best response to the question or statement and mark the letter (A), (B), or (C) on your answer sheet.

7. Mark your answer on your answer sheet.

8. Mark your answer on your answer sheet.

9. Mark your answer on your answer sheet.

10. Mark your answer on your answer sheet.

11. Mark your answer on your answer sheet.

12. Mark your answer on your answer sheet.

13. Mark your answer on your answer sheet.

14. Mark your answer on your answer sheet.

15. Mark your answer on your answer sheet.

16. Mark your answer on your answer sheet.

17. Mark your answer on your answer sheet.

18. Mark your answer on your answer sheet.

19. Mark your answer on your answer sheet.

20. Mark your answer on your answer sheet.

21. Mark your answer on your answer sheet.

22. Mark your answer on your answer sheet.

23. Mark your answer on your answer sheet.

24. Mark your answer on your answer sheet.

25. Mark your answer on your answer sheet.

26. Mark your answer on your answer sheet.

27. Mark your answer on your answer sheet.

28. Mark your answer on your answer sheet.

29. Mark your answer on your answer sheet.

30. Mark your answer on your answer sheet.

31. Mark your answer on your answer sheet.

PART 3

Directions: You will hear some conversations between two or more people. You will be asked to answer three questions about what the speakers say in each conversation. Select the best response to each question and mark the letter (A), (B), (C), or (D) on your answer sheet. The conversations will not be printed in your test book and will be spoken only one time.

32. What does the woman need help with?

(A) Organizing a workshop
(B) Using a computer program
(C) Making a presentation
(D) Finding a report

33. Why is the man unable to help?

(A) He is leaving work soon.
(B) He lost some documents.
(C) He missed a training session.
(D) He has to meet a client.

34. What will the speakers probably do next?

(A) Speak with a coworker
(B) Complete a project
(C) Prepare some forms
(D) Send out some emails

35. Where are the speakers?

(A) At a car rental business
(B) At a travel agency
(C) At a public library
(D) At an electronics repair shop

36. What will the man do next week?

(A) Attend an autograph signing session
(B) Participate in a tour
(C) Renew a membership contract
(D) Depart for a business trip

37. Why does Tammy talk to Ms. Chin?

(A) To refer her to a service
(B) To get approval for a purchase
(C) To inquire about a rule
(D) To check on the status of a delivery

38. What event are the speakers discussing?

(A) A guided tour
(B) A luncheon
(C) A training session
(D) A client meeting

39. What problem does the man mention?

(A) Some items are unavailable.
(B) There are not enough seats.
(C) Reservations have not been made.
(D) More staff is needed.

40. What does the woman decide to do?

(A) Send an email
(B) Postpone a gathering
(C) Use a company facility
(D) Hire a new employee

41. What does the woman say she has heard about?

(A) The renovation of a building
(B) The acquisition of a company
(C) The construction of a new facility
(D) The launch of a new product

42. What benefit is expected?

(A) Lower rental rates
(B) More employment opportunities
(C) Increased tourism
(D) Clearer company guidelines

43. What does the man suggest the woman do?

(A) Tell her son to call him directly
(B) Forward a résumé
(C) Visit a company's Web site
(D) Speak with a manager

GO ON TO THE NEXT PAGE

TEST 10

44. What special feature does the woman request for the card holders?

(A) Water-resistant material
(B) A company logo
(C) Specific colors
(D) An extra-large size

45. What does the man say she must do?

(A) Order from a Web site
(B) Make a deposit
(C) Provide a sample
(D) Speak to a craftsperson

46. What does the man say about discounts?

(A) They must be approved by a supervisor.
(B) They require a membership card.
(C) They are not available for customized items.
(D) They are only offered for online orders.

47. What type of business does the woman want to work for?

(A) A translation firm
(B) A law firm
(C) A marketing agency
(D) A publishing agency

48. What job requirement is mentioned?

(A) A degree in business
(B) Knowledge of a specific product
(C) Event organizing skills
(D) International experience

49. What does the man ask the woman to do?

(A) Prepare a presentation
(B) Fill out a questionnaire
(C) Return at a later time
(D) Submit a reference letter

50. Where does the man work?

(A) At a law firm
(B) At a printing center
(C) At a recycling plant
(D) At an advertising agency

51. What would the man like to do?

(A) Register for a training session
(B) Purchase new equipment
(C) Store some merchandise
(D) Get rid of old electronics

52. What will Kathy probably do next week?

(A) Deliver a package
(B) Give the man a tour
(C) Participate in a workshop
(D) Visit the man's office

53. Where will the speakers be on November 21?

(A) At a job fair
(B) At a store opening
(C) At a technology conference
(D) At an anniversary celebration

54. What does the man mean when he says, "That's a good idea"?

(A) The location of an event should be changed.
(B) The start date of an internship should be moved.
(C) The length of a training session should be shortened.
(D) The order of speakers should be switched.

55. What will the man probably do next?

(A) Talk to an HR employee
(B) Make a reservation
(C) Prepare a contract
(D) Look for a piece of equipment

56. What does the man want to do?

(A) Buy some furniture
(B) Return some supplies
(C) Replace a broken item
(D) Organize a warehouse

57. What does the woman say about some merchandise?

(A) A color is not in stock.
(B) A size is not available.
(C) The prices have been reduced.
(D) The products are handmade.

58. What does the woman caution the man about?

(A) Complicated installation procedures
(B) Costly shipping charges
(C) An easily damaged item
(D) A long waiting period

59. What is the woman calling about?

(A) A damaged phone
(B) A pool service
(C) A travel itinerary
(D) A promotional deal

60. What does the woman imply when she says, "I've tried that"?

(A) She spoke with a technician earlier.
(B) She is pleased with some results.
(C) A coupon code was applied.
(D) An idea was not effective.

61. What does the woman decide to do?

(A) Place another order
(B) Visit a business
(C) Talk to the man's supervisor
(D) Cancel a trip

Order Form	
Menu Item	**Quantity**
Cheeseburger	5
Fruit Bowl	7
Shrimp Pasta	9
Chicken Sandwich	15
Beverages	36

62. Look at the graphic. Which quantity on the order form must be revised?

(A) 5
(B) 7
(C) 9
(D) 15

63. Who most likely is Mr. Burke?

(A) A custodian
(B) A researcher
(C) A chef
(D) A musician

64. What will the woman probably do next?

(A) Mail a package
(B) Forward a file
(C) Contact a store
(D) Update a schedule

GO ON TO THE NEXT PAGE

GALAXY WAY MOVIE THEATER

VOUCHER

$7 OFF FILMS ON MON-THU
$5 OFF FILMS ON FRIDAY
$3 OFF FILMS ON WEEKENDS

23872983472
(EXPIRES 4/5)

Warranty Restrictions

The following are not covered under warranty:

1. Products owned for more than one year
2. Products damaged by an accident
3. Products that get lost
4. Products with parts from different manufacturers

---

65. What does the man mention about *Marvelous Fiction*?

(A) Its actors are all famous.
(B) It is sold out for the weekend.
(C) Its first screening is on Friday.
(D) It has received positive reviews.

66. Look at the graphic. Which discount did the woman receive?

(A) $3
(B) $5
(C) $7
(D) $9

67. What does the man recommend?

(A) Bringing a receipt
(B) Checking out a restaurant
(C) Arriving early to a theater
(D) Using a credit card

68. What kind of product is being discussed?

(A) A phone
(B) A television
(C) A computer
(D) A watch

69. Look at the graphic. Which restriction does the man refer to?

(A) Restriction 1
(B) Restriction 2
(C) Restriction 3
(D) Restriction 4

70. What does the woman say she will do?

(A) Check a user guide
(B) Speak to a manager
(C) Test some other items
(D) Compare some costs

PART 4

Directions: You will hear some talks given by a single speaker. You will be asked to answer three questions about what the speaker says in each talk. Select the best response to each question and mark the letter (A), (B), (C), or (D) on your answer sheet. The talks will not be printed in your test book and will be spoken only one time.

71. What is the speaker giving instructions about?

(A) Updating a system
(B) Completing some documents
(C) Entering some work hours
(D) Ordering office supplies

72. According to the speaker, what could happen if a deadline is missed?

(A) A delivery could be delayed.
(B) A vacation request could be denied.
(C) A payment could be postponed.
(D) A budget proposal could be rejected.

73. What does the speaker say he can do?

(A) Address some inquiries
(B) Contact a department
(C) Check some equipment
(D) Provide a tour

74. What is the focus of the workshop?

(A) Management skills
(B) Investment tips
(C) Advertising solutions
(D) Sales strategies

75. What are the listeners encouraged to do at home?

(A) Design a cover letter
(B) View a video
(C) Make a daily schedule
(D) Write a review

76. Why does the speaker say, "Francine has more than 25 years of experience"?

(A) To recommend Francine's services
(B) To announce Francine's promotion
(C) To discuss Francine's retirement
(D) To support Francine's decision

77. What is the broadcast about?

(A) A public holiday
(B) A new stadium
(C) Results of a sports competition
(D) Improvements to public transportation

78. According to the speaker, why has a change been made?

(A) To promote local shops
(B) To attract more tourists
(C) To respond to complaints
(D) To comply with new laws

79. What does the speaker encourage listeners to do?

(A) Buy tickets in advance
(B) Consult a map
(C) Volunteer at an event
(D) Vote in an election

80. What is the topic of the talk?

(A) An industry convention
(B) An advertising proposal
(C) A worksite regulation
(D) A revised brochure

81. What are the listeners asked to do?

(A) Examine some paperwork
(B) Work additional hours
(C) Clean an area
(D) Distribute some beverages

82. What will the speaker do next?

(A) Review a schedule
(B) Conduct an interview
(C) Test some products
(D) Meet some clients

GO ON TO THE NEXT PAGE

83. Where does the speaker most likely work?

(A) At a bookstore
(B) At a laboratory
(C) At a museum
(D) At a café

84. Why does the speaker say, "talk to Heather"?

(A) To check the availability of an item
(B) To check the number of visitors
(C) To check the choices on a menu
(D) To check the payment of an invoice

85. What will the listeners do next?

(A) Fill out a form
(B) Go to lunch
(C) Tour an office building
(D) Watch a demonstration

86. What type of event is taking place?

(A) A retirement dinner
(B) A community fundraiser
(C) A business opening
(D) An awards ceremony

87. What will Arnold Vans be in charge of?

(A) Renovating a public property
(B) Designing new products
(C) Managing a branch office
(D) Improving marketing strategies

88. What are the attendees asked to do at the end of the evening?

(A) Take a group picture
(B) Register for membership
(C) Submit comments
(D) Pick up a gift

89. Where does the speaker most likely work?

(A) At a bank
(B) At a factory
(C) At a software developer
(D) At a telephone service provider

90. What does the speaker mean when she says, "but we're still getting a lot of calls"?

(A) More employees are required.
(B) Complaints are still being received.
(C) A marketing strategy was successful.
(D) Some orders have not been fulfilled.

91. What will the listeners probably do next?

(A) Review a file
(B) Sign a contract
(C) Contact some clients
(D) Upgrade a program

92. What product is the speaker discussing?

(A) A finance software program
(B) An assembly machine
(C) A storage container
(D) An inventory barcode scanner

93. What does the speaker say the product will help avoid?

(A) Having incorrect data
(B) Causing product defects
(C) Experiencing system failures
(D) Losing important documents

94. What will the speaker do next?

(A) Distribute some brochures
(B) Print a document
(C) Answer some questions
(D) Give a tutorial

Rita Matsumoto's Friday Appointments

10:00 A.M.	Management meeting
11:00 A.M.	Budget review
12:00 P.M.	Client consultation
1:00 P.M.	HR presentation

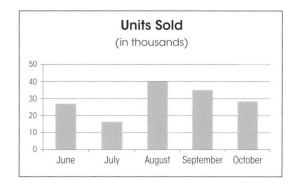

95. What does the speaker want to talk about?

(A) A production deadline
(B) A new TV series
(C) A job opening in Osaka
(D) A construction proposal

96. Look at the graphic. Which of the speaker's appointments was postponed?

(A) Management meeting
(B) Budget review
(C) Client consultation
(D) HR presentation

97. What does the speaker ask the listener to send?

(A) An application form
(B) A travel itinerary
(C) A guest list
(D) A price estimate

98. Where does the speaker most likely work?

(A) At a sporting goods store
(B) At an electronics maker
(C) At an accounting firm
(D) At a broadcasting station

99. According to the speaker, what caused a decrease in sales?

(A) A consumer gave a poor rating.
(B) A manufacturer raised its prices.
(C) A factory closed down.
(D) A competitor released a new product.

100. Look at the graphic. When did the company discount a product?

(A) In June
(B) In July
(C) In August
(D) In September

This is the end of the Listening test.

Scripts

TEST 1

PART 1

1. (A) She's cycling through a park.
   (B) She's securing a bicycle to a post.
   (C) She's leaning against a tree.
   (D) She's walking down a road.

2. (A) The men are installing electrical wiring.
   (B) The men are working on a roof.
   (C) The men are repairing a window.
   (D) The men are laying tiles on the floor.

3. (A) They are sitting at opposite workstations.
   (B) They are adjusting a computer monitor.
   (C) One of the people is cleaning a desk.
   (D) One of the people is pulling open a file drawer.

4. (A) The woman is waiting at a counter.
   (B) The woman is putting groceries into a bag.
   (C) The woman is lifting a basket.
   (D) The woman is studying an item.

5. (A) Potted plants have been placed on a desk.
   (B) A laptop is covered with some papers.
   (C) Some cabinets are filled with books.
   (D) Some magazines have been scattered on a desk.

6. (A) A woman is storing her camera in a carrying case.
   (B) A woman is taking a picture out of the frame.
   (C) Some structures are casting shadows on the ground.
   (D) Photographic equipment has been set up by a fence.

PART 2

7. Who arranges the store's display shelves?
   (A) Tanner usually does that.
   (B) Those items are on sale.
   (C) Some new furniture.

8. How long is your presentation on leadership?
   (A) At 3 o'clock.
   (B) Just for the managers.
   (C) About 15 minutes.

9. When can we get started on the new product design?
   (A) Right after this meeting.
   (B) With the product development team.
   (C) Due to its smaller size.

10. Is there a printer in this room?
   (A) The ink cartridges in the supply cabinet.
   (B) There are no empty rooms on this floor.
   (C) Actually, it needs to be repaired

11. Easter Café is closing, right?
   (A) Turn left at the next street.
   (B) Yes, they didn't get enough customers.
   (C) I'd like a coffee with cream, please.

12. How much should we charge for the new sweater?
   (A) I'll talk to the manager.
   (B) Do you have it in blue?
   (C) The fall clothing line.

13. Which laptop belongs to you?
   (A) No, I put it on top of the table.
   (B) The black one with an orange sticker.
   (C) Is the battery charged?

14. Could you put the extra computers in the storage room?
   (A) Yes, but after I send this email.
   (B) We don't need any more office equipment.
   (C) Thank you for your input.

15. Didn't you sell your bike recently?
   (A) The new trail in the park.
   (B) That's a nice model.
   (C) No, I still have it.

164 해설지 다운로드 (유료) • http://www.pagodabook.com

16. Where can I adjust the volume of this speaker?
(A) There are buttons on the left side.
(B) It has the best sound quality.
(C) We've made an adjustment to the process.

17. Would you prefer to go to the Japanese or Chinese restaurant for lunch?
(A) I'd rather get Chinese.
(B) A table for six.
(C) No, my friend referred me.

18. Did you set the timeline for the renovation project?
(A) The recent renovation of the Belleview Complex.
(B) A new construction manager.
(C) Yes, I just sent you an email about it.

19. Why don't I get you a drink while you wait for your interview?
(A) That'd be great, thanks.
(B) I'll call the waiter.
(C) I brought my résumé.

20. The company sports festival was postponed, wasn't it?
(A) Yes, at the stadium.
(B) The team wearing blue.
(C) Where did you hear that?

21. Shouldn't you get your mobile phone repaired?
(A) A wireless internet service provider.
(B) I'm waiting for the new model to come out.
(C) You'll be contacted by email soon.

22. Why is the department hiring?
(A) The application is on the Web site.
(B) At the end of the month.
(C) We've acquired more clients recently.

23. Could I borrow a pen for the meeting?
(A) I took notes for you.
(B) No, I couldn't attend.
(C) It's almost out of ink.

24. I sent you the contract, didn't I?
(A) Standard terms and conditions.
(B) The internet is not working.
(C) The conference room next door.

25. Our recycling bin is full again.
(A) I'll empty it out today.
(B) I ride my bicycle to work.
(C) Thanks, but I'm still full.

26. Do you know which room the IT Department office is at?
(A) It's on my desk.
(B) Don't forget to turn off your computer.
(C) I just started working here.

27. Don't we need more volunteers to finish handing out the flyers?
(A) Jonah is checking the list right now.
(B) I took the direct flight back home.
(C) We recently hired a new engineer.

28. When will Ms. Egert leave for Japan?
(A) Four hours from Tokyo.
(B) She's at the airport right now.
(C) The moving company is here

29. There's an opening for the shipping director position.
(A) Yes, I live quite close.
(B) The shipment arrived today.
(C) How do I apply?

30. Who will be leading the workshop session on project management?
(A) Here's the program.
(B) It will start right after the break.
(C) About communication.

31. Let's find a cheap supplier, so we can minimize our costs.
(A) We have a lot in stock.
(B) Try maximizing the window on the screen.
(C) The Purchasing Department is looking into it.

PART 3

Questions 32-34 refer to the following conversation.

W: I think it was the right move to have bands perform at our coffee shop on Saturday nights. Our sales have really increased over the last few weeks.

M: Yeah. Although I don't really enjoy rearranging the chairs and tables frequently to create space for the performances, it's still worth it.

W: Right, and we're attracting a lot of attention. Have you read the online article in *Galveton Entertainment Magazine*? It has a list of our town's top 10 live entertainment venues. And we're number four on the list.

M: Oh, I didn't know that. I think we should put the article in a frame and hang it where customers can see it.

W: I'll print it out right now.

Questions 35-37 refer to the following conversation with three speakers.

W1: I have to get a new briefcase. One of the locks broke on my old one. Can either of you recommend a brand?

M: Why don't you check out Luxmore Accessories? I purchased a Luxmore leather bag, and it's really nice—a lot more stylish than most other brands I've seen.

W2: Yeah, and they're also offering a special deal on their Web site. If you order a Luxmore briefcase, you will receive a small traveling pouch free of charge.

W1: Oh really? Can you give me the link to their home page, Valerie?

W2: Sure.

Questions 38-40 refer to the following conversation.

M: Hi, my name is Patrick Simms, the director of the Meadow Philharmonic Orchestra. We'll be traveling abroad next June to begin our concert series in Europe. And my colleagues highly recommended you for the tour arrangements you made for other orchestras.

W: Thank you. I'd be happy to assist you. I have over 10 years of experience in the tourism industry, and prior to that, I was actually a professional violinist, so I understand what you need.

M: That's good to hear. I'm a bit worried about our instruments, though. They're very expensive, and I want to make sure that they're not damaged during travel.

W: Well, most of your instruments should be fine as carry-on luggage, but larger instruments take up much more space, so you'll probably need to buy additional tickets for them. It might be costly, but it's the best way to transport those instruments.

Questions 41-43 refer to the following conversation.

M: Hey, Celia.

W: Hi, Robert. I'm so glad you picked up. I wanted to see if you could give me a ride to the office today.

M: Actually, I just got to work a few minutes ago. I had to come in earlier than usual this morning to get ready for our product demonstration. Can you still make it in time for the demo?

W: Hmm… I don't know. My car won't start.

M: Oh, I hope it's nothing serious. Well, I would pick you up, but the representatives from JRA, Inc. are arriving soon. Why don't you ask Lisa? She's coming in later today, and I believe she lives near you.

W: Alright, I'll do that now. Let's hope I can make it to the demo.

Questions 44-46 refer to the following conversation.

> **W:** Hi, my name is Suzanne Rouse. I'm here to see Mr. Winfield for a job interview. It's for a sales position. Could you please let him know that I'm here?
>
> **M:** Oh, I'm afraid his flight home was canceled last night. So unfortunately, he won't be back here until late tonight. Would it be OK if I rescheduled your interview for tomorrow morning?
>
> **W:** Actually, I'm busy all day tomorrow so that won't work for me.
>
> **M:** Well, Mr. Winfield's assistant sometimes handles his interviews for him when he's away. Why don't I give her a call and see if she's available now?

Questions 47-49 refer to the following conversation.

> **W:** Hello, my name is Kimberly Hughes, a sales representative at Millennium Electronics. I wanted to talk to Mr. Alvez about the tablet PC he ordered last week. May I speak to him, please?
>
> **M:** I'm sorry, but he's not in the office at the moment. Would you like to leave a message?
>
> **W:** Yes. Could you tell him that his computer is here? I told him that it wouldn't arrive at our store until next week, but we received an early shipment this morning.
>
> **M:** OK. He's supervising a construction site right now, but I'll make sure he gets the message when he comes back.

Questions 50-52 refer to the following conversation.

> **M:** Hi, I want to take the professional pilot training program at your school, but there isn't any information about the enrollment fee on your Web site.
>
> **W:** That's because it varies depending on what each student's experience level is and what their needs are. But it's normally between 25 and 40 thousand dollars. The total cost includes renting a plane, fueling it, and paying the instructor.
>
> **M:** I guess that makes sense, but I had no idea it was that expensive. I think I'd better look into other commercial flight schools and compare the fees. Is there anything in particular I should be aware of when checking out different programs?
>
> **W:** Well, the fees are about the same at most flight schools, but you should be aware that not every school guarantees job placement like we do. I'm sure you'll agree that's probably the most important thing. So be sure to ask about their placement services.

Questions 53-55 refer to the following conversation with three speakers.

> **W1:** Clark, Lois, I'm glad I ran into you both. It looks like preparations are going well for next week's yearly reception party for our theater's donors.
>
> **M:** Yes. Arrangements for the dinner have been finalized. Do you need us to do anything else?
>
> **W1:** I just got off the phone with one of our donors, Mary Romo.
>
> **W2:** If I recall, she was responsible for getting us the new sound system, right?
>
> **W1:** Yeah. Anyway, she initially told me that she would be going on vacation this week, but it got canceled at the last minute. So now, she is saying she would like to attend.
>
> **M:** Alright. I'll put her name on the attendance sheet right now.

Questions 56-58 refer to the following conversation.

W: Hello, Mr. Shubert.

M: Good morning, Ms. Bolton. The City Council wanted to know how far along you are with the landscaping work on the Town Hall Garden. Is everything going smoothly?

W: Yes, we're actually a bit ahead of schedule, so it should be done by August.

M: Wow, I didn't expect that. Now, we don't have to worry about making the deadline.

W: Yes. I'm happy about it as well. Residents probably can visit the garden earlier than anticipated.

M: Hmm... I still need to check with the local nursery. They are providing all of the plants and flowers, so it really depends on their delivery schedule. They promised to give me an update by the end of the week.

Questions 59-61 refer to the following conversation.

W: Hi, Larry. We need to talk about all the extra orders that have been coming in for the Manufacturing Department recently.

M: Ah, I heard you were getting a lot more orders. Is it an issue?

W: Yeah, the volume of orders we need to fulfill has increased dramatically, and my crew can't keep the same levels of quality control if we try to speed up production.

M: Hmm, OK. We can't install more equipment right now, but I may be able to get authorization to add more employees to our assembly lines.

W: Oh, that would be great. Is there anything you need from me?

M: If I could get you to create a chart comparing the number of orders now to last quarter's, that'd help me out a lot.

Questions 62-64 refer to the following conversation and schedule.

M: It's great that we have the afternoon off from this training workshop. I heard from one of our instructors that we should take a tour of the Chateau Archives. It's the oldest library in this region.

W: Yeah, I can't wait to see it.

M: Same here. But let's not forget that we agreed to be back at the hotel tonight to eat dinner with our other team members.

W: Right, of course. OK, let's read more about the tours on Chateau Archives' Web site on my laptop. Alright, it shows that there are still three spots left at this time.

M: That's perfect. I'll call them now and reserve our places.

Questions 65-67 refer to the following conversation and bill.

W: Thank you for calling Westfield Credit Card Services. How may I help you?

M: Hi, there. My name is Chris Walker, and I've got a question about my monthly account statement. I noticed on May 9, I was charged a foreign transaction fee, but I never made an overseas purchase.

W: OK, let's have a look. Ah, we had a system error that day, and it must have affected your account. I'll take out that charge right away.

M: Thank you.

W: Now, Mr. Walker, we take all of our customer concerns very seriously. If you don't mind, would you remain on the line for a few minutes to take a brief survey about your experience today?

Questions 68-70 refer to the following conversation and office park map.

M: Hello, Ms. Crowlie. It's Martin Sanchez from Nertech, Inc. After careful review of your job application, we have decided to call you in for an interview. Does next Wednesday at 10 A.M. work for you?

W: I'm so glad to hear back from you. Just a minute, I'll check my schedule. Yes, that time should be fine.

M: Great. Now, Nertech is on the west side of town. Our office building is located on Redwood Street, right by the community center.

W: Alright. And can I just park anywhere in the lot, or do I have to get a pass?

M: As long as you're in a spot that's marked "guest", you won't have a problem.

PART 4

Questions 71-73 refer to the following broadcast.

W: This is K-wave Radio with your local news. Oceanside City officials announced that this year's annual charity soccer tournament has been postponed. It was originally scheduled to be held tomorrow afternoon, but due to thunderstorms in the weather forecast, it has been rescheduled for next week. For those who want to register your team, there is still time to do so. Simply visit the city Web site, and click on the tournament registration link.

Questions 74-76 refer to the following announcement.

M: Good morning, ladies and gentlemen. On behalf of Captain Gonzalo and the rest of the flight crew, we welcome you aboard Flight 927, flying directly from Miami to Barcelona. There are some vacant seats on today's flight, and several passengers have inquired about changing their seats. You are free to do so, but we ask that you wait until the fasten seat belt sign has been turned off. Also, please let one of the flight attendants know if you require a headset for the in-flight movie. Meanwhile, make yourself comfortable, and have a look at our brochures and magazines which are located in the pocket of the seat in front of you. We are scheduled to arrive in Barcelona at 12 P.M. local time.

Questions 77-79 refer to the following excerpt from a meeting.

M: I've asked all the food service staff to gather this morning to explain a change in the way we are going to serve meals to our residents at Fairview Nursing Home. The facility will now be using a system whereby residents can phone in their meal orders and have the food delivered to their rooms. To ensure that residents' dietary restrictions are adhered to, the food service coordinator on duty will check the database before any meal is prepared. The system, which has already been successfully implemented in local hospitals, has many advantages, the most significant of which is that far less food is wasted.

Questions 80-82 refer to the following telephone message.

W: Ms. Johanson, this is Sally. I'm calling to let you know that due to your recent promotion, you will be moving from your cubicle into a manager's office on the 3rd floor. I know you're happy with where you're sitting right now, but you're right next to the staff lounge. It's a lot quieter on the 3rd floor. Also, as we often have management meetings on the 3rd floor, it would be convenient for you to be here. I'll send someone down to help you pack up tomorrow morning. On Friday, the IT Department will set up a new computer and printer for you at your new workspace.

Questions 83-85 refer to the following speech.

W: Hello, everyone, and welcome to tonight's celebration of BH Industries' Entrepreneur of the Year Awards Show. It is my honor to recognize Maggie Olmstead of Olmstead, Inc. Maggie's company first entered the spotlight for its anti-virus program, Mag-O, which has received great reviews from users everywhere. Olmstead is now working on another application that compresses files to save space on all mobile devices. If it is anything like Mag-O, it will surely sell well. With Olmstead, Inc. looking to grow and expand, Maggie has plans to move her company's offices to Nickel Hills at the start of next year. Now, let's all give a big welcome to Maggie Olmstead.

Questions 86-88 refer to the following advertisement.

M: If you want to use the best business meeting facilities in the city, then Lloyd Conference Center has everything you need. We have a wide range of small and large meeting rooms, and state-of-the-art electronic equipment. And starting this year, our copying services are available 24 hours a day. For detailed information about our services and rates, call 555-3578. Tell us about this ad when you make your next reservation, and you will receive 15 percent off our regular rates.

Questions 89-91 refer to the following excerpt from a meeting.

M: Now, the next thing we need to discuss is the ScanMaster 3000, our hand-held scanning device. You're all aware of last quarter's sales performance. We have to work on getting more customers to purchase it. Raymond has done some research, and according to his report, the main issue is that consumers see no difference between the ScanMaster 3000 and our largest competitor's product, which

looks almost exactly the same. There are five unique features we need to make clear in all our advertisements, so buyers can make the distinction. I'll go over them one by one, but first, let's take a few minutes to review this data chart.

Questions 92-94 refer to the following excerpt from a meeting.

W: Good afternoon, everyone. Before your shifts start tonight, I'd just like to say a couple of things. As always, we received a lot of positive feedback last month on the quality of the dishes. However, we did not get such positive feedback on the speed of service. Some customers complained that they had to wait up to 40 minutes for their meals, especially between courses. As we cater to a lot of business customers, particularly at lunchtime, we need to ensure that meals are prepared and served quickly. All waiting staff, please make sure that orders are immediately sent to the kitchen. And kitchen staff, make every effort to get orders cooked as fast as possible. I know you can do it. Thanks.

Questions 95-97 refer to the following telephone message and inspection report.

W: Good afternoon. It's Becky Hamlin from The Boxton—the caterer on Pearl Street. You conducted a health inspection at our business this morning, and I have a question regarding the report. The top section looks fine, but at the bottom, we were not given any details as to why we didn't pass the inspection. I would like to know the reason why our freezer's condition was unacceptable, so we can get it repaired right away. I'm worried because we need to complete a large order for a party in a few days, and we have to get ready for it soon.

Questions 98-100 refer to the following excerpt from a meeting and diagrams.

> **M:** Welcome to our first planning session for this year's Public Health Conference. This conference will feature presentations by some world-renowned experts in the public health industry. As a result, all advance tickets have sold out, and we are anticipating that a lot more people will sign up for the event in the upcoming weeks. Sanjiv Singh, the dean of GSU's School of Public Health, will be our main speaker. He'll be presenting in Malone Auditorium. He wants us to arrange the room so that he is in front of as many people as possible, rather than having people on all sides of him. We'll put two tables in front of him, and then set up chairs in rows. Who can take care of setting that up?

PART 1

1. (A) A woman is cutting grass.
   (B) A trash bin is being emptied.
   (C) A man is sweeping the floor.
   (D) A chair is being adjusted.

2. (A) The man is pouring a drink into a glass.
   (B) One of the people is wearing glasses.
   (C) The women are holding their forks.
   (D) The people are waiting to be seated.

3. (A) They are watering flowers in the garden.
   (B) They are strolling through a walkway.
   (C) A trolley has been filled with items.
   (D) Potted plants have been loaded onto a truck.

4. (A) A flight attendant is checking tickets.
   (B) A fence is being installed outside a building.
   (C) Boxes are being carried along the runway.
   (D) People are walking toward an entrance.

5. (A) She is unpacking a package.
   (B) She is wheeling a baggage cart.
   (C) An airline employee is loading some luggage.
   (D) A suitcase is being removed from an overhead compartment.

6. (A) A worker is pulling up a blind over a glass door.
   (B) Some desks are positioned one in front of the other.
   (C) Some chairs are stacked in a storeroom.
   (D) Light fixtures are being hung over a meeting table.

PART 2

7. Does this subway go to city hall?
(A) No, it doesn't.
(B) I saw it on the bus.
(C) The station was crowded.

8. Where did you purchase these concert tickets?
(A) At the box office.
(B) Last weekend.
(C) Some instruments.

9. How was the annual trade exposition?
(A) I traded it in for a new one.
(B) Not as good as last year's.
(C) Yes, at the same location.

10. Who's responsible for ordering the office supplies?
(A) It's a big responsibility.
(B) That's not my order.
(C) That would be Ms. Kroll.

11. When will the yearly sales figures be available?
(A) Yes, the data is still available.
(B) Sometime tomorrow.
(C) A monthly subscription.

12. Which branch did you send the package to?
(A) I paid for it this morning.
(B) The express option.
(C) The Remington office in New York.

13. Would you like some assistance preparing your proposal?
(A) Yes, he did.
(B) It does occasionally.
(C) I just emailed it to our manager.

14. How far away is your office from your home?
(A) I can walk there.
(B) OK. I'll give you a ride.
(C) On the 5th floor.

15. Why is Grover Avenue blocked off this morning?
(A) For the bike race.
(B) At the next street.
(C) In three hours.

16. Have the discount coupons for August been printed yet?
(A) Twice a month.
(B) I appreciate the update.
(C) Robert in Marketing should know.

17. Where do I apply to participate in the art competition?
(A) For a museum exhibit.
(B) At the main booth.
(C) A trophy will be awarded.

18. Why don't we recycle our used plastic bottles?
(A) Oh, she already did?
(B) OK, I'll tell the others to do the same.
(C) Our new packaging process.

19. Aren't we supposed to submit the budget report to Mr. Rogers' assistant?
(A) A financial advisor.
(B) I was asked to email it directly to him.
(C) No, the train is late.

20. I heard that Barbara will be transferring to the Huntington branch.
(A) The new branch manager.
(B) No. I'll transfer the money now.
(C) Yes, they're short on staff.

21. Are you going to hold the training workshop at our office or do it online?
(A) Most likely early next week.
(B) There isn't a meeting room big enough here.
(C) What did you think about the presentation on international markets?

22. Could you prepare an agenda for tomorrow's conference call?
(A) I'll have it ready by lunchtime.
(B) A call from the company president.
(C) We'll need to repair the projector.

23. How many planners should I bring to the new staff orientation?
(A) Let me review the list.
(B) Yes, I've seen them.
(C) A charitable organization.

24. Do you have any seats available for this show?
(A) His best performance yet.
(B) No, that's an old seating chart.
(C) All of the tickets are sold out.

25. You've visited Italy before, haven't you?
(A) I went there just last year.
(B) I've tried that pasta before.
(C) Many historic sites and monuments.

26. Who should I talk to about getting a new ID issued?
(A) I'll take you to my supervisor.
(B) Would you like to discuss this issue?
(C) No. I don't have an ID card.

27. Shouldn't we interview additional applicants?
(A) Yes, it's a beautiful view.
(B) I think we met enough.
(C) Through an online application.

28. How frequently does Ms. Chung want to hold the professional development seminars?
(A) The lecture at 6 o'clock.
(B) It will be in seminar room B.
(C) What did she do last year?

29. We'll most likely have to work extra hours this month, right?
(A) I attended the workshop last month.
(B) It took almost two hours to get to work.
(C) Actually, the project has been put on hold.

30. Should we repair this printer or just buy a new one?
(A) I don't think it can be fixed.
(B) The paper is in the supply closet.
(C) An online store.

31. I think it's too early to enter the theater.
(A) You're right. The movie was great.
(B) I see some people going in now.
(C) Two general admission tickets, please.

PART 3

Questions 32-34 refer to the following conversation.

M: Hi, Alison. Have you seen this week's *Business World Net Magazine*? There is an online article that says we're the fastest growing mobile phone company in the country.

W: Yes, I just read it. In fact, it would be great if you could post a link on our Web site that directs people to the article. That kind of media coverage will definitely help our campaign to recruit new employees.

M: It will certainly attract more prospective job applicants to our company. I'll go to my computer right now and add the link.

Questions 35-37 refer to the following conversation.

W: Mr. Mason, I just went over our plant's health and safety records, and it looks like some of our employees' safety certificates have expired.

M: Really? I thought we had a training session a few months ago, and all of our workers were certified. And aren't the certificates good for one year?

W: Yes, they are, but that session was only for our new employees. Now, we need to do another session for those who were certified last year. But all they need to do is attend a short refresher session for their recertification.

M: I see. Could you send me a list of the employees who need to get recertified? Then we can organize a session for them.

Questions 38-40 refer to the following conversation.

> **M:** Hi, Donna. The company is sending me to Prague in two weeks to cover a fashion show at the Moda Exhibition Center. They want me to write a special article about it for our magazine. Weren't you there recently?
>
> **W:** Yes, and a close friend of mine is one of the designers whose clothing line will be displayed at the event. Would you like to get in touch with him?
>
> **M:** Yes, It'd be great to get as much information as I can about the designers that will be featured before attending the show.
>
> **W:** OK, I have his business card in my office. Let me go get it for you.

Questions 41-43 refer to the following conversation.

> **W:** You've reached Rally Rental Cars. How may I assist you?
>
> **M:** Hello, I returned a rental car at your Bixby location two days ago, and a representative dropped me off at the nearest train station. I'm looking at the bill right now, and I was wondering why there's an extra fee for the drop-off service. This is the first time I've had to pay for it.
>
> **W:** Ah, due to the increase in gas prices this year, our agency had no choice but to add a fee for that service.
>
> **M:** Oh, I wasn't aware of that...
>
> **W:** I apologize that you weren't told about this earlier. I'll remove the fee this time, but starting next time, we'll have to charge for the service.

Questions 44-46 refer to the following conversation.

> **W:** Hey, Ron. Would you like me to help you carry those boxes up to our storage room? There are quite a lot.
>
> **M:** I would appreciate that very much! The elevator isn't working right now, so we'll need to take the stairs.
>
> **W:** But it stopped working last week. Why hasn't Maintenance fixed it yet?
>
> **M:** Well, I heard that the control system had to be reconfigured.
>
> **W:** That makes sense. Well, it's a good thing the storage room is just on the third floor, so we won't need to carry these too far.
>
> **M:** Yeah. Thanks again for helping me with these boxes. It would have taken a long time if I had to do it myself.

Questions 47-49 refer to the following conversation with three speakers.

> **W:** Thank you both for meeting me today. How well did our cosmetics sell this month?
>
> **M1:** Um... Sales have increased by 4 percent, but I don't think our spring promotional event attracted as many customers as we had hoped.
>
> **W:** Hmm... That's a bit worrisome. Chris, what do you think is the reason for these disappointing sales figures?
>
> **M2:** We probably didn't sell as many cosmetics because we have a smaller marketing budget this time. I think we should request that our budget be increased.
>
> **W:** Well, why don't we wait a few more weeks? If we're still not drawing in many customers, we'll look into requesting more funds. But for now, I'd like to wait on this decision.

Questions 50-52 refer to the following conversation.

> **M:** Good morning, Angela. It's been a few months since you've been with us. I was wondering how your internship has been so far.
>
> **W:** It's been a lot of fun, and I've learned a lot about marketing strategies. Coming up with campaign ideas is challenging, but I enjoy doing it.
>
> **M:** That's great. I know you still have a few months left in your internship, but since your work has been so outstanding, we're going to increase your hourly rate by 10 percent starting next month.
>
> **W:** I'm thrilled to hear that. Thank you so much!

Questions 53-55 refer to the following conversation.

> **M:** Lettie, we're excited to have you over here at our Tokyo branch next week. We're looking forward to seeing the updated design of our RV400 laptop.
>
> **W:** Me, too. I'm especially pleased about one feature of the laptop.
>
> **M:** Oh, which one?
>
> **W:** This is the lightest model we've ever produced. It only weighs 1 kilogram!
>
> **M:** Wow, that's amazing! I'm eager to find out more about the other features during your talk. And if you're free, several of us from the office will be going out to dinner that night.
>
> **W:** Hmm… I'm watching a play that evening.
>
> **M:** Ah, I see. I'll see you next week then!

Questions 56-58 refer to the following conversation with three speakers.

> **M1:** Welcome to Cadalisk Resort. I'm in charge of event planning, and this is my assistant, Roy. Are you interested in holding an event at one of our facilities?
>
> **W:** Yes. I represent Lepton Manufacturing. We're organizing a company anniversary party for November—around 150 people will be attending.
>
> **M2:** OK. I think the Sapphire Hall would be the perfect venue for your event. Many companies have used it for their anniversary celebrations in the past.
>
> **W:** Great. Also, about 50 guests will be visiting from other cities. Will there be enough vacant rooms for all of them?
>
> **M1:** I think so. Let me see what's available and what group discounts we offer.
>
> **M2:** Oh, and we provide complimentary bus rides back and forth to the airport.

Questions 59-61 refer to the following conversation.

> **M:** Iris, I need to talk to you about last week's shipments of our computers. Apparently, 11 orders weren't delivered on time.
>
> **W:** Yes, we experienced a problem with our online ordering system. Some of the confirmation emails that were sent to customers included incorrect delivery times.
>
> **M:** Has the issue been resolved?
>
> **W:** Yes. But you know, I think we should add one more step to our process to ensure that customers receive the most up-to-date information regarding their orders. How about if we have our drivers give every customer a call before they deliver a package?
>
> **M:** That's a good idea! We'll update our drivers on this change tomorrow morning during our meeting.
>
> **W:** Alright.

Questions 62-64 refer to the following conversation and table.

W: Hey, Liam. I'm preparing an invoice for Dr. Park's patient this morning, but whenever I enter this code, an error message pops up.

M: Ah, the invoice codes were updated a few days ago. You're probably looking at the old chart.

W: Oh, where can I get the new one?

M: I have one on my desk. What kind of procedure was it?

W: Gum surgery.

M: OK. This is the code you have to use.

W: Thank you. Can I make a copy of that chart?

M: Of course. But they're going to be inputting all of the codes into our invoice program next week, so we won't have to use paper charts anymore.

Questions 65-67 refer to the following conversation and chart.

M: Thank you for calling Mon Chapeau Fashions.

W: Yes, hi. I'm browsing through the catalog on your Web site, and I'm hoping to order several hats. But it's for a friend who is living in South America at the moment. Do you ship there?

M: Hold on, let me check... Yes, we do. It's in our Overseas Zone A.

W: Ah, good. I want five black cowboy hats and three Russian fur caps, please.

M: OK. I've entered your order and added the fee for shipping to that destination.

W: Thank you. I'll give you my credit card number.

Questions 68-70 refer to the following conversation and tag template.

M: Bunmi, we've gotten a lot of calls about that new collection of men's jackets we're launching this fall. I think we're going to have a lot of orders, so we should increase inventory so that they don't sell out.

W: OK, why don't we call the Manufacturing Department and let them know we'd like to double production?

M: Yes, I'll talk to them right now.

W: Good. I'm getting the tags for those jackets ready now. Here's the template I'm going to use for those.

M: Oh, let's see. Hmm... The jackets are made of nylon, so I don't think they need to be dry-cleaned.

W: Ah, you're right. I'll change that part right now.

PART 4

Questions 71-73 refer to the following telephone message.

W: Hi, this is Jessica Finch calling from Finch Home Furnishings. I actually went over our billing records, and... It looks like you were right. We did charge you extra for the kitchen chairs you recently ordered. I made a mistake. I've resolved this issue, and you've been fully refunded for the additional charge. Also, I will email you a coupon, which is good for a 30 percent discount on your next purchase. Please do not hesitate to contact me if you have further questions. Once again, I apologize for the error.

Questions 74-76 refer to the following radio advertisement.

M: Join us this weekend in celebrating the grand opening of Jerome's Oceanside Restaurant in Gulliver Bay. You'll be able to experience the same excellent service and mouthwatering dishes as our Jarome's downtown restaurant, a local favorite for over a decade. Our specialty dishes are made from the freshest fish caught in the bay. Whether you are hosting a company dinner or eating out with close friends, Jarome's Oceanside Restaurant is the perfect place. Tell us that you heard this ad, and we will give you any one of our desserts at no extra cost.

Questions 77-79 refer to the following speech.

W: It's nice to see that so many people have come here tonight to help celebrate Travis Kim's last day with our company before his retirement. Over the years, my client numbers have increased considerably thanks to my friend's hard work and dedication. He has secured the most number of business contracts in the history of the firm, which has been his most outstanding achievement at Primeau Company. We thank you, Travis. At this time, we'd like to ask you to come up to the stage so that we can present you with a special engraved watch. Now, let's give Travis a big, warm welcome.

Questions 80-82 refer to the following broadcast.

M: Alright, it's time for the Avocado Valley weekly events update. This Saturday, the AV Youth Arts Club will be holding their yearly art sale fundraiser, and they could use all of our help. If you have any paintings or other art objects that you'd like to donate to the cause, please bring them to the community center by Friday morning. Also scheduled for this weekend is Avocado Valley's yearly outdoor film festival, which

will be held at South Lake Park. But check our Web site for updates, because we may be looking at some heavy rain on those days. To find out more, let's hear from Dave Contreras in our Weather Department.

Questions 83-85 refer to the following talk.

W: Hello, I am Camila, and I'll be your server today. It looks like it's your first time at our café, so let me tell you a little bit about us. All of the fruits used in our dishes are grown organically at our very own farm. Marco, the owner of this restaurant, is dedicated to serving fresh and chemical-free meals. Now, this evening's special is a great Indian dish. It's a delicious chicken curry salad with fresh mangoes and apples. All my friends come here to eat this. Now, can I get you anything to drink while you look at the menu?

Questions 86-88 refer to the following talk.

M: Thank you for attending this year's first managers' meeting. When we met last time, Gloria requested that the company purchase a computer program made specifically for training textile machine workers. I met with several software developers to look at their products, and the one I think would be the most useful for our company is from the Witro Tech Company. They emphasized how quickly the program prepares workers to do their jobs. They also guaranteed a significant increase in work efficiency and productivity. So I propose that we start using this program with the four new workers who will be joining us next week.

Questions 89-91 refer to the following excerpt from a meeting.

W: I called everyone to this meeting to talk about... um... a serious problem. As you all know, Durham Publishers prides itself on publishing top-selling books and maintaining an excellent reputation. So we were very surprised when we found out that four manuscripts of unpublished works have disappeared. To prevent similar occurrences from happening, you will now be required to complete a form asking for authorization when you take out manuscripts from the office. This will help us keep track of the documents. If there are any questions or concerns regarding this matter, please talk to your department manager.

Questions 92-94 refer to the following tour information.

M: Welcome to Flatiron National Park. My name is Liam, and I'll be your tour guide today. I was raised in Flatiron, so I'm very familiar with the region. The path we're taking today has some steep areas, so you'll have to pay extra attention while walking. And just so you know—we're going to stop several times throughout the walk, so you will have the opportunity to sit down and rest. Also, a photographer will be accompanying us today to take some pictures of the tour. They will be made available for download on the park's Web site tomorrow. If you have any questions during the hike, please let me know.

Questions 95-97 refer to the following announcement and directory.

M: Attention, Arca Department Store, shoppers. For this week only, we are selling select laptops and desktop computers at 40 percent off. You can identify which items are on sale by looking for a small yellow sticker attached to the price tag of the laptop or computer. Remember this deal only applies to products with a yellow sticker. Also, if you're an Arca Loyalty Club member, you can earn twice the number of points when making purchases at our store. Not a member? You can register for a card at our customer support center on the first floor.

Questions 98-100 refer to the following telephone message and identification card.

W: Hello, this is Wendy Parker leaving a message for Eric Mendes, the Personnel Manager. I was in your office earlier today to pick up my new company ID card and business cards. I just got back to my office and noticed that the job title on my card is wrong. Aside from that, everything is fine. If you could, please call me back at 555-3824 when you get this message, I'd appreciate it. Thank you.

TEST 3

PART 1

1. (A) He's cutting up some ingredients.
   (B) He's turning on a blender.
   (C) He's hanging up some utensils.
   (D) He's looking in a drawer.

2. (A) A woman is approaching an archway.
   (B) A woman is grasping a handrail.
   (C) A staircase leads up to a hillside.
   (D) Fountains are casting a shadow.

3. (A) A fence runs along the edge of the yard.
   (B) A railing separates some steps.
   (C) A man is repairing a sidewalk.
   (D) Lampposts line both sides of a staircase.

4. (A) A picture is positioned above a bed.
   (B) A rug has been laid near a door.
   (C) A ceiling fan has been taken down.
   (D) A night stand is being repositioned in a corner.

5. (A) Some people are organizing items on a desk.
   (B) Some people are stacking folders in a corner.
   (C) One of the women is closing a cabinet.
   (D) One of the women is distributing papers.

6. (A) Some tables have been arranged in a row.
   (B) Some furniture is being assembled outside.
   (C) Some customers are ordering a meal.
   (D) Some people are taking their seats.

PART 2

7. When did you begin your job as a medical assistant?
   (A) At the medical center.
   (B) That's right.
   (C) Just last year.

8. Who's in charge of the Browley marketing campaign?
   (A) No, I can't tell.
   (B) It's Mr. Gordon.
   (C) The commercial is finished.

9. Did you contact the caterer for the anniversary dinner yet?
   (A) I'm not responsible for the catering.
   (B) For over 45 years.
   (C) He made a reservation at the restaurant.

10. Where should I leave this spare set of keys?
    (A) On top of the front desk.
    (B) Please close the door.
    (C) Sure, you can.

11. Can I get you something to drink while you wait?
    (A) No, I'm fine, thanks.
    (B) I couldn't find it.
    (C) Check the final weight.

12. Haven't you kept in touch with the architectural firm?
    (A) I'm waiting for a response.
    (B) No, don't touch the glass.
    (C) The new building design.

13. Jeff has been promoted to operations manager, hasn't he?
    (A) It's operating fine.
    (B) Just enter the promotional code.
    (C) I think it was Norah.

14. I have an appointment at 3 P.M. today.
    (A) You should go now then.
    (B) No, I can't.
    (C) We will appoint a new CEO.

15. Don't you need to give another presentation tomorrow?
    (A) No, this was the last one for the week.
    (B) That was a great demonstration.
    (C) I thought the presenter was too quiet.

Scripts | TEST 3   179

16. How much is the seminar registration fee?
(A) It should say on the flyer.
(B) About an hour more.
(C) I'd rather register online.

17. Would you care for some tea?
(A) In the beverage section.
(B) They were very caring.
(C) Sure, that'd be great.

18. Was there a problem with the subway last night?
(A) I see. I'll just drive.
(B) Get off at the next station.
(C) Yes, I had to take a taxi.

19. The research states that our numbers have dropped this year.
(A) I'll take another look at the report.
(B) Here's my account number.
(C) He searched online.

20. Where can I purchase a desk fan?
(A) You can use mine.
(B) He's at his desk.
(C) The purchase was just approved.

21. Should I buy the sports equipment at the shop or from the Web site?
(A) Please get it from the shop.
(B) Some new soccer gear.
(C) It was an amazing game.

22. How do I log in to the company system using my smartphone?
(A) Install the mobile app.
(B) On the cabinet, right next to the wall phone.
(C) The company workshop is next week.

23. I need to assemble some furniture in the conference room.
(A) How long will that take?
(B) A brand-new couch.
(C) Today on the news.

24. What restaurant do you recommend for the company dinner?
(A) Someone with a lot of experience.
(B) I can't remember its name.
(C) The food was delicious.

25. Didn't you buy some extra ink cartridges?
(A) They haven't arrived yet.
(B) By next month.
(C) Put them in the cart.

26. Can you sign for my package on Friday?
(A) I'll be working at another location.
(B) Let's hang this sign up.
(C) The delivery service.

27. It's difficult to say when the exact completion date of the construction project will be.
(A) Exactly two months ago.
(B) That's true. I'll ask for more details.
(C) It was an easy question.

28. Do you want to walk around the park more or take a break?
(A) The parking lot around the corner.
(B) I can take it for you.
(C) Actually, I'm a little tired.

29. The sunglass advertisement is nearly done, isn't it?
(A) The agency is making additional changes.
(B) Behind the department store.
(C) The monthly reviews.

30. I'm not sure how to connect this printer to the network.
(A) One for each person.
(B) I'll show you.
(C) At the online store.

31. Why was the team dinner moved to next Monday?
(A) I can reschedule it to tomorrow.
(B) I moved to Seoul last weekend.
(C) Yes, I'll be there.

PART 3

Questions 32-34 refer to the following conversation.

> **W:** Hey, Troy! I just found out that the Chinese restaurant near the local library closed last week. I really liked their food.
>
> **M:** That's unfortunate. But a new Chinese restaurant just opened on Sanhee Lane yesterday. It's only 10 minutes from here. Why don't you check it out?
>
> **W:** Oh. That sounds great. Sanhee Lane is close to my home, so I wouldn't have to take my car. I can just walk there. Trying to find parking around here is always a hassle.
>
> **M:** Right. And they have a promotion where you can receive a 15 percent discount if you go there this week.

Questions 35-37 refer to the following conversation.

> **W:** I want to reserve two spots for tomorrow's All Day City Tour.
>
> **M:** Of course. We still have some spots left. Just so you know, this tour will make stops at six local attractions and finish at Marley's Bistro.
>
> **W:** Sounds great! My cousin is here on vacation. She'll definitely enjoy it.
>
> **M:** That's good. Also, you'll have to place your restaurant order in advance. You can choose between two options: the fish special or the creamy garlic pasta.
>
> **W:** We'll both get the fish.
>
> **M:** OK, these are your tickets. Also, the weather forecast says that it's going to be a little windy tomorrow. You should probably wear some warm clothes. You wouldn't want to catch a cold.

Questions 38-40 refer to the following conversation with three speakers.

> **W1:** Hey, Ciara. I've printed out all the documents for the training seminar. Are you almost done setting up the room?
>
> **W2:** My slides aren't displaying on the projector screen. Could you get in touch with the maintenance supervisor? He'll know what to do.
>
> **W1:** Of course. I'm calling him now. Hello, Jack? Ciara and I are in meeting room B. We're unable to connect the computer to the projector.
>
> **M:** Ah, the cables in that room haven't been working properly. You'll have to go to another one.
>
> **W1:** Hmm, there isn't any other place available right now.
>
> **M:** Well, actually, the conference in meeting room C was postponed. I'll go there right now to check if everything is working.

Questions 41-43 refer to the following conversation.

> **M:** Hello, I received a notice today, and it said some repairs have been scheduled for my apartment on Thursday, the 15th.
>
> **W:** Yes, that's right. The owner of the building has arranged to put in new kitchen floor tiles in all apartments.
>
> **M:** Hmm, I was planning on finishing up a report at home on that day, and I'm afraid I won't be able to concentrate with all the noise from the work.
>
> **W:** OK. The times are flexible, so I'll reschedule you for Tuesday, the 20th then.

Questions 44-46 refer to the following conversation.

> W: Good to see you, Earl. Did you enjoy the medical conference?
>
> M: I did, and I picked up some useful information.
>
> W: Oh, like what?
>
> M: Well, one of the presenters, Riya Shah, suggested that doctors such as ourselves take online courses to keep up with the latest trends in medical science and technology.
>
> W: Ah, that's a good idea. It's difficult for us to make time to attend classes in person.
>
> M: Yeah. Oh, and also, there is a mobile app we can download. It was developed by the Seneca Medical Society.
>
> W: I see. Isn't that expensive?
>
> M: I'm not sure. I'll look into how much it costs and let you know by tomorrow.

Questions 47-49 refer to the following conversation with three speakers.

> M: Hi, Leslie. Hi, Donna. It's nice seeing you two at this company luncheon.
>
> W1: Ah, it's been a while, Matt. The last time I saw you was at the training workshop in April. It's been a busy month.
>
> M: Yeah, I know that your department is revising the fall clothing catalog.
>
> W2: "Revising" isn't the word I'd use. We're actually recreating the whole thing. The new one will be much simpler.
>
> M: Oh, that's good. I was in charge of reviewing customer feedback last quarter. Many customers who participated in the questionnaire said that our catalog was too confusing to read.

Questions 50-52 refer to the following conversation.

> M: Hello, I'm calling from Jonathan Lim's office regarding Mr. Lim's interview with your newspaper on Friday. Do we need to arrange anything else before you arrive?
>
> W: Actually, there is one request. I'd like to put some pictures of Mr. Lim in our article. So would it be OK if I brought our photographer to the interview?
>
> M: Sure. Just give me your photographer's name so that I can make ID badges for both of you. I'll leave the badges at the front desk in the main lobby of the building.

Questions 53-55 refer to the following conversation.

> M: Hi, George. Do you have some time to check out the charts in my slides?
>
> W: I went through them this morning. They were very detailed. Great job!
>
> M: Thanks! I think I'm all set for the convention now. I'll purchase my train ticket today. Would you like to me purchase yours as well?
>
> W: Um, actually, the deadline for the Routaber project was moved up, so I don't think I can attend the convention. You'll probably have to present on your own.
>
> M: Hmm... I haven't been here long, and it's a big presentation.
>
> W: It's OK. No one knows that material better than you.

Questions 56-58 refer to the following conversation.

W: Mr. Johnson, thank you for meeting me today. I am planning to write a newspaper article on popular trends in men's casual wear. As head designer of ALBATA Fashion, could you give me a preview of the upcoming clothing line for the fall?

M: Yes, I would love to. Using different colors is the most popular fashion trend right now in men's casual wear. We are currently redesigning all our standard casual jackets to have a wider variety of colors. We anticipate that this will be popular among men between the ages of 20 and 30.

W: How interesting! I see you've got some samples of your new jackets from the showroom. Would it be OK if I took some photographs for the article I'm going to write?

Questions 59-61 refer to the following conversation.

M: Hey, Mindy. I just got off the phone with Mr. Callahan. He visited the job site earlier today to check on the landscaping work, and he was pleased with everything but the stairway lights. He said he would like round ones instead of the square ones.

W: Hmm... But those are the lights he selected at our store.

M: I know, but he didn't think they looked good, so he wants different ones. I was going to order them, but the earliest we'd receive them would be next Thursday.

W: Well, according to the contract, we need to finish everything by this week.

M: Right. OK, I'll send him a text message right now to see if he's fine with next week.

Questions 62-64 refer to the following conversation and table.

M: Rachel, I'm glad we're nearly done organizing the company's year-end party. Ms. Anderson also sent me the confirmed budget for the expenditures this morning, so we can start finalizing everything.

W: Sounds good. Alright, now, we need to select the venue for the party. Here are some places we could choose.

M: Hmm, I was at Bistro 324 last week, and it has a nice atmosphere. But we're probably going to have more than 150 guests attending the party, so it'll be good to have a venue with a lot of space. Let's book the largest one.

W: You're right. OK, once you set the exact date, I'll call our agency and arrange for the live music show at the party.

Questions 65-67 refer to the following conversation and invoice.

W: Good afternoon, Mr. Posner. Did you come to pick up the paintings you wanted restored?

M: Yes. I appreciate you completing the work so quickly. We're planning on auctioning them off at a fundraiser next week.

W: Ah, I see. I wish you the best of luck with that. Let me give you your invoice.

M: Thank you. Um... Something is not right. I asked for three paintings to be restored, not four. I shouldn't be charged for this 20-by-24-inch painting.

W: Hmm... Yes, you're right. I'll remove that right now and give you a new invoice. In the meantime, my assistant will take your paintings out to your van.

M: Oh, I'd appreciate that. Thank you.

Questions 68-70 refer to the following conversation and schedule.

W: Speedline Railways, how can I assist you today?

M: Hello, I have to get from Boston to Chicago tomorrow. I'm trying to purchase a train ticket through your Web site, but I keep getting an error message.

W: I'm sorry for the inconvenience. All tickets bought less than one day before departure must be ordered over the phone. I can help you with that now. When would you like to leave?

M: Any departure time is fine, if it gets me to Chicago before noon the following day. I'm enrolled in a seminar on that day.

PART 4

Questions 71-73 refer to the following excerpt from a meeting.

M: I'd like to say a special thanks to the design team for your amazing work on the RK990 smartphone's user interface. You all did a wonderful job in designing the product, and we're now ready to move on to the next step of our project. We will present the interface to several groups of people who have never seen it to find out what they think. So we need a person to call other departments and ask if anyone would like to participate in the upcoming product tests. Do we have a volunteer?

Questions 74-76 refer to the following telephone message.

W: Hi, I'm calling from Jack's Uniform Boutique. We have some information regarding your order. The shirts have been altered as requested. According to the memo on your order form, you asked for them to be shipped by the end of the week.

Unfortunately, some of our drivers are out sick at the moment. Also, we're still waiting on the pants that you wanted. To make up for this delay, we'll take 20 percent off on your next order.

Questions 77-79 refer to the following broadcast.

M: In business news, Fairways, the country's leading manufacturer of commercial aircraft engines, has been contracted as the supplier of engines for the newly developed Bering X20 airplane. In order to meet the required production numbers of the engines, Fairways has decided to open an additional factory at the start of August. The new manufacturing plant will be built in the town of Willington. During a press conference this afternoon, the mayor of Willington expressed his excitement about the construction of the facility, emphasizing that it will create an estimated 400 new skilled jobs in the community.

Questions 80-82 refer to the following advertisement.

W: Every year, homeowners waste thousands of dollars using central heating systems that need maintenance. To make sure your system is working properly, call Cen-Tech Repair Services at 555-8162 and arrange for a free energy efficiency checkup. Our central heating expert will visit your home to inspect your system and explain in detail what needs to be done. And until the end of the month, take advantage of our 25 percent discount on any parts you order from us. Don't hesitate—contact us today!

Questions 83-85 refer to the following talk.

W: Now, we've reached the last part of our tour, the packaging area, which is also the final step for Heaven Cookies. After the cookies have been baked and cooled, they arrive here where they're put in sealed bags and sent to retail stores across the country. Over here, we've got a small bag of our most popular cookies for each of you. While you're enjoying your delicious gift, feel free to look around the area and take pictures. And don't forget to return your visitors' pass to the security desk when exiting the factory.

Questions 86-88 refer to the following excerpt from a meeting.

M: Hello, everybody. Thanks for joining our production meeting. Before we start, though, just a reminder to finish up your task reports and hand those in to your supervisor by the end of the day today. OK, first, I have some good news to share with you all. There has been a significant increase in our manufacturing output compared to last year, and that's thanks to the excellent work all of you have been doing. Now, I was originally going to have everyone's work schedules for next month prepared for today's meeting, but as you know, we've been hosting visitors from Japan for several days. You should have your schedule by tomorrow morning.

Questions 89-91 refer to the following talk.

W: Thank you for attending today's introduction to the Hartman Arts Program. My name is Whitney Brown, and I'm the lead coordinator. As you're aware, this program assists hopeful artists in achieving their dreams by providing financial assistance. In exchange, we require members to commit some of their time by holding events, such as extracurricular activities at schools, in their local area. I've asked two former participants who became famous artists with the help of this program to join us tonight. They'll be talking to you about their experiences in the industry, and how the program has helped launch their careers.

Questions 92-94 refer to the following telephone message.

M: Heather, this is Rich. I'm calling because I need to postpone our meeting later. My train back to Tokyo has been delayed, so I won't be able to make it into the office in time. I was, however, able to look over the research proposal you created for expanding our client base. You noted that some design changes would be required to our logo, but it would still be recognizable. It's a good idea, but I'm afraid it will confuse our current customers. Let's discuss this in more detail.

Questions 95-97 refer to the following telephone message and list.

M: Hello. This message is for Rachel Preston. This is Robert calling from Risbon Telephone. We are sorry to hear that you are discontinuing your service with us. Before we terminate your service, you should review the list of fees on the contract you signed. Since you are terminating early, you will be subject to a penalty fee. We also ask that you visit our Web site and fill out a survey to let us know if there is anything we can do to improve our service. Thank you.

Questions 98-100 refer to the following telephone message and conference schedule.

W: Hello, it's Boram Lee from TRD Motors. We spoke briefly at the Innomax Convention three weeks ago. I listened to your informative talk, and we discussed TRD's upcoming vehicle line for a moment afterwards. I'm contacting you because I want to hire you to advise us on how to make our cars more fuel efficient. I know that this is your area of specialty, so I'd really like you to join us for this project. Would you mind sending a chart of your consulting fees to me here at blee@ trdmotors.com? Thank you.

TEST 4

P. 66

PART 1

1. (A) A man's making a photocopy.
   (B) A man's turning on some lights.
   (C) A woman's putting on eye glasses.
   (D) A woman's typing on a laptop computer.

2. (A) She is stirring liquid in a container.
   (B) She is picking up a paint can.
   (C) She is standing in front of a fence.
   (D) She is looking at her reflection in a mirror.

3. (A) The man is getting into a vehicle.
   (B) The man is operating a forklift.
   (C) The man is moving some cartons on a cart.
   (D) The man is cleaning the floor of a warehouse.

4. (A) A pavilion is being built in the park.
   (B) A picnic area is empty.
   (C) The trees have lost most of their leaves.
   (D) There is a water hose on the path.

5. (A) A bicycle is being secured to a pole.
   (B) Some people are resting on the bench.
   (C) Some people are walking side by side.
   (D) Trees are being cut in a park.

6. (A) A sculpture is being cleaned.
   (B) A line of shops stretches along a shoreline.
   (C) Some vendors have closed their awnings.
   (D) Stalls have been erected outdoors.

PART 2

7. When are you interviewing the applicant?
   (A) For the HR Department.
   (B) It's been canceled.
   (C) Because there is a job opening.

8. Which express train did you book?
   (A) The Web site is bookmarked.
   (B) The one that leaves at 5.
   (C) It received great reviews.

9. Would you like to try the chef's special pasta?
   (A) I'll just get a salad.
   (B) A table for four, please.
   (C) Can you try calling again?

10. How old is the downtown theater?
    (A) Twenty movies every day.
    (B) It was built 70 years ago.
    (C) My birthday was last week.

11. Do you think we should use a new marketing technique?
    (A) I haven't been to that market.
    (B) I used to shop there.
    (C) What did you have in mind?

12. Where is the electronics trade show being held?
    (A) No problem. I'm an engineer.
    (B) In late June.
    (C) I heard it's in Seoul.

13. There's a package for you in the lobby.
    (A) Thanks, I've been expecting it.
    (B) Did you finish packing yet?
    (C) Multiple box sizes.

14. Who played the doctor in that film you saw?
    (A) A new actress, Chun Hua.
    (B) But I am friends with the producer.
    (C) She's feeling better now.

15. The lease on our office can be extended, right?
    (A) Have you checked with the building owner?
    (B) Call extension number 473.
    (C) I've been working here for a long time.

16. Do I need to set up four or five computers for the new employees?
    (A) Only four people were hired.
    (B) I am not available for training.
    (C) Several new desks.

17. How much does it cost to repair the keyboard on a laptop?
(A) An extra pair of keys.
(B) Around 20 minutes.
(C) It depends on the model.

18. Make sure you turn off the heater before you leave the office.
(A) No, it's at my desk.
(B) Over 30 degrees.
(C) Of course. I always do.

19. Why is the front entrance of the building locked today?
(A) They're installing a security system.
(B) Probably not until tomorrow morning.
(C) It's not my locker.

20. This smartphone comes with a set of earphones, doesn't it?
(A) No, they're sold separately.
(B) It sounds clear to me.
(C) I will come alone.

21. Haven't you already signed up for the conference?
(A) A conference call at 3 P.M.
(B) The sign on the window.
(C) I'm going to do it after lunch.

22. Are the clients going to visit our new manufacturing plant?
(A) A new safety manual.
(B) It's still under construction.
(C) I've never visited it.

23. This is the newest model of the smartphone, isn't it?
(A) No, that one came out last year.
(B) It comes with an extended warranty.
(C) Would you like to buy a case?

24. Hasn't the budget proposal been approved yet?
(A) We just emailed it.
(B) The annual expenses.
(C) That's what I proposed.

25. We need to purchase a file cabinet to store these documents.
(A) Which drawer are they in?
(B) I prefer a hard copy.
(C) Order it with the company credit card.

26. Can you email me the contract for the construction project?
(A) The new office building downtown.
(B) A world-famous architect.
(C) I sent it this morning.

27. Do you want Jane or Su-Young to attend the client lunch meeting today?
(A) You're not going?
(B) The product launch was successful.
(C) They arrived last night.

28. How will you present your research results?
(A) With a slideshow.
(B) Yes, a slight increase.
(C) A famous researcher.

29. Do you have time to look over my report?
(A) We all had a good time.
(B) I have a lot of work to do.
(C) Around 30 pages.

30. Where in the break room are the paper cups?
(A) I'll be careful with it.
(B) Did we purchase more?
(C) Sure. Let's get some coffee.

31. Are you having problems connecting to the internet, too?
(A) It's connected to the computer.
(B) Two new Web designers.
(C) Someone from IT will be here soon.

PART 3

Questions 32-34 refer to the following conversation.

W: Excuse me, sir. I'm an employee of the company that currently manages this shopping mall, and we're conducting a brief customer survey. Do you have a moment to answer some questions?

M: OK, I guess I can spare a few minutes. Does this have anything to do with the recent announcement about renovating the mall?

W: Yes, it does. So what do you think needs to be improved or added as far as facilities are concerned?

M: Well, it would be better if there were a wider selection of restaurants. My office is nearby, so if there were more dining options to choose from, I'd probably come here more often for lunch and even shop a little.

Questions 35-37 refer to the following conversation.

M: Hi, Leslie. How's the landscaping work going so far?

W: It's going well, Mr. Huntley. I'm almost done planting the flowers around your house, but there's a slight problem.

M: What's wrong?

W: I don't have enough fertilizer for the flowers in the back yard. I was about to drive to Panetta's on Johnston Avenue to get some more.

M: I was just around that area, and there was heavy traffic on Johnston Avenue. You might want to take Walnut Lane instead.

W: I'll do that. Thank you.

Questions 38-40 refer to the following conversation.

W: Jerry, our summer computer sale is really attracting a lot of customers. We've only been open a few hours, but look at how busy we are.

M: I know. I think displaying RDK's laptops out in front was the right move. Have you seen the shelves?

W: I have. It looks like only three boxes are left.

M: Yeah. RDK is a relatively new company, so I hadn't expected this. I think we should consider entering a partnership with them.

W: I agree. Why don't I call their Sales Department and discuss their other product lines? This would be a good opportunity to improve our market share.

Questions 41-43 refer to the following conversation.

W: Tyler, do you mind helping me find some printers? It seems like a lot of the merchandise in our stockroom was rearranged while I was on vacation last week, so I'm not sure where to look.

M: No problem. We're expecting a large shipment of brand-new printers tomorrow morning in preparation for our store's summer sale. That's why we moved so many things around. What exactly are you looking for?

W: There's a customer in the showroom who wants to compare the G series and X series models. If you could point out where they are, I'll grab a cart and take them out to him.

Questions 44-46 refer to the following conversation.

M: Hello, it's George Muntz calling from Muntz's Dessert Shop. I wanted to talk about my recent order of apples.

W: Of course. How can I help you?

M: Well, my order arrived today, and I received only three boxes of apples. I was supposed to get five.

W: Alright. I'll pull up your information on my computer right now. Ah, it looks like there was an error. I apologize.

M: Do you know when I can expect to receive the rest of the boxes?

W: Hmm... I'll ship them out via expedited delivery, so they should arrive at your business by 3 P.M. tomorrow.

M: OK, I appreciate that.

W: Also, to make up for the mistake, I'll send you a complimentary box of fresh oranges.

Questions 47-49 refer to the following conversation.

W: Hello, I'm trying to order a camera on your Web site, and I have a coupon for 25 percent off. The problem is, it doesn't say whether it can be used for online purchases.

M: Hmm... There should be a 13-digit code on it. Just enter it when you're asked to during the online checkout process.

W: I don't see a code anywhere, but according to the expiration date, the coupon should still be valid.

M: It must be an old one if it doesn't have an online code. I'm afraid the only way to get a discount with that coupon is to come to our store.

Questions 50-52 refer to the following conversation.

W: James, how are we doing with the expansion of our store's produce section?

M: It's going well. But we have to let our food supplier know that we need to place additional orders for broccoli and tomatoes. Can you get in touch with them?

W: Yeah, I'll give them a call after lunch.

M: I appreciate that. Oh, by the way, I made some posters to inform our shoppers of our upcoming sale. I'll put them up by our store's entrances right now.

W: Great! Sounds like everything is progressing smoothly.

Questions 53-55 refer to the following conversation.

W: Gerard, I know you've been busy lately with the photo editing program for smart devices. How is that coming along?

M: Not too bad. The product development division and I have been trying to ensure that the program is released without any problems. But there seems to be an issue when it tries to save an edited image.

W: Hmm, I see. Do you know when the program will be completed?

M: You'll need to ask someone in the IT Department about that. I'm sure it'll be resolved soon.

W: OK. I'll get in touch with them. I'm concerned since we're supposed to launch the product at the beginning of next month, and we have to conduct market testing before then.

Questions 56-58 refer to the following conversation.

W: Hello, I want to book a flight to Rome for April 15. Are there any direct flights that arrive in Rome in the early afternoon?

M: Well, we have one that lands in Rome at 3:45 P.M.

W: Hmm, that's too tight. Do you have anything earlier? I need enough time to prepare some materials for my 5 P.M. presentation.

M: In that case, your only option is to book a connecting flight through London. If that's OK with you, we have a flight that can get you to Rome earlier.

Questions 59-61 refer to the following conversation with three speakers.

M: Good afternoon. I'm Henry Yoon, a journalist for the *Marketing Digest*. I'm here to interview Ms. Gomez. My appointment with her is at 2.

W1: Ah, yes, Mr. Yoon. I'll notify her right away. While you wait, could you fill out this form? We keep a record of all our visitors.

M: Of course.

W1: Ms. Gomez will be with you shortly. Oh, here she is. Ms. Gomez, Henry Yoon is here for your 2 o'clock appointment.

W2: Hello, Mr. Yoon. I'm sorry, but I'm afraid I need you to wait just a little longer. I have to make a quick phone call, but I'll be right with you.

Questions 62-64 refer to the following conversation and chart.

W: Hello, Franklin. I'm just about to purchase seats for the dance performance. Where would you like to sit?

M: Well, I usually like seats in the front row. That way, I'm able to see the performance better.

W: Me too. How about these seats in the front row, to the left, near the west exit?

M: Looks good to me. Did you want to carpool after work?

W: Hmm... There's going to be a lot of traffic around that time. We should probably take the subway.

Questions 65-67 refer to the following conversation and menu.

M: Hey, Sharon. Before you begin serving our customers today, can you please update the list for today's specials? We had so many customers during the lunch rush, and now, we don't have any more sausages.

W: Of course. What change should I make?

M: Our head chef will prepare some chicken wings instead of the sausage platter.

W: OK. Is the price still the same?

M: Yes, it'll be the same as the sausages.

W: Alright. I'll make the change right now.

Questions 68-70 refer to the following conversation and flow chart.

M: Good morning, Ms. Ludwitz. Welcome to Glamist Marketing Solutions. Let's start off by talking a little about your business.

W: Yes, of course. I operate a small online store that sells vintage clothing.

M: I see. Have you visited our Web site and checked out the marketing planning chart?

W: Yes, and it was pretty useful. I aim to reach out to customers in other regions of the country in the next three years.

M: That's good to hear. So where should we start?

W: Hmm... I'm still in the process of creating a detailed plan to attract my target group. I actually came in today to go over this step with you.

PART 4

Questions 71-73 refer to the following advertisement.

M: Ready to relieve stress and get healthy? Core Yoga Fitness has just opened multiple studios in your town. Our qualified instructors will help you meet all your fitness goals, including strengthening your muscles, losing weight, and getting flexible. But wait–there's more! Beginning in October, your membership will allow you to use our database of online tutorials. So on days you're out of town for work or just too busy to get to class, you can still keep up your workout program. Go on our Web site to download our app so that can you preview some of these tutorials.

Questions 74-76 refer to the following excerpt from a meeting.

W: The first thing I want to do is thank all of you for all the extra hours you've devoted to making sure our new textbook series would be ready to publish. The result of all that hard work is that now we'll be able to present the series at the book fair scheduled for later this month in New York. It'll be presented along with all of our existing series, but that's fine. We've got a display case on the ground floor, and there's plenty of room.

Questions 77-79 refer to the following broadcast.

M: Thanks for tuning into *You and Your Business* on QMOE Radio. We have a special guest today, Martin Greenwald, founder of Productivity Squared Consulting. His company teaches department leaders how to train their employees to be more productive. He believes that having an efficient scheduling system is a great way to improve workplace productivity. On today's show, he'll reveal how reducing meeting times can lead to getting more work done. Unfortunately, we'll only be able to talk to him for a short period, so I recommend you all to check out his video seminars on our Web site.

Questions 80-82 refer to the following telephone message.

W: Mr. Brown, I'm calling from Alcon Airlines. I'd like to apologize on behalf of our company for the confusion we have caused as a result of our mistake with your reservation. I discovered that when your booking was being made last week, the wrong flight code was entered into our system. We have corrected this, and we'd like to compensate you for our mistake by offering you a complimentary in-flight meal. Should you have any questions, do not hesitate to call our customer service hotline.

Questions 83-85 refer to the following telephone message.

M: Hi, this is Keith. I'm one of your delivery drivers. I have some new office furniture that I'm supposed to drop off at our shop in Memphis, but I'm having trouble finding it. The shop is supposed to be at 61 Iris Way. I've been driving down this street for a few minutes now, and I've only seen houses. I'll take care of my other orders first, but when you get this message, can you find out the correct address and call me back as soon as possible? Thanks.

Questions 86-88 refer to the following excerpt from a workshop.

M: I would like to thank you for attending the Sales Department's yearly training workshop. It's no secret that with the continuous traveling, negotiating, and catering to clients, you are bound to get really stressed. In today's session, we'll talk about some relaxation techniques to relieve some pressure during work. Studies have shown that meditation reduces tension and can ease health concerns. By spending some quiet time alone, you will be able to clear your mind and calm down. Now, I will play a video for you showing some common meditation techniques to help you get started.

Questions 89-91 refer to the following telephone message.

W: Hi, Kristy, how are you? It's Madison. I wanted to talk about how we're going to celebrate Lance's retirement. If we want to have a surprise party, we'll need to get together to plan out the details, such as where it should be held. More importantly, we need to keep this is a secret from Lance, unlike the party we had for our manager last year. I still can't believe what happened. Anyway, I'm meeting a friend at the restaurant that just opened on Larimer Street after work. I heard the food is good and that it's big enough to accommodate large groups. If the place is nice, I'll see if I can make a reservation. Call me when you get this message.

Questions 92-94 refer to the following broadcast.

M: Good morning, and welcome to my program, *Business in a Flash*. I'm Michael Alvarez, and I've been running my store for over 15 years. I'm going to share with you some fast, effective tips for promoting your business. Today, we'll be looking at expos. Now, having a booth at an expo isn't cheap, but expos are great for meeting many new buyers for your products in one location. Also, they're an excellent networking opportunity and a good way to see what your competitors are doing. Coming up, I will suggest four ways to ensure that your expo booth gets a lot of attention.

Questions 95-97 refer to the following news report and weather forecast.

W: In other news, the always entertaining Greenwich Community Softball Tournament is upon us. This year, the event will be held at Caster Park. Contestants from a variety of local businesses and organizations will play a series of games. Winners will receive gift certificates for local businesses in the neighborhood. This day is filled with excitement and fun for the whole family. To see a list of the teams that are taking part this year, visit the city's Web site. On the day of the event, the weather forecast predicts a sunny day. There won't be a cloud in the sky, so don't forget to pack your sunglasses!

Questions 98-100 refer to the following excerpt from a meeting and chart.

W: Let's finish today's production meeting by looking at our first quarter output numbers. As you know, the company just started selling dress shoes, so we don't have a lot of orders yet. This is no surprise. But this output of 6 million is a bit troublesome. This is our most popular product line, and the sales team thinks that they could sell a lot more if we could just keep up with the growing demand. So to resolve this issue, we have decided to buy more machines for the assembly lines to increase production.

PART 1

1. (A) Utensils have been piled up in the sink.
(B) Dishes are being wiped on the counter.
(C) A tray is being put into an oven.
(D) A pot is being lifted from the stove.

2. (A) Some people are cutting trees.
(B) Some seats are being set up outdoors.
(C) A performer is entertaining an audience.
(D) A musician is walking onto a stage.

3. (A) A cyclist is viewing a town from a distance.
(B) A tourist is taking a picture of the landscape.
(C) A man is seated on the grass.
(D) A man is setting his backpack on a ledge.

4. (A) A worker is washing the windows.
(B) Some plants are hanging next to each other.
(C) The roof of a home is being repaired.
(D) Some flowers are being watered in a garden.

5. (A) A carpet is being rolled up.
(B) A picnic table is being assembled.
(C) Cushions have been placed on sofas.
(D) Some chairs have been stacked on top of each other.

6. (A) One of the people is strolling past the bench.
(B) One of the people is leaning on a lamppost.
(C) They are facing away from each other.
(D) They are entering a hallway.

PART 2

7. When did you purchase your computer?
(A) The shop across the street.
(B) I still use the monitor.
(C) Four years ago, when it first released.

8. Do you know where Conference Hall C is?
(A) The keynote speaker.
(B) There's a map over there.
(C) A conference call on line 3.

9. That was quite a long concert, wasn't it?
(A) The venue is really small.
(B) I don't know where it is.
(C) Yes. It was over three hours.

10. Where can I find the information desk?
(A) In three days.
(B) On the other side of the building.
(C) I'm OK, thanks.

11. Who's going to manage the sales team?
(A) I managed to finish the report.
(B) Yes, he works in sales.
(C) Probably Mary Jensen.

12. How was the client lunch?
(A) An Italian restaurant.
(B) That's correct. At 1 P.M.
(C) He agreed to sign a contract.

13. You've shopped at Burlington Mall before, right?
(A) Is that the one on Rocker Avenue?
(B) No, it's on the left.
(C) I work the night shift.

14. Wasn't yesterday the deadline for this report?
(A) No, a decline in production.
(B) It took us longer than expected.
(C) The reporter won an award.

15. Whose turn is it to order lunch?
(A) The salmon sounds good.
(B) In the break room.
(C) I ordered yesterday.

16. Where will the corporate workshop be next month?
(A) In May I guess.
(B) No, I haven't been there.
(C) It will be determined later.

17. Let's talk about the office relocation this afternoon.
(A) Does she work in this office?
(B) For my vacation to Europe.
(C) Why don't we do it now?

18. Why are there balloons out in the lobby today?
(A) The newspaper on the table.
(B) Because Ms. Webber is retiring today.
(C) I'll see who's here.

19. How are we supposed to set up our display booth in time?
(A) In room 501.
(B) The newest kitchen appliances.
(C) Maggie said she'd help.

20. Have you taken the employee development program yet?
(A) I didn't know I had to.
(B) An employee appreciation dinner.
(C) Sure. I can take her there.

21. Why don't we expand the products we carry at our store?
(A) Extend the business hours.
(B) I think that's a good idea.
(C) Put them in the storage room.

22. What type of laptop do you have?
(A) Are you planning to get one?
(B) At a computer store.
(C) I have some time to help you.

23. Wouldn't you rather get some food during your lunch break?
(A) I have a project to finish today.
(B) It's quite delicious.
(C) A table for four, please.

24. You sent the clients the invoice, didn't you?
(A) She has a great voice.
(B) Haven't they made the payment yet?
(C) A fast delivery service.

25. How soon can you get started on the building design?
(A) She's a new graphic designer.
(B) Try the rear entrance.
(C) I'll begin this afternoon.

26. Did you bring your current résumé with you for this interview?
(A) It's in my bag.
(B) She's a qualified candidate.
(C) Previous job experience.

27. The last day to book a reservation is on Wednesday.
(A) That's a nice hotel.
(B) No, I haven't read it yet.
(C) How do you know that?

28. Your train to Moscow has a dining car, doesn't it?
(A) Yes, and the food is good.
(B) The airport is nearby.
(C) It's easy to find parking.

29. Are you planning to buy the car you checked out yesterday?
(A) No, I can't pick you up.
(B) It's too pricey.
(C) Our check-in time is 2 P.M.

30. Would you like wireless internet for your flight today?
(A) A window seat, please.
(B) Is it free of charge?
(C) It departs in two hours.

31. Should I print out the meeting agenda or email it to everyone?
(A) Everyone will bring their laptops.
(B) The first page of the report.
(C) In Conference Room B.

PART 3

Questions 32-34 refer to the following conversation.

M: Hello, I'm Justin, the facilities supervisor. Thanks for coming. This is our company cafeteria, which needs to be completely remodeled.

W: Thank you for hiring my design firm. OK, it looks like we'll have to get rid of everything. After we replace the floors, we can put in new tables and seats.

M: Alright, but we're holding a celebration banquet for our R&D Division during the first week of February, and we're planning on using the cafeteria. Will you finish before then?

W: If my team begins right away, it's definitely possible. If I email you an invoice this afternoon, will you be able to make a faster decision?

M: Yes. Our CEO should approve it immediately if it's within our budge

Questions 35-37 refer to the following conversation.

W: The chef just informed me that he's used up a lot of the ingredients for our meatball dish—the special today. We should tell the servers to stop taking orders for it from customers.

M: Good idea. As you know, we have a large party arriving soon at 7 o'clock. I think a few of those customers pre-ordered the meatball special, so we should make sure to have enough for them.

W: OK, but it's still being advertised on our menu board. Shouldn't I take it off?

Questions 38-40 refer to the following conversation with three speakers.

M: OK, that's the end of the company building tour. Now, we'll walk over to the personnel office so that you can fill out your new hire documents. Are there any questions?

W1: Do we need to submit a special form to use the leisure center and sauna?

M: No. The center and sauna are open daily from 7 A.M. to 9 P.M. You can access them with your staff ID badge. Anything else?

W2: Yes. I was just curious when we'd be going to the sales team's office. I'm eager to finally meet our colleagues.

M: Oh, we'll go right after lunch. I'm sure the department members are also looking forward to meeting you two.

Questions 41-43 refer to the following conversation.

M: Hello, it's Gordon Stevens, Manager of the Accounting Department. Water from the ceiling has been dripping onto my desk, so I had to move my computer to another area of the room. Do you know what the cause of the leak is?

W: One of the pipes on the floor above your office must be leaking. I'll send someone from my team to check it out right away.

M: Thank you. Do you think it will be possible for you to repair it before noon today? I'm expecting an important client at 3 o'clock in my office today.

W: Yes, it shouldn't take too long.

Questions 44-46 refer to the following conversation.

W: Hey, Chris. I know you're taking this Friday off, but we need additional workers for that day. We're providing catering services for a party at the Performing Arts Center, and I was just told that more guests would be attending.

M: Hmm... I'm expecting an important package this Friday. It's supposed to be delivered around 6 P.M.

W: Oh, the party is a dinner banquet, so I don't think it'll be possible then.

M: Yeah, I'm sorry about that. You might want to talk to Corinna, though. She told me she wanted to work extra hours.

Questions 47-49 refer to the following conversation.

W: Hello, my name is Irene Marquéz, and I'm calling from Mahal Engineering. Our company will be hosting some investors from Seoul, and we have some documents that need to be translated before they arrive. You do English to Korean translations, right?

M: Yes, that's correct. But I'll be interpreting at a conference both days this weekend, so I won't be available to do your work until next week. Would that be OK with you?

W: Actually, our meeting is scheduled for next Monday, so we need our annual earnings report translated by this Saturday at the latest.

M: Ah, in that case, I can recommend a colleague of mine. Her specialty is financial documents. Let me get your email address, and I'll ask her to contact you.

Questions 50-52 refer to the following conversation.

W: How far have you gotten on your presentation for the Finance Committee tomorrow? This presentation is essential to getting enough funding for our investment. So it's crucial that we clearly describe our plans for investing in Gio-tech's eco project.

M: It's nearly complete, but I'm missing the recording of Giotech's welcome message. I'm not sure who has the video file.

W: Oh, that's right. I was supposed to email that to you. I'll go to my desk right now and send it to you.

M: Thanks. Also, we should make sure the file is compatible with the software in our computer. Do you mind going to the conference room after your lunch break today to make sure the computer plays the file?

Questions 53-55 refer to the following conversation with three speakers.

W: Hello. My name is Vivian Hurns. I'm here to pick up a research paper Professor Chun edited. I need to review the edits before submitting it for publishing next week.

M1: Sure. Let me check. Which professor was it again?

W: Dr. Chun.

M1: OK. I believe my coworker, Drew, met with him this morning. Just a moment, please. Drew?

M2: Yes?

M1: Did Dr. Chun leave a paper with you this morning?

M2: Yes. Ms. Hurns, I just need to see your student ID before I hand this over to you.

W: Certainly. Here you are.

Questions 56-58 refer to the following conversation.

M: Crystal, I'm concerned that we didn't sell many winter vacation packages this month. I don't think our travel agency is doing enough to attract more customers.

W: Well, we're going to launch a new marketing campaign next week. That should help increase our sales.

M: Maybe, but winter's nearly over.

W: Yeah... Last year, we had a lot more winter vacations reserved around this time.

M: Hmm... Why don't we get in touch with our transportation companies and hotels, and discuss two- to three-day packages? This might draw more customers looking to go on a short break.

W: That's a good idea. I'll give our vendors a call right now.

Questions 59-61 refer to the following conversation.

M: Hi, it's Jason from Grapper Industries. I'm calling to follow up on your inquiry about renting our Pro-X Gauge.

W: Thanks for the call. I manage a small factory, and I know your gauge keeps track of a machine's internal pressure. I'm looking for a device that can provide reliable information for our new mixing tanks.

M: Then the Pro-X Gauge is ideal for you. It will accurately measure the pressure levels of your tanks throughout the day so that you'll be able to make sure your machine is operating well.

W: Great. I'm a little worried about the cost, though.

M: It's just $95 a month.

W: OK. But I'll have to check our budget, so why don't I call you back tomorrow?

Questions 62-64 refer to the following conversation and report.

M: I've reviewed expenses for our computer manufacturing plant and prepared a report. Do you mind reading it over?

W: Sure. Hmm... Most of our expenditures have increased this month. I think we should focus on lowering costs on packaging materials.

M: Well, the packaging design for our new office computers is a bit complex. We should try to simplify it.

W: I agree. I'll look into how much this can save us.

Questions 65-67 refer to the following conversation and GPS application.

W: Larry, thank you for coming to get me today. I really appreciate you driving me to work while my van is being fixed.

M: No problem. We live in the same neighborhood, so it's easy! Oh, I just remembered that today's the day of that race. The street that I usually take to the office is closed off for the cyclists.

W: Ah, I forgot about that. Well, I'm looking at my smartphone's GPS app, and there are three alternative routes you could use. I suggest taking this one because it will get us to work in just 25 minutes.

M: Alright. Sounds good to me.

Questions 68-70 refer to the following conversation and schedule.

W: I think the management meeting we just had with the executive board went well.

M: Yeah. It won't be easy building additional manufacturing plants, but it's the right move.

W: Oh, by the way, before going into the meeting, I read your email regarding our new plants' completion dates. We need to make one change. The work on the Westmark plant won't be finished on schedule.

M: Got it. What's the reason?

W: That region has been experiencing heavy snowfall, and the storm's been delaying the construction work. We need to move the completion date for the Westmark facility to sometime around mid-October.

M: Ah, I see. Well, at least this will give us additional time to find qualified factory workers.

PART 4

Questions 71-73 refer to the following broadcast.

M: You're tuning into 104.5 FM, Atlanta's number one radio station. It's time for your weekly community news. It's been announced that the annual dance competition at Candler Park, scheduled for this weekend, has been postponed until further notice. I know that many of you were looking forward to this, but some underground pipes burst, so technicians need to fix them. You can check out our Web site for updates regarding the new date for the competition. And now, here's Nancy Bates with a look at your local traffic report.

Questions 74-76 refer to the following broadcast.

M: Thanks for tuning into Channel 8's evening news. Earlier this afternoon, Bradbury Theater, the 125 year-old structure in downtown, was finally sold. It's one of the most recognizable buildings in our city, and plans are to have it converted into a shopping complex. Wight and Company has been chosen for the job. With proven expertise in renovating old buildings, they were the ideal candidate for this difficult project. City council members hope to generate more revenue for the town, and the new shopping complex will certainly contribute to the cause.

Questions 77-79 refer to the following speech.

W: I'm so happy to see you all here for the 9th annual Heartland Agricultural Management Convention. This is actually the largest turnout we've ever had for the convention, and you'll get chances to meet various people in the field. I hope everyone brought plenty of business cards. Now for me personally, this is kind of a sad moment. As I'm sure you're aware, I've been running this event for many years in hopes of creating a better future for our region and our industry. And I honestly believe that I have been making a difference. So it was not an easy decision to leave my position as Convention Director. At the same time, however, I know that my replacement, Otto Hamilton, will keep up the good work.

Questions 80-82 refer to the following telephone message.

M: Hello, this is Arthur Johnson from Office 881. I'm supposed to have some carpets delivered to me this morning. I know that I have to notify the building manager to use the back entrance of the building, and that's why I'm calling you. The name of the company is Modern Office Furniture, and the people making the delivery should be here between 10 and 11 o'clock. Could you please let them into the building when they arrive? If you need to contact me, I'll be in the office organizing files all morning until noon. Thank you very much.

Questions 83-85 refer to the following announcement.

W: Attention, all travelers. As there are a large number of people traveling through our airport today, there are significant delays at the check-in counters of all gates. To speed up the process, make sure to have your passport and ticket ready for our agents when your flight is called. Also, attendants with yellow badges will be coming around to identify those passengers who require special assistance and check their departure times to make sure that they get on their flights on time.

Questions 86-88 refer to the following notice.

M: Welcome to today's concert here at the Bach Auditorium. We apologize for the late start. There was an unexpected turn of events. We seem to be having some difficulties with our speaker system. Our technicians are currently working on the problem, and we expect the concert to start momentarily. In the meantime, we suggest you visit the front desk in the lobby where copies of the orchestra's new album are available for purchase. Also, don't forget to take a look at the posters by the exit advertising future shows for this fall.

Questions 89-91 refer to the following announcement.

W: Just one thing before we start our delivery routes for the day. I know that you all have a lot of deliveries to make and a tight schedule, but we need to follow protocol when delivering packages. It's critical that you get a signature from each recipient before moving on to the next location. We have been hearing that many packages are simply left on doorsteps, and that cannot be tolerated. All of this information is coming from our customers. As Dispatch Manager, it's my responsibility to make sure that we are making deliveries quickly, but without sacrificing security. Starting immediately, a new client relations manager will be contacting random recipients and checking if you are properly following this procedure.

Questions 92-94 refer to the following announcement.

M: Last on the schedule today, I'd like to discuss the matter of moving our patient records that are on paper to an electronic database. All of the records will now be stored electronically like many other health clinics in the city, and there's one main benefit I'd like to mention. Removing all the paper files that are in our office will create a lot more space that we can use for other purposes. I've asked the office manager to get in touch with a recycling company that specializes in document disposal to come next week and take away all of the paper records so that we can use the space.

Questions 95-97 refer to the following excerpt from a meeting and schedule.

W: Good morning, everyone. As you know, the company will be holding several informational sessions for employees next week. Although they are not mandatory, as members of the marketing team, I would like to urge every one of you to attend the session on social media. I am confident that this class will help give you a better idea of the needs of our consumers. Also, participants in each session will be provided with lunch, compliments of the company. If you're interested, please let me know by tomorrow afternoon.

Questions 98-100 refer to the following excerpt from a meeting and neighborhood map.

W: As you all know, we've been receiving more requests for our recycling pickup services, thanks to our community awareness program. We'll now be making more than one stop in several neighborhoods. We'll start by changing our Monday route. Since this route has experienced the biggest increase in customers, we're going to spread the work over two days—Monday and Tuesday. This is a good thing. I hope that by gaining more customers, we'll finally be able to buy better machines that can process recyclables more quickly.

TEST 6 P. 94

PART 1

1. (A) The woman is seated by a tree.
(B) The woman is organizing some folders on a table.
(C) The woman is drinking from a water bottle.
(D) The woman is closing a laptop computer.

2. (A) A woman is pouring a beverage.
(B) A man is setting down a plate.
(C) A customer is sipping from a glass.
(D) A diner is reading a menu.

3. (A) She is arranging glass bottles on a shelf.
(B) She is placing plastic containers on the floor.
(C) She is wearing laboratory gloves.
(D) She is setting up video equipment.

4. (A) Some shirts have been laid out on a shelf.
(B) Some merchandise is on display outside a store.
(C) Leaves are scattered on a walkway.
(D) A sign is being taken down from an awning.

5. (A) A man is handing out some documents.
(B) Some people are attending a meeting.
(C) A woman is pointing at a screen.
(D) Some people are taking their seats.

6. (A) A bicycle is being wheeled into a building.
(B) Some women are jogging through a park.
(C) There's a woman polishing a statue.
(D) There are shadows on a path.

PART 2

7. When's the new Greek restaurant opening in our town?
(A) A renowned chef.
(B) Ten job openings.
(C) Sometime in May.

8. Pardon me. Is this seat taken?
(A) Yes, it's on my desk.
(B) Yes. Someone's sitting there.
(C) I'll take it down now.

9. Why did you buy a compact car?
(A) Because it's easy to park.
(B) It's a new credit card.
(C) At the auto dealership.

10. Where do you get your hair cut?
(A) Yes, it was too long.
(B) At a salon near my work.
(C) About once a month.

11. Who's the new floor supervisor?
(A) They're on the 2nd floor.
(B) I didn't know that either.
(C) A former coworker of mine.

12. Should I ship this package to the head office?
(A) More delivery drivers.
(B) Bruce will drop it off later.
(C) I sent them by email.

13. These wrist watches are handmade, right?
(A) Actually, they're not.
(B) Here's the guest list.
(C) I'm not sure what time it is.

14. Can you help me load these boxes into my truck?
(A) In the storage room.
(B) I've already downloaded them.
(C) Sure. Where's your truck parked?

15. Why are you setting up a computer on that desk?
(A) A part-time employee is starting today.
(B) Yes. Put it on my desk, please.
(C) Every morning before work.

16. When will the keynote speech begin?
(A) By the CEO.
(B) In Conference Room 3.
(C) Let me check the schedule.

17. What material is this bag made of?
(A) A mix of different fabrics.
(B) It's a luxury brand.
(C) This is a smaller size.

18. How was the movie yesterday?
(A) It was very entertaining.
(B) About one and a half hours.
(C) Sorry, I'm busy.

19. Didn't you attend the company party last night?
(A) Make a right at the next light.
(B) I had to finish an assignment.
(C) We'll be there by 8.

20. I'm traveling to Amsterdam for my next business trip.
(A) When will you be leaving?
(B) Get off at the next stop.
(C) The flight has been delayed.

21. Where should we install this photocopier?
(A) All the software is included.
(B) We don't have room in this office.
(C) A well-known photographer.

22. The number of people taking your exercise class increased, didn't it?
(A) Group aerobics classes on weeknights.
(B) Yes, the online ad was effective.
(C) Contact the new fitness center.

23. Do you have time to review the budget report before noon?
(A) A decrease in spending.
(B) I'm in meetings all morning.
(C) On the accounting team.

24. Should we drive or take the subway to the conference center?
(A) A business management seminar.
(B) I'm OK, thank you.
(C) It's right by the subway exit.

25. We will have to reschedule the meeting to June 23.
(A) When will you finish?
(B) It was delivered on the 21st.
(C) I'll mark it in my calendar.

26. I can show the slides again from the beginning if you want.
(A) There's no time for that.
(B) Sign on the left side of the paper.
(C) We'll take some, if you have extras.

27. Are you enrolled in the marketing strategy course?
(A) I took it last year.
(B) I have a small role in the play.
(C) A local business school.

28. Who's picking up the buyers from the train station?
(A) Traveling to Los Angeles.
(B) A 2:50 arrival.
(C) It should say on their itinerary.

29. Which store location has the best sales numbers so far?
(A) No, an in-store discount.
(B) The data will be released this afternoon.
(C) It's sold at all participating locations.

30. You ordered the extra supplies, didn't you?
(A) Their food is delicious.
(B) Sure, I'll have a few more.
(C) The manager said we won't need them.

31. How did the executive director like the project proposal?
(A) The annual sales projection.
(B) He talked to Lawrence about it.
(C) I hope to, in the future.

PART 3

Questions 32-34 refer to the following conversation.

M: Welcome to Sansor's Law Office. What can I assist you with?

W: Hello, my name is Carrie Lin, and I'm here for my 2 P.M. meeting with Jeffrey Bowers.

M: Hmm... I can't find your name in the system.

W: Well, I set up the meeting over the phone yesterday morning.

M: Ah, our server experienced some issues yesterday, so there's a good chance your reservation did not get entered into the schedule. I'm sorry for the inconvenience. If you're willing to wait, I can arrange a meeting for you within 30 minutes.

W: That should be fine.

M: Thank you for understanding. By the way, feel free to visit our lounge area, and pick up some snacks and beverages.

Questions 35-37 refer to the following conversation.

W: Hi, Will. I'm planning to open a consulting firm, and I was thinking of renting an office in the Telco Complex on Memphis Avenue. You have a shop there, right?

M: Yeah, and it's right in the middle of the downtown area, so it should be easy for your clients to get to your office.

W: That's exactly why I'm considering this location. I actually checked out an office there last week, but it was in the basement. I set up another appointment to check out one on the 3rd floor.

M: Ah, great. Actually, the tenants and I are going to have a luncheon this Sunday at the complex's barbecue area. You should join us if you're interested.

Questions 38-40 refer to the following conversation with three speakers.

M: I'm sure you're all aware that our museum hasn't been getting many visitors recently. I've called everyone to this meeting to brainstorm ways to solve this problem. Mara, you told me you had a suggestion to draw more visitors, right?

W1: Well, we should consider replacing our current audio equipment with small mobile players. What are your thoughts, Tiffany?

W2: I agree with you. Our audio tours are still delivered at the exhibits' kiosks. Other museums in the city are using portable equipment.

W1: It'll be a little pricey to purchase these audio players, but we can start charging guests a rental fee.

M: That's a good idea. I'll contact one of our vendors and arrange a consultation.

Questions 41-43 refer to the following conversation.

M: Hey, Julia. I need you to drop by a client's office on Nader Avenue. It's Berman's Newspaper Company. They want to replace the floor tiles in their lobby.

W: Didn't the office manager say they didn't need new ones?

M: Well, he decided that the current tiles were too old. Please go over to their office once you're done installing the wallpaper at Hearth Software, Inc.'s headquarters.

W: Um… The work here will take me all day.

M: Ah, OK. Well, I'll check what appointments Kenneth has today and see if he can make some time.

W: Alright. If not, I can stop by tomorrow.

Questions 44-46 refer to the following conversation.

W: Hi, I recently dropped a management course at the Wayne Institute of Business because of a scheduling conflict. I thought my registration fee would be refunded within one week. But it's been over three weeks, and I haven't received it yet.

M: I'm sorry for the delay. There were some problems with the computer system, and some refunds weren't processed correctly. Can you please tell me your name?

W: My name is Mito Shizuma. When will I be able to receive my refund then?

M: Well, according to our records, we processed your refund today, so you should get it by Thursday. You can track your refund status online at www.wayneib.com.

Questions 47-49 refer to the following conversation.

M: Hello, I wanted to tell you that I really enjoyed listening to your lecture on publishing. I've been trying to publish a book based on my travels, but I didn't know where to begin. I never knew I could do it on my own online.

W: Thank you. I'm happy that it was useful to you. I know there was a lot of information. I hope I covered everything you wanted.

M: Yes, everything was explained well. I did have an issue, though. You posted a list of Web sites that you recommended for self-publishing, but there wasn't much time to write down every address while you went through your slides.

W: Oh, I'm really sorry about that. That list is quite long. I'm going to email the links to you and all the other attendees tomorrow.

Questions 50-52 refer to the following conversation.

W: Hello. I'm a delivery driver for Stadwell Kitchen Appliances, and I'm here to drop off the stoves you purchased.

M: Oh, they arrived sooner than expected! I'm looking forward to using them for a long time.

W: Well, we're well-known for producing stoves that last longer than any other brand. Anyway, just sign this confirmation receipt, and we'll move these stoves into your kitchen.

M: OK. Wait a minute—this invoice lists only two stainless steel stoves, but I'm certain that we ordered three. I'm pretty sure this isn't correct.

W: Hmm... I'll have to contact the warehouse. Please give me a few minutes while I try to figure out what happened.

Questions 53-55 refer to the following conversation.

W: Good afternoon. This is the Barrel Lounge.

M: Hello. I'm putting together a farewell party. Someone referred me to your café, but I wanted to see if we could bring in some bottles of wine.

W: Unfortunately, outside beverages are not permitted here. However, you can choose from our wide selection of wines.

M: Hmm... How much do you charge for a bottle of red wine?

W: Our most affordable one costs $40.

M: Oh... Gallagher's Tavern's cheapest bottle is $25.

W: I see. OK, why don't I put you hold so that I can talk to my supervisor and see if we can work something out?

M: Alright. Thank you.

Questions 56-58 refer to the following conversation.

M: Excuse me, Cecilia. Since you're our Department Manager, I was hoping I could get your approval to use five of my vacation days at the start of May. And in case you're wondering, I've completed my portion of the Kaiser Flight project already.

W: That's good to hear. But there are still a few more tasks that must be finished before the end of the month, and I'm worried that the project won't be completed on time without you.

M: That won't be an issue. I'm willing to take on extra work and finish it before I leave.

W: Great. That would be very helpful. I'll see to it that you receive the necessary assignments right away. Then there shouldn't be a problem if you're gone during that time.

Questions 59-61 refer to the following conversation with three speakers.

W: Hello, Jeremy. Hello, Ernie. I wanted to go over the magazine ad we're designing for Fergus Accessories.

M1: Let's take a look. Hmm... The background is so bright that the pictures of the jewelry aren't clearly visible.

M2: Jeremy's right. 60 They just look like part of a background. We need to do something about this.

M1: Daisy, can you take care of this issue soon? We need to get this printed by next Thursday.

W: Yes, I can. I'll use a darker color for the background so that jewelry stands out better. I'll make a new draft of the layout by the end of the day today.

M1: Thanks.

Questions 62-64 refer to the following conversation and product list.

M: Good afternoon! Is there anything you're looking for in particular?

W: Oh, I'm glad you asked! I'd like to buy a winter coat, but I'm not quite sure which one is best.

M: Hmm… What exactly did you have in mind?

W: Well, I go skiing a lot, so I want to get something nice and warm. But it can't be too expensive.

M: I understand, and we have some really reasonably-priced padded jackets at the moment. Check out this catalog.

W: Ah, I like them a lot. Do you have that red one in a women's medium size?

M: I'll search our computer database to find out if we have that color in that size. Give me a moment.

Questions 65-67 refer to the following conversation and price list.

M: Hey, Rebecca. I know you wanted to order USB flash drives with your firm's name to distribute to everyone at your company's 30th anniversary dinner. Here are some samples and a price list of our products.

W: Thank you. We don't have a big budget for the anniversary dinner, so I'll just go with the cheapest option.

M: Of course. That's understandable.

W: But even this price is still more than we had expected. Do you think you could give us a discount?

M: The prices listed here are for an order of at least 50 items. If you'd like to order more than 100 items, I can take 10 percent off the total. You could keep the remaining flash drives for a future occasion.

Questions 68-70 refer to the following conversation and ferry schedule.

M: According to the ferry schedule, Michelle Funakoshi is due to arrive about an hour late.

W: I'm not surprised. The storm earlier caused several boats to slow down.

M: That means there's no rush to drive over to the port.

W: Actually, Highway 702 is undergoing some emergency repairs. So we'll have to take side streets, meaning it will take longer to get to the port. Let's leave in the next five minutes.

M: Alright. But there'll still be a bit of extra time before she arrives, so let's grab a coffee there.

PART 4

Questions 71-73 refer to the following telephone message.

M: Good morning, Hye-young. This is Adam Yardley from Marketing. As you know, we're supposed to have a meeting tomorrow afternoon to discuss RXO Footwear's new advertising campaign. But unfortunately, we're going to have to move it to another day. Some potential clients are visiting tomorrow, and management has asked me to give a presentation about our current projects. I understand that you had some interesting ideas, so why don't you bring them up with Karen? She's involved in the campaign as much as I am.

Questions 74-76 refer to the following introduction.

W: As chairman of the Global Health Association, I would like to introduce Mr. Sawada. Mr. Sawada has been a medical professional for over four decades. He recently received an award for the creation of a software program that automatically arranges patient health records by category. This allows doctors and nurses to easily locate their patient's files at any time and helps to facilitate faster service. And now, Mr. Sawada will give a demonstration on how the software works and go over its key features.

Questions 77-79 refer to the following telephone message.

M: Hey, this is Chris. I'm driving in for our meeting, but there seems to be a lot of construction on the highway. I've forgotten whether or not I gave you the final copy of the proposal, but let me send it to you now so that you can begin the budget meeting. And we'll need Jeanell to draft the post-meeting summary. I'll let her know. She's prepared that report before. OK, talk to you soon.

Questions 80-82 refer to the following advertisement.

W: Do you record a lot of videos but don't know how to make them look professional? Then what you need is Expert Movie Designer, the best software program for video editing and special effects. Expert Movie Designer is the only video editing software that includes online tutorlals, which allow users to easily learn how to edit their own videos. By following these step-by-step tutorials, you will be creating amazing material in no time. Still not convinced about our product? Then check out what all of our satisfied customers have to say about our product at www.expertmoviedesigner.co.uk.

Questions 83-85 refer to the following excerpt from a meeting.

W: Everyone, please take a seat, so we can start. I want to pick up from our last discussion regarding the plans for June's technology expo. It's been over three months since we started accepting requests for booth space, but we've received fewer than 100 applications. I'm a little worried because we need to have a lot of booths to attract more attendees. But just remember that the application deadline is at the end of the month. OK, moving on... I'm putting together a group to create a satisfaction questionnaire that will be sent to participants after the expo is over. If you're interested in being a part of this team, please come see me once the meeting ends.

Questions 86-88 refer to the following talk.

M: Good afternoon. I hope all of you are enjoying your first day at work. My name is Clay Bernard, and I'm the trainer for all new IT personnel here at Rossmore Corporation. This afternoon, I will teach you how to use our company's database. I had planned on starting by showing you a video that gives an overview of the database, but the projector seems to be out of order, so we'll have to wait until someone brings us a new one. Meanwhile, since all of you need ID badges, I'll take you to the administration office now to get that taken care of. Hopefully, when we get back, we can get on with the training.

Questions 89-91 refer to the following excerpt from a meeting.

M: Welcome to the monthly branch managers meeting. I want to talk about our existing accounts. Our acquisition of Dos Mundos will bring in a lot of new clients, but we won't have access to their information until all the details of the purchase are set. Who can say how long that will take? Meanwhile, we need to generate more revenue by talking to current clients. I want each of you to create a plan for contacting your top customers and increasing the amount they are investing with us by at least 30 percent. Over the next few weeks, I'll be making some time to discuss the plans with each branch manager individually.

Questions 92-94 refer to the following news report.

W: Let's move on to the local news. Yesterday, Kaufman County Board members authorized the construction of new apartment buildings on Peakview Road. The project will start this March and is scheduled to be completed by next fall. The location's biggest advantage is that it is right across the street from the community recreation center. Tenants who wish to exercise at the center need only walk a few minutes. Listeners are encouraged to check the Kaufman County's Web site to download floor plans of the buildings. Units will be available for rent or to buy.

Questions 95-97 refer to the following telephone message and chart.

M: Hi, this is Steve from Roland's Baked Goods. I'm calling about the revolving ovens you sold us a few months ago. This equipment is fantastic, and it's made a huge difference for our business. Since we installed the machinery, the production of one of our baked goods has gone up by 40 percent. As a result, I was hoping we could purchase ovens for other branches. I'd like to start with the one in Sussex, since at the end of the month it will be getting remodeled. Please call me back when you get a chance.

Questions 98-100 refer to the following excerpt from a meeting and label.

W: Hello, I called all of you here because I wanted to go over the first month's sales figures for our new Powercharge energy bar. Unfortunately, we were not able to meet our sales goal due to many customer complaints. According to Wally Cruz, the owner of Fresh and Good, many of his supermarket's customers have expressed concern with the first ingredient—there are more than 200 milligrams, and that's quite a lot. So I'll talk to the operations manager in charge of our manufacturing plant to see if they can adjust the bar's ingredients for the next batch.

TEST 7

P. 108

PART 1

1. (A) He's shutting a garage door.
   (B) He's mowing the lawn.
   (C) He's handling a ladder.
   (D) He's entering an office building.

2. (A) She's looking into a display case.
   (B) She's paying for an item.
   (C) She's opening a jar.
   (D) She's examining a product.

3. (A) Some papers are laid on the floor.
   (B) Some workers are painting a table.
   (C) A man is pointing at a laptop.
   (D) A woman is holding a drinking glass.

4. (A) A passenger is getting out of a car.
   (B) A tree is being planted.
   (C) A vehicle is being sprayed with water.
   (D) A man is rolling up a hose.

5. (A) A truck is being towed away.
   (B) A bike is mounted on the bus.
   (C) People are entering a store.
   (D) Some signs are being installed on a wall.

6. (A) A customer is putting produce into a basket.
   (B) Cartons of fruit are being delivered to a warehouse.
   (C) Shopkeepers are setting up a canopy.
   (D) An awning is shading some merchandise.

PART 2

7. Where should I store these tablecloths for the charity banquet?
   (A) Not everyone can make it.
   (B) In the supply closet over there.
   (C) Some grilled chicken and vegetables.

8. When should I drop off my car?
   (A) You dropped it on the floor.
   (B) Sometime after 3 P.M.
   (C) At the car park.

9. Who has been chosen to give the opening speech at the workshop?
   (A) They'll announce that today.
   (B) In Conference Room 1A.
   (C) It starts at 11

10. Why don't we try to call Ms. Cruz again in about an hour?
    (A) Around this time last month.
    (B) Because it wasn't there.
    (C) Yes, she should be back by then.

11. Won't you be at the merger negotiation next Monday?
    (A) An important decision.
    (B) No, I'll be away on business all week.
    (C) My major was in Psychology.

12. Why isn't my laptop starting?
    (A) Is the battery charged?
    (B) In a few seconds.
    (C) Through the Web site.

13. How did you assemble this cabinet?
    (A) Much longer than I thought.
    (B) To organize our files.
    (C) I just followed the instructions

14. This tape dispenser is Alice's, isn't it?
    (A) Yes, you should give it back to her.
    (B) In the supply cabinet.
    (C) Would you be able to do that?

15. Could you update this employee list?
    (A) Kim, Sun-Hee, and Mark.
    (B) I'll find some time today.
    (C) The software update.

16. When will the production of the new model be finished?
    (A) Fashion models in magazines.
    (B) Let's see the final product.
    (C) Not before November.

17. Where can I get a copy of the presentation?
(A) There's coffee in the break room.
(B) Did you check your email?
(C) Tomorrow morning at 11.

18. Can the packages be shipped now, or do they need to be labeled?
(A) I'm making the labels right now.
(B) I picked them up this morning.
(C) No, I am not taking my car.

19. How did you enjoy your dessert?
(A) Just a slice of chocolate cake.
(B) It was delicious. Thanks for recommending it.
(C) Yes, to share with my friend.

20. Did it seem like there were more attendees this year than before?
(A) This was my first time participating in the conference.
(B) It's going to be held this Friday.
(C) I already emailed you the guest list.

21. Where did Mr. Kim work when he first joined the firm?
(A) There is one across the street.
(B) In the Accounting Department.
(C) More than 10 years ago.

22. Isn't Nisha Rowshan the most qualified applicant?
(A) No, she's new to this field.
(B) Several openings on the sales team.
(C) An impressive résumé.

23. Should I send out the invitation to everyone or just the new employees?
(A) Business strategies for next year.
(B) Any time before noon.
(C) We only have a few seats available.

24. Can I show you my report before the meeting starts?
(A) Your presentation was great.
(B) Sure, but we don't have much time.
(C) I'll meet you at 1 o'clock.

25. Scott wants us to attend a meeting with the publishing team this afternoon.
(A) I have to visit a client today.
(B) I bought that book, too.
(C) Yes, it's a sample issue.

26. We have a guest performer at the anniversary event, don't we?
(A) I'd love to go to the concert.
(B) We were founded 30 years ago.
(C) Yes, she's right over there.

27. The technician said the new computers will be installed tomorrow.
(A) That's when our project is due.
(B) An increase in storage capacity.
(C) The computer lab is over here.

28. Did you read the email about the updated safety guidelines?
(A) No. When did we get it?
(B) I'll lead the meeting.
(C) It's a temporary password.

29. Will you send this invoice to Ms. Jensen?
(A) I'll do it right away.
(B) A shipping company.
(C) No, it didn't.

30. Have you read what the food critics said about that restaurant?
(A) Well, we could eat somewhere else.
(B) A reservation for four at noon.
(C) I'll read the menu to you.

31. Can you contact the marketing team and give them an update?
(A) Isn't that the newer model?
(B) It arrived a month late.
(C) I have a meeting with them at 1.

PART 3

Questions 32-34 refer to the following conversation.

M: Hi, Giselle. Some important packages are arriving at my home tomorrow morning, and I really have to be there to receive them. Do you think I could work from home?

W: Sure, but how is the renovation budget you've been working on for the new recreation center coming along? The project's deadline is getting closer, and I'm worried that we might be late sending in our work.

M: I'm almost done with it. I can send you the final draft by tomorrow morning.

W: OK, as long as the budget is finished by tomorrow, we should be fine. The proposal won't be presented to our clients until late next week.

Questions 35-37 refer to the following conversation.

M: Excuse me. Do you have any travel guides for tourists? You know, brochures that contain information about local attractions. Most hotels usually have them.

W: Oh, yes. I know what you're talking about. There should be some in your room.

M: Are you sure? All I saw was a telephone directory. Anyway, I'm looking for a bus tour company. I heard that there is one in the area. Can you tell me where it is?

W: Sure. There's a business called Gem Sightseeing a few kilometers away from here. I'll call their office and ask when their tours are scheduled for.

Questions 38-40 refer to the following conversation.

M: Thank you for calling Wally's Computer Store. How may I assist you?

W: Hello, I own a small graphic design agency, and two of our printers broke down. Are you able to repair printers?

M: Yes, we'd be glad to fix them. Just come by today, and we'll have them ready for you by this Friday.

W: Hmm... I'll be out of town meeting a client on Friday, so I can't visit then. Is it OK if drop by on Saturday to pick them up?

M: That's fine.

W: You're located at 1500 James Avenue, right?

M: Yes. Just remember to come before 4 P.M. We close early on weekends.

Questions 41-43 refer to the following conversation.

M: Ms. Reynolds. All the tables are set up, and the restaurant is ready to open at 9 o'clock. Would you like me to take care of anything else?

W: Actually, yes. I got a call from the city's Maintenance Department yesterday, and they said a crew will be coming today to repair the sidewalk right outside our restaurant. Customers might think we're closed because of the work, and I'm worried that we may lose business.

M: Well, I'll put out a sign to let customers know we're open for business, and that they should use the side door to come in.

Questions 44-46 refer to the following conversation with three speakers.

W1: OK, I think we've covered everything about the 20-year anniversary party. I think it's going to be the best one yet.

M: I agree. Donna, you really have done well planning the event so far. I'm excited about taking over for you.

W1: Donna, can you think of anything else Jay should be aware of?

W2: Actually, yes. Remember that we have very strict rules about entertainment expenses. So please be sure to watch spending and make sure that we don't go over budget.

M: Understood. And Donna, congratulations again on your promotion!

W2: Thank you. I can't wait to travel abroad and meet all of our foreign clients face-to-face!

Questions 47-49 refer to the following conversation.

M: Welcome to Stanson Insurance. Do you have an appointment with one of our agents?

W: Actually, I'm with NCB Courier, and I have a package for Ms. Dorsett.

M: OK. You can just leave it with me, and I'll make sure it gets to her.

W: Sorry, but Ms. Dorsett has to be the one to receive this package directly.

M: Well, Ms. Dorsett has just stepped out for lunch.

W: Alright. I'll be back later in the afternoon then.

Questions 50-52 refer to the following conversation.

M: Good evening, Ms. Decker. I'm sorry for not responding to the voicemail message you left me yesterday. I'm just getting ready to return from my business trip to Milan. You said that you wanted to discuss the marketing campaign for the Roscar Corporation.

W: Yes. Roscar will be sending their representatives to our company on Tuesday to talk about the campaign. And I have told Bomin to create a presentation for them. But she needs your video files.

M: Oh, I thought I had already given them to her. I'll send them to her once I get into the office tomorrow morning.

W: You know, I think it might be better if the two of you worked together on the presentation. The Roscar Corporation is a very important client, so we must impress them on Tuesday.

Questions 53-55 refer to the following conversation.

M: Hi. I have a morning membership here at the swimming pool, but can I come in the evening sometimes?

W: May I ask why?

M: I just changed jobs, so I won't have time to come to the pool in the morning on certain days.

W: Well, we normally don't allow that. But I suppose we could make an exception depending on which days of the week they'll be.

M: They'll be Tuesdays and Thursdays. So it'll only be twice a week.

W: I think that should be OK. It doesn't get too crowded on those evenings.

M: Thank you. I appreciate it.

W: If you give me your membership number, I'll make a note of it in your file.

Questions 56-58 refer to the following conversation with three speakers.

W: I called this meeting so that we can discuss where we're going to stay when we travel to Tokyo for the conference.

M1: What about the hotel in Shibuya we reserved last year?

W: That place ended up putting us over the budget, so we have to find another location this year.

M1: Well, there's this inn called Jiro's House that provides affordable rates, even during the peak seasons. I've stayed there a few times, and they offer great amenities and spacious rooms.

W: OK. Michael, as you're responsible for our team's finances, can you please find out more about Jiro's House?

M2: Of course. I'll also check whether they offer any special discounts.

Questions 59-61 refer to the following conversation.

W: Mark, I think I know a less expensive way to order our office supplies.

M: Really?

W: Yes. I came across this site on the internet, and their prices are 30 percent lower than our current supplier.

M: Hmm… But you have to keep in mind that even though online stores offer cheaper prices, they charge a lot for shipping.

W: Well, that's only on small orders. This store doesn't charge for delivery on bulk purchases of over $300.

M: But that doesn't really apply to us since that's a lot more than we usually purchase at one time.

W: I didn't think about that.

M: If we're going to order that much at once, we'll have to get the staff to complete the request forms ahead of time.

Questions 62-64 refer to the following conversation and train timetable.

M: Good afternoon, passengers. Kindly be prepared to present your tickets as I walk by.

W: Hello, this is my ticket. Did I get on the right train? I need to get to Faverton.

M: Unfortunately, no. You're on the XB10 Train. It won't stop at that destination.

W: Oh, this is not good. What can I do?

M: Hmm… We've already departed from Hemsforth Station, so you should transfer to the other train at our next stop.

W: Alright. Will it take long for the train to arrive? I'm in a rush because I have to make a presentation at a conference at 3:40.

M: Not really—about 15 minutes. I think you'll have enough time to get to your conference.

Questions 65-67 refer to the following conversation and list.

M: Hello, Ms. Roberts. My name is Brad Ford, and I'm the Vice President of the Reinheim Consulting Group. I'd like to congratulate you on winning the Investment Management Award tonight.

W: Thank you, sir. It's an honor to meet someone from such a famous firm.

M: Well, I've wanted to meet you for a while. Listen, we're looking for someone to fill our senior analyst position, and we think you'd be a perfect fit for the job.

W: I appreciate the offer. But I'm not interested in switching companies at the moment.

M: I understand. I'll see if the winner of Corporate Finance Award is interested in the offer. Anyway, congratulations again.

Questions 68-70 refer to the following conversation and coupon.

> **M:** Hi, I'm Brad York from Florence Technologies. I ordered for 300 business cards last week. I need 200 more, and I was wondering if I could get all of them by Friday.
>
> **W:** I'm afraid not. We're really busy, and we won't be able to print the additional business cards until late next week.
>
> **M:** That's fine. I'll just place another order. But you can still send the first 300 cards to me by Friday, right?
>
> **W:** Of course. Those are ready to go.
>
> **M:** Thank you. By the way, I forgot that I had this coupon. Could I use it for the new order?
>
> **W:** Of course. I'll use the same credit card information as last time.

PART 4

Questions 71-73 refer to the following broadcast.

> **W:** This is PABC Radio with your local morning update. We have some wonderful news for those planning to go to the concert in Braxton Stadium this afternoon. The current rain should stop by the morning, leaving clear skies for OB Rock Band's performance at 3:00 P.M. But right now, the rain is causing more traffic, especially towards the city center. Make sure you allow more time if you're driving into that area. And now onto the show, Money Matters. Here with us today is renowned financial expert Michael Robinson, author of Spend Smart. He'll be answering questions from our listeners on money issues, so stay tuned.

Questions 74-76 refer to the following telephone message.

> **M:** Iris, this is Martin calling. I wanted to thank you again for opening up the store this morning while I'm out attending a conference. However, I just passed by the store, and I saw that there's still some trash by the entrance. I'm driving to the convention center now. Do you think you could clean it up before customers start coming in? By the way, a technician will be stopping by later in the afternoon. He'll be setting up the new security cameras we ordered last week. Keep me updated on how things go. Thank you.

Questions 77-79 refer to the following excerpt from a meeting.

> **W:** Before we bring this meeting to an end, I'd like to give everyone a heads up about some upcoming changes to our current menu. Our restaurant's corporate office notified me that they plan on adding several low calorie choices to our menu. And our head chef, Harold, will lead the team that will develop the recipes for the new dishes. Once the recipes are set, we will offer the new dishes at our restaurant. By doing so, we hope to attract more health-conscious diners and increase our business by 20 percent next year.

Questions 80-82 refer to the following excerpt from a talk.

> **M:** Now, I'd like to discuss a problem with how we record our working hours here at the accounting firm. We have recently found out that the project codes we've been using are outdated. It's very important that we use the correct codes when entering our hours because these codes are used to calculate the time spent on a client's account. To resolve this issue, I want all of you to re-enter your working hours for the last month. I'll pass around new timesheets

with the revised project codes. If you are unable to find your project code, please see Perry Kay, and she'll look it up for you.

Questions 83-85 refer to the following introduction.

W: Hello everyone, and welcome to the 3rd annual National Professional Engineers Conference. Our first guest speaker today is Charlene Young, who is one of the foremost environmental engineers in the world. She is renowned for her innovative designs in the development of water distribution systems, recycling methods, sewage treatment plants, and other pollution prevention and control systems. She has won several awards in recognition of her continued efforts to seek new ways to reduce pollution. There'll be a small break outside the lobby after her presentation, and juice will be provided, compliments of Barry's Corner. Now, please welcome Charlene Young.

Questions 86-88 refer to the following excerpt from a meeting.

W: OK, let's talk about the final item on the agenda: customer responses to the feedback forms that were sent out this month. We had a lot of positive reviews and several surprises as well. There were many customers who were disappointed by our universal notebook chargers and made negative comments about them. Most of them said that the charger gets too hot, while others have mentioned that the plug bends too easily. So Brian, I want you to take the lead and put together a team to find solutions to these problems and report back to me in three days.

Questions 89-91 refer to the following advertisement.

M: Do you want a comfortable fitness watch? Englewood Tech recently released one that is durable as well. The Y4 tracks every step during activities, such as running or hiking, and due to its shock resistant feature, you don't have to worry about dropping it! This product is perfect for those who enjoy outdoor sports in all kinds of conditions. Head over to our Web site where you can read some user testimonials.

Questions 92-94 refer to the following news report.

W: Welcome, and thanks for tuning into Channel 2's *Your City*, where we update you on community events and activities. We've got a story for you today about the city's new agriculture project, which will provide vegetables, meat, and dairy products to local restaurants. The lead farmer, Marissa Gomez, is confident that the project will provide many benefits, but the most important one will be having less expensive produce. Because all goods will be coming from farms in this area, there will be significant cost savings. Ms. Gomez says she still isn't sure when the project will be completed. After all, this is an enormous task.

Questions 95-97 refer to the following telephone message and coupon.

M: Hello, this is Roberto. I wanted to give you an update about the dinner we're planning for the new employees. Now, the date of the event is still October 22, and I've just confirmed that 35 people will be attending. However, I'm afraid we won't be able to use that coupon from Sushi Heaven as planned. I'm going to look into a couple of different locations. Oh, also, Bill is going to host a talent show after everyone's eaten. Could you put together a list of people who are interested in participating?

Questions 98-100 refer to the following telephone message and timetable.

> M: Hello, it's Nicolas Damira calling from Oakwood Avenue Realtors. Don't forget that you still need to sign one more form before I can give you the keys to your apartment. You also said that you plan on using public transportation to get to work on Orchard Road early in the afternoon. The Market Lane bus stop is just a three-minute walk from your apartment complex, and you'll want to take bus 909. I'll have a copy of the afternoon timetable waiting for you when you drop by to complete the remaining paperwork. Talk to you soon.

TEST 8 P. 122

PART 1

1. (A) He is adjusting a shelf.
(B) He is replacing a light.
(C) He is cleaning a countertop.
(D) He is hammering a nail.

2. (A) Some workers are repairing a road.
(B) A man is kneeling to check the tire of a car.
(C) A driver is getting out of a vehicle.
(D) Some men are securing a car for towing.

3. (A) Some people are enjoying a performance.
(B) Some musicians are putting away their instruments.
(C) A guitar is being placed on a stand.
(D) A group is exiting a stage.

4. (A) The woman is looking through a drawer.
(B) They are exchanging a document.
(C) The woman is reaching for a keyboard on the desk.
(D) They are seated near an entrance.

5. (A) A bridge leads to a platform.
(B) A train is stopped at a station.
(C) Some commuters are waiting in line.
(D) Some lampposts are being repaired

6. (A) A sign is hanging from an awning.
(B) There are potted plants along a wall.
(C) Some paint is being applied to the building.
(D) There are curtains over the windows.

PART 2

7. Do you know where the nearest café is?
(A) Yes, it's across the street.
(B) Two cups of tea.
(C) She's on her way.

Scripts | TEST 8   **215**

8. When is Mr. Cho's last day at work?
(A) Next Friday.
(B) With the finance team.
(C) He drives his car.

9. How much do you pay monthly for your home internet?
(A) Around 45 euros.
(B) Sure, I'll sign up for it.
(C) Only once or twice.

10. Would you like something to drink?
(A) Yes, I like it.
(B) No, thanks. I'm not thirsty.
(C) The menu on the Web site.

11. Weren't the auto parts sent out last week?
(A) A new car dealership.
(B) We had to delay the delivery.
(C) Mr. Banner is.

12. Has the museum picked out the artifacts for the exhibit?
(A) That's a beautiful sculpture.
(B) It opens on the 15th.
(C) I'm going to call them now.

13. Is our assembly line working again?
(A) Not yet, but it should be soon.
(B) Yes, it was.
(C) It's a tight deadline.

14. Where will the jewelry convention take place next month?
(A) At the end of the month.
(B) In Atlanta, like last time.
(C) She's the keynote speaker.

15. Why don't we hand in the budget report?
(A) No, we don't.
(B) Sure. I'll submit it now.
(C) Yesterday morning.

16. Mr. Anderson landed at 6 this morning, didn't he?
(A) All flights were canceled.
(B) No, at the landscaping company.
(C) Well, there's a two-year warranty.

17. Why are the guests arriving so late?
(A) Let's go ask Mr. Rogers.
(B) No. The earlier train.
(C) The delivery already arrived.

18. Who's leading the McAllister project?
(A) It hasn't been decided yet.
(B) She'll lead you to the building.
(C) On the 1st of May.

19. Hasn't this month's workshop been canceled?
(A) No, it's been postponed.
(B) I had no problems with it.
(C) An employee training session.

20. When is the payment due?
(A) I have one too.
(B) 500 dollars a month.
(C) It needs to be sent by Thursday.

21. The air conditioner should be fixed by tomorrow, right?
(A) OK, I'll take a few.
(B) Actually, it was done this morning.
(C) Poor weather conditions.

22. Are you printing this on one side only, or do you want it doublesided?
(A) No, the printer is out of ink.
(B) Load the paper in this tray.
(C) Double-sided, please.

23. I'd better keep my jacket on in here.
(A) I can turn on the heater.
(B) We'll keep your bag for you.
(C) At a department store.

24. Who'll be the interpreter at the International Economics Forum?
(A) I heard it's being held in March.
(B) You bought an electronic dictionary?
(C) Ms. Allen from the RMK Agency.

25. How many times have you visited Korea?
(A) I've never been there.
(B) Round-trip tickets, please.
(C) I moved last month.

26. Do any of you have time to help me move the bookshelves?
(A) Up on the 12th floor.
(B) I finished reading that yesterday.
(C) The part-time worker should be here soon.

27. I'm not sure how to send documents with this new fax machine.
(A) To an important client.
(B) I haven't used it yet either.
(C) Thank you for helping me.

28. Are you available for a meeting this Wednesday?
(A) All the department managers.
(B) OK. I'm not busy this weekend.
(C) I should be free later in the day.

29. How do I install this software?
(A) Of course you can upgrade it.
(B) I have enough, thanks.
(C) Have you asked Mr. Walker?

30. The moving van just arrived in front of our office building.
(A) I'll go get the manager.
(B) Who moved the chairs?
(C) To the new headquarters.

31. You saw the notice for the management workshop, didn't you?
(A) It's a new shop.
(B) He was just promoted.
(C) Yes, I already signed up.

PART 3

Questions 32-34 refer to the following conversation with three speakers.

W: Mr. Wong, Mr. Hoover, I know I haven't been doing a good job keeping the museum neat recently. But it's because I've been so busy sorting through the new historical documents that I don't have much time to clean.

M1: No worries! We've all been busy lately, so it's getting more difficult to find the time to wipe the display glass.

M2: We should consider hiring a cleaning company.

W: Yeah. I can get in touch with several local companies if you'd like.

M2: Oh yes, that would be very helpful. Thank you.

Questions 35-37 refer to the following conversation.

W: Good morning. Thank you for calling Gellar Gas Company. May I please have your name and account number?

M: My name is Scott Prentice. I just moved here, so I don't have an account with your company yet. Can you help me set one up now?

W: Actually, another department handles new customers. I can transfer your call to that department, or you can do it yourself on our Web site. Do you have the address?

M: Yes, I do. I didn't know an account could be set up online. I'll go ahead and do that then. Thanks.

Questions 38-40 refer to the following conversation.

> W: Hello, I want to book a ticket for the train that departs to Chicago at 4 o'clock this afternoon.
>
> M: Let me look in the computer system. The blizzard has forced many people to make sudden changes to their travel arrangements. There aren't many seats left today.
>
> W: Yeah, I figured. I was just told this morning that I have to inspect our Chicago factory tomorrow. That's the reason I'm in such a rush.
>
> M: I'm checking for available seats for the 4 P.M. train. Ah, there's a train that leaves at 8 o'clock.
>
> W: Hmm... OK. I'll get a ticket for that one. I just need to get there today.

Questions 41-43 refer to the following conversation.

> M: Hi, it's Eric Shuuman from the apartment management office. You left a message about a problem in your bedroom.
>
> W: Oh, yes. Thank you for calling me back right away. I just discovered a large water stain on my bedroom's ceiling. I think there might be a leak coming from the apartment right above me.
>
> M: Actually, there is a dripping water pipe in that apartment, so our maintenance crew is up there fixing the problem right now.
>
> W: I see. Do you think you could send the workers over to my place when they're finished? I'd like them to check my ceiling to see how bad the damage is.

Questions 44-46 refer to the following conversation.

> M: Hello, I'm calling from the Cedar Fitness Club. I saw your ad online, and we'd like to have some T-shirts made to advertise our business. Could I get some information about the prices?
>
> W: Of course. They're 6 dollars each. However, if you order them in bulk, we will give you up to 20 percent off the total price depending on the quantity.
>
> M: That sounds reasonable. We also want to have our gym's logo printed on the front of the shirts. Is that possible?
>
> W: Sure. All you have to do is visit our Web site and upload an image of the logo when placing your order.

Questions 47-49 refer to the following conversation.

> W: Dustin, have you heard that the company is going to try to make our offices more energy-efficient? They recently set up a Strategy Committee and are asking employees to participate.
>
> M: Yes, I received an email about it last week. It sounds quite promising. Are you planning on getting involved with the committee?
>
> W: Well, I'll attend the first meeting this Thursday to get further details before I decide to join. Since I'm currently between projects, I have some free time. How about you?
>
> M: I want to go, but I'll be busy that day. I'll be doing the marketing presentation at the Tourette Corporation, so I probably won't have any time. But please let me know what you learn at the meeting.

Questions 50-52 refer to the following conversation.

M: Hi, Chung-Hee. Someone told me you wanted to speak to me about our upcoming staff party. How are the preparations coming along?

W: Well, we're not going to have live musical performances this time. Instead, we are buying new audio equipment so that we can have recorded music playing at the party. Do you mind picking up the equipment on Sunday morning and bringing it to the reception hall?

M: I'm afraid I can't. My son has a baseball game that Sunday morning, and I promised him that I would be there. So I won't have time before the party.

Questions 53-55 refer to the following conversation with three speakers.

W1: Good afternoon, Mr. Anderson, Ms. Walsh. I'm pleased you've decided to take another look at this commercial space. Like I said over the phone, the price has been lowered again.

M: Well, it's perfect for our store, but we have one major concern.

W2: We don't have the budget to pay for any serious repair work. This floor for example... How long has it been since it was replaced?

W1: It's only been three years. And the building underwent extensive remodeling last year.

W2: That's good to hear. I'm surprised that the landlord is selling this place at such a low price.

W1: Well, he's moving to another country, so he needs to sell the place as soon as possible.

Questions 56-58 refer to the following conversation.

M: Olga, I just came back from the mixing room, and there seems to be something wrong with the ingredients for our ice cream. The texture is too thick.

W: That's not good. I also noticed yesterday that our ice cream wasn't as creamy as it normally is. I wonder what's causing the problem. Do you think it might be the mixer?

M: Hmm... That machine is very old, and it's been repaired quite a few times. Maybe it's finally time to buy a new one.

Questions 59-61 refer to the following conversation.

W: Hey, Francesco, an important client is visiting from Thailand later this week. Do you think you could show them around our headquarters on Friday afternoon?

M: Actually, I'm leading a workshop all day on Friday.

W: Oh, that's right. Do you know if Leslie's available?

M: Maybe... I can talk to her about it if you want.

W: That'd be great. Just keep me updated.

M: Sure. It seems like we've been getting a lot more business in Southeast Asia these days. That's exciting!

W: Yeah. And if we keep getting more business like this, it might be possible for us to construct a new plant in the region by the end of this year.

Questions 62-64 refer to the following conversation and voucher.

W: Good morning, Ken. You heard about Shirley's transfer, right? She'll be taking over the branch manager position in Washington next week.

M: This is the first time I've heard about it. That sounds like an exciting opportunity!

W: I agree. Anyway, a few of us are planning to treat her to lunch this Friday at Mallie's Place. You should join us.

M: Sure, thanks for inviting me. As a matter of fact, I have a voucher for that café. Here, you'll see that they have some nice dessert deals this month.

W: Oh, let's see. Shirley really likes strawberry pie. We can get a pie to share after the meal.

M: Great! By the way, we should make sure they'll have space that day. Why don't I book a table for us?

Questions 65-67 refer to the following conversation and graphic design.

M: Hey, Violet. I'm finally done with the initial design for the new Max Energy Bar, and I'd like your opinion on it.

W: Let's see... Oh, it looks nice. But I'm not sure the bar's name is being displayed effectively. As you know, we're marketing Max Energy Bar as a helpful fitness supplement.

M: OK, how do you think I should change it then?

W: Well, you could place the firm's logo at the bottom next to the price, and then, move up the name of the bar. By doing that, you should grab the attention of those who are looking for something to improve their fitness workouts.

M: Ah, thank you for the suggestion!

W: No problem. The clients aren't coming in until next Friday, so you still have time.

Questions 68-70 refer to the following conversation and flyer.

M: Hello, Mandy. I'm in charge of our firm's upcoming Health Awareness Week. Here's a flyer.

W: Thank you. I'm excited that everyone is getting multi-vitamin bottles this year. They are manufactured by a well-known company. There were no presents last year.

M: I'm looking forward to that. Which event are you planning to go to?

W: Hmm... I do want to learn more about nutrition, but I'll be visiting a client that day. Oh, Wednesday's event sounds really fun! My schedule should be open that day.

M: I see. By the way, can you take some more flyers and give them to your employees in Publishing? That way, we can hand them out faster.

PART 4

Questions 71-73 refer to the following talk.

W: I've asked all of you to gather here this morning to tell you about the new packaging machines. They are a lot faster than the previous model that we were using here at our factory. They can package items at twice the speed of the old machines. Now, please look at the checklist that I've just handed out and follow along while I show you how to operate the machines.

Questions 74-76 refer to the following recorded message.

M: You've reached the Culliver Hills Department of Parks and Recreation. Please be aware that we have changed the application procedure for booking community picnic areas. Because of the recent high volume of applications, reservations will now take at least seven business days to process. Make sure to submit a complete description of your event along with the reservation form. A department spokesperson will be with you in just a moment. Thank you for your patience.

Questions 77-79 refer to the following excerpt from a meeting.

W: I called today's meeting because I have some news to share. I know all of you are busy with your training sessions at our gym. But don't worry, you won't be late for any of your appointments. If you remember, we had an expert come in on Monday, Jeffrey Polumbus, to evaluate our fitness center. Although a lot of members are satisfied with our personal trainers, Jeffrey pointed out that we could still do better. He said we could generate more money if we sell more vitamin products to gym members. I know that selling vitamin supplements isn't your area of expertise. That's why Jeffrey is back today to hold a brief activity to practice some useful sales tactics.

Questions 80-82 refer to the following talk.

M: OK, let's begin today's team meeting. I'm going to go over a new procedure that will be implemented at our post office. Right now, all packages that come in are given a label with the name and address of the recipient. However, beginning next Monday, all packages will also include barcodes. We will scan the barcodes every time we receive a piece of mail. This will help us

record the exact date and time a package comes in and goes out. Alright, to get you all familiar with this process, I'll pass out scanners to everyone so that you can try scanning some packages yourself.

Questions 83-85 refer to the following introduction.

W: Thank you all for coming to today's digital advertising presentation: Making your Product Stand Out Above Others. I'm Ashna Faraj, the content manager at JCB. I'm sorry that we weren't able to begin on time. I missed my train and had to wait for the next one. We've got a lot to cover, so let's begin. Oh, it looks as though not everyone has gotten the handout. I have extras here in the front.

Questions 86-88 refer to the following announcement.

W: I'm pleased to announce that Retro-Fit Designs has just purchased a new printer. We can now offer our clients the highest quality design images while maintaining our commitment to being environmentally friendly. This latest model uses vegetable oil-based inks, so it doesn't pollute the environment. Also, the inks are completely recyclable. On Wednesday, we will be providing training on how to properly maintain and use the new printer. And to make sure that all workers can attend, we'll be offering two training sessions, one at 9:00 A.M. and one at 4:00 P.M.

Questions 89-91 refer to the following introduction.

M: Hello, everyone, and welcome to the convention. I hope you didn't have too much trouble finding this room. I'm sorry for any confusion. The program should have included the new location of the event, but I guess it didn't. Anyway, I'm excited to introduce today's speaker: Hunter Griffin. Mr. Griffin is a senior consultant at Midway Bank. His job is to help his clients create smart savings and investment plans. He has a lot of experience in teaching people how to be more organized with their money. I'm sure you all agree that careful planning is crucial to maintaining financial stability. To learn more, let's welcome Mr. Griffin.

Questions 92-94 refer to the following talk.

W: Thanks again for letting me visit your construction company to explain the Mundial Videoconferencing Software. Since you all are involved in major global design projects, I have no doubt that you need to coordinate with engineers around the world. With this program, you can cut back on the number of face-to-face meetings required, which should bring travel expenses down. Suppose you are working with an engineer in India on a project there. You can conduct a meeting online to complete your initial planning instead of traveling to India. Now, I'm sure you'd like to know how to use the program. Did everybody turn on their laptops?

Questions 95-97 refer to the following excerpt from a meeting and product information page.

M: Thank you for attending this morning's meeting. We're going to begin by going over some comments regarding our custom dress shirts. Our shop allows people to design dress shirts by choosing an option from each of the four style components: color, fabric, collar, and sleeve length. A large number of customers have mentioned that they would like more fabrics to choose from, so beginning in February, we'll be adding two additional fabrics options. Now this next part really worries me. Some customers have complained that their shirts have had small tears. This issue needs to be fixed immediately.

Questions 98-100 refer to the following telephone message and order form.

M: Hello, it's Jun from BSA, Inc. I'm calling in regards to the catering order request for the Innovative Leader's Conference. One of our employees found a lot of unused utensils in our storage room. So we won't need any for this event. Please take out this item from the order and adjust the total amount accordingly. Once you've done so, please email the revised invoice to me. Thank you.

TEST 9

PART 1

1. (A) A woman is hammering a nail.
    (B) A woman is setting down some tools.
    (C) A woman is wiping a wall.
    (D) A woman is using a power tool.

2. (A) One of the people is putting down his bag.
    (B) One of the people is cleaning a window.
    (C) Some people are grasping a railing.
    (D) Some people are descending some steps.

3. (A) Some chairs are stacked on top of each other.
    (B) A table has been set for a meal.
    (C) A curtain is being drawn.
    (D) Some plates are drying on a rack

4. (A) A man is drinking from his cup.
    (B) A woman is talking on her mobile phone.
    (C) People are seated in separate booths.
    (D) People are looking out the windows.

5. (A) She's washing some dishes.
    (B) She's pouring liquid into a pot.
    (C) She's reaching for a cupboard.
    (D) She's cleaning the kitchen.

6. (A) A stairway is divided by a handrail.
    (B) A man is holding onto a pole.
    (C) The people are climbing up the staircase.
    (D) Some banners are being removed from the ceiling.

PART 2

7. When will the project be completed?
    (A) Will you have time around then?
    (B) By the end of May.
    (C) For an overseas client.

8. Do you have a spare pen I can borrow?
    (A) Is a blue one OK?
    (B) The pen wasn't that expensive.
    (C) I borrowed this book from Kevin.

9. Why is Marcia not at her desk today?
    (A) I left it on your desk.
    (B) No, it was yesterday.
    (C) Because she's visiting the Seattle office.

10. We need to prepare more copies of our presentation handouts.
    (A) A training session.
    (B) How many people will be attending?
    (C) It's in room 2A.

11. Would you like to try a bowl of our new salad?
    (A) I'll try to be there.
    (B) It was very informative.
    (C) Does it have any nuts?

12. Was it Nadia or Harry who updated the presentation slides?
    (A) A multimedia projector.
    (B) Sorry, I'm not quite sure.
    (C) Let me confirm the date.

13. Who's working the night shift tonight?
    (A) He's a good worker.
    (B) By tomorrow morning.
    (C) It's my turn.

14. Has the air conditioner been repaired yet?
    (A) About 25 degrees.
    (B) Yes, I'll accept the conditions.
    (C) The technician's still here.

15. I'm here to see Dr. Baker for an examination.
    (A) Yes, 3 o'clock is OK.
    (B) He's not available at the moment.
    (C) I'm afraid we don't accept cash.

16. When are you going to return the library books?
    (A) She's the librarian at the local university.
    (B) The rooms were already booked.
    (C) They're due early next week.

17. Where can I receive my authorization card?
(A) The security desk has them.
(B) By 8 o'clock.
(C) After the training orientation.

18. You're being moved to the HR Department, right?
(A) No, they changed their mind.
(B) Some revisions to my résumé.
(C) A new apartment.

19. Why don't I add pictures to the menu?
(A) Here is the revenue report.
(B) I'm not very hungry.
(C) That's a really good idea.

20. Who's opening the store this Saturday?
(A) A special sales event.
(B) I'll display the sign.
(C) I'll take a look at the calendar.

21. Isn't the press conference with the CEO today?
(A) Over 20 reporters.
(B) A public statement.
(C) It's been rescheduled.

22. Would you like some dessert, or should I get you the check?
(A) What kind of cakes do you have?
(B) They liked it, too.
(C) Thank you for checking.

23. I need the quarterly sales report as soon as possible.
(A) A new product promotion.
(B) I'll email it to you in a minute.
(C) It wasn't for sale.

24. What's the cost of this box of whiteboard markers?
(A) It might be on sale.
(B) A marketing firm.
(C) A board of directors.

25. There's no fee for parking at the company building, right?
(A) For almost five years now.
(B) I take public transportation.
(C) Would you like the receipt?

26. Which songs should I play for the ceremony?
(A) She's ordered two cakes.
(B) It's up to you.
(C) I just listened to them.

27. I'm really disappointed with the quality of Mr. Lee's report.
(A) I had an appointment with the director.
(B) Yes, it contains too many mistakes.
(C) Please repaint it this week.

28. Should we buy more vegetables at the Sunday farmers' market?
(A) I agree. It wasn't easy.
(B) OK, let's drop by the pharmacy.
(C) We still have some left from last week.

29. Where are the expense reimbursement forms?
(A) You should ask Mr. Chan.
(B) On a business trip.
(C) A dinner with a client.

30. Will you be driving to the sports stadium?
(A) It's the last game of the year.
(B) The subway is more convenient.
(C) I joined the company baseball team.

31. Why is the marketing proposal taking so long?
(A) By the marketing team.
(B) Hasn't Jamie sent it to you?
(C) I'd like to propose a toast to the presenter.

PART 3

Questions 32-34 refer to the following conversation.

M: Excuse me. I just saw an ad posted on the notice board in your gallery for art classes. I was wondering if it's possible to sign up for the oil painting class on Monday nights.

W: Unfortunately, the classroom is quite small, so it can't accommodate more than 10 people, and the class has already been filled.

M: Oh, that's too bad. Do you think you'll be offering a second class?

W: Actually, we're considering having another one on Thursday nights. I can put your name on the waiting list if you'd like.

Questions 35-37 refer to the following conversation.

W: Hi. I found a note on my apartment door, and it says that there is a package for me here at the security office. My name is Rena. R-E-N-A.

M: Hmm, are you a resident of the building? Your name is not on the list of tenants in our database.

W: Oh, that's probably because I just moved here last weekend. I'm in Apartment 445.

M: OK, but I would have to see some form of verification that you live there before giving you the package. Do you mind showing me your lease agreement?

Questions 38-40 refer to the following conversation.

M: Excuse me, I'll be opening up my own café next month, and I'm looking for some outdoor furniture to buy for the patio area at my shop. The only issue is that I have a very limited budget.

W: Oh, I see. Why don't you apply for our installment plan then? That way, you only have to pay a portion of the total amount each month. All you have to do is complete this application form.

M: That sounds good. But how long does it take for the application to be processed? Will it be approved right away, or do I have to wait a while?

W: It should only take about 20 to 25 minutes. Once you're approved, you can take your purchase home today.

Questions 41-43 refer to the following conversation with three speakers.

W1: Welcome to the Annual Electronics Expo. Did you register beforehand?

M: Yes, I received my registration packet in the mail, but I lost my visitor's badge.

W1: Ah, well, if you show me another valid form of ID, I can let you into the event.

M: Here you go.

W1: OK, Mr. James Won. You're on the list. You can go in.

M: Thanks! But could I get a new badge?

W1: Yes, let me talk to my manager about that. Ms. Park, Mr. Won here needs a new visitor's badge.

W2: Hello, Mr. Won. I can take care of that for you, but I'll need some time. Why don't you visit our desk again in about one hour? I should have your badge ready by then.

Questions 44-46 refer to the following conversation.

M: Hi, Colleen. Do you happen to know anyone who's fluent in Japanese? I started doing business with a new client in Japan. I know some Japanese, but I'd still like someone to check the translation for a sales presentation I'll be giving there.

W: Actually, I do. Her name is Yuriko Sugimoto, and she works at a publishing company, but she's on vacation now and won't return until next Thursday.

M: That's OK. My presentation is in three weeks, so I have time. I just need my slides proofread before I depart for Japan. By the way, has Ms. Sugimoto done this kind of work before?

W: I think so, but I'll talk to her when she comes back and have her contact you directly.

Questions 47-49 refer to the following conversation.

W: Hi, George. It's Helen. I sent an email to you yesterday regarding the construction budget for the new Westvale Shopping Center, but I'm not sure whether you got it or not. I hope I sent it to the correct email address.

M: Hi, Helen. You sent it to the right address, and I got your message. I'm sorry I didn't reply to you yesterday. I'll answer your questions and email you back by noon today.

W: I appreciate it. I have a meeting with the shopping center project supervisors at 3 P.M., and I'd like to report the approximate budget to them at the meeting.

Questions 50-52 refer to the following conversation with three speakers.

M1: Hello, my name is Jay Collins. I had a 3 P.M. legal consultation with Mr. Workman, but I couldn't make it because I was stuck in heavy traffic. Is it still possible to see him today?

W: I'm not sure... His schedule is a lot tighter this week. His partner, Laura Feinstein, is traveling for the holidays, so he's been meeting with some of her clients. But actually, here he comes right now. Hello, Mr. Workman.

M2: Hi, Linda.

W: Mr. Collins missed his scheduled consultation earlier, but would you be able to meet with him now?

M2: Sure. Just give me a couple minutes to fax these documents.

Questions 53-55 refer to the following conversation.

M: Cindy, this is Reggie Hemsley from the production team. I'm calling because one of the lights in our studio went out.

W: I'm sorry to hear that. I'll send Jimmy down right away to fix that for you.

M: Um... Actually, someone is coming here for an interview in 10 minutes. I think we're fine for now, but if you can send him later on...

W: Of course. Once you're done, just send me a text message. Should he check for anything else while he's there?

M: No, I don't think so. Anyway, this is the first time I'll be interviewing someone through our video conference system, so it should be interesting.

Questions 56-58 refer to the following conversation.

M: Hello. My name is Shamus Emory. I have an appointment to check out a rental unit at this office building for my art classes.

W: Welcome, Mr. Emory. Thank you for coming. I'm Wendy Kim, and I'm the complex's property manager.

M: Pleased to meet you. I'd like to get some space on the top floor. That way, my students can look out at the wonderful scenery around here while doing their work.

W: Of course. We'll look there first. Also, did I tell you that there is a large cafeteria on the first floor? It can only be used by tenants and employees of this complex. Your students would have access to it as well.

Questions 59-61 refer to the following conversation.

W1: Hello, Giselle. I looked over our manufacturing schedule. Aren't we supposed to begin making the uniforms for Tarco Bistro this week?

W2: Actually, I wanted to discuss that with you...

W1: We guaranteed that the uniforms would be completed by the 25th of this month, right?

W2: We did. But the thing is, we still haven't gotten the nylon fabric. I contacted our supplier to see what is causing the delay.

W1: Oh, what happened?

W2: Well, I'm meeting with them in our office in 20 minutes.

W1: Alright. Keep me informed. If the shipment is delayed any longer, we'll most likely have to use another company to supply the fabric.

Questions 62-64 refer to the following conversation and sign.

M: Good morning. What is the reason for your visit to the Terreston Department of Transportation?

W: Hello. I'd like to register for the driver's license exam.

M: It'll be $45 to sign up.

W: Oh, that's more than I expected. OK, when is the earliest date I can take it?

M: Give me a moment to check the system. Alright, it looks like there is an available slot on May 27.

W: Hmm... I'll be out of town for a business trip during the last week of May.

M: Then, how about June 4?

W: That'll work!

M: Great. Just fill out this form so that I can make a reservation for you. Afterward, go to the next window to submit your payment.

Questions 65-67 refer to the following conversation and floor plans.

M: Hello, I'm planning to move to Cerksville during the first week of July. My firm is transferring me to our branch there, and the HR manager referred me to your agency. I'm looking for an apartment with two rooms.

W: Alright. Let me show you some of our available listings.

M: Thank you. Oh, it looks like there are three-room places, too.

W: Yes, both of them are actually located downtown and are very roomy.

M: Hmm, but I'd like to keep it under $800 a month.

W: Well, how about this two-bedroom apartment? It's $750, so it should be within your budget.

M: OK, I want to check it out. Can I make an appointment to do that next week?

W: Let me look at my schedule.

Questions 68-70 refer to the following conversation and Web page.

M: Hey, Daniela, it's great to see you. Are you still working at the same place?

W: Yes, for the moment. I like the job because it pays pretty well. But I really want my work to involve visiting different cities around the world. My current company hasn't expanded abroad yet, so I'm hoping to find something new.

M: Well, you should visit the job advertising Web site: employnet.com. You can narrow the search parameters by the type of travel that the position requires.

W: Oh, nice. I'll check that out later. What about you? How's your job treating you?

M: Well, my last day of work is actually next Thursday. I'm planning to go into business for myself next month. I'm looking forward to being a boss!

PART 4

Questions 71-73 refer to the following announcement.

M: I'd like to move on to the last item on our agenda today. Our company is committed to helping staff members maintain a healthy lifestyle, so we're going to be providing complimentary exercise classes. A fitness trainer will be holding a session once a week in our event room. Participating employees will get complimentary healthy snacks and drinks after every session. If you're interested, visit the company's Web site to download a registration form. Once you've completed it, just hand it in to me by next Friday.

Questions 74-76 refer to the following telephone message.

W: This message is for Greg. My name is Pam, coach of the Fairview Bruins soccer team. I just received the schedule for the use of the soccer field next month. My team has the field from 7 to 8 P.M. But here's the thing: most of my players live on the other side of town, which means some won't get home until after 9. Your team has the field from 6 to 7. Do you mind giving me a call when you have some time? My number is 555-9284.

Questions 77-79 refer to the following announcement.

W: We still need more volunteers to help clean up the front of the library on Saturday, May 12. This is a great chance to do your part to support the community. If you would like to lend a hand, come to the main entrance of the library by 10 A.M. This year, we're going to focus on the large planters outside the building. We'll be pulling out weeds and ivy, and trimming overgrown shrubs and bushes. Bring yard tools if you have any, and make sure to wear gloves. I think we could make the library look nice and neat in a few hours. Obviously, the more workers we have, the faster we will finish. And just like last year, sandwiches will be provided by Dom's Deli and will be given out to all volunteers at noon.

Questions 80-82 refer to the following news report.

M: Now for today's community news. This Saturday, the yearly Harvest Festival will take place at downtown Riverton's outdoor market from 7 A.M. to 11 P.M. There will be live performances, refreshments, and a variety of contests and drawings for prizes. To find out more about the list of events, please go to www.KC102.com. We anticipate heavy traffic all weekend, so driving and parking will be more difficult than usual. If you're heading to the downtown area, there are a few subway lines.

Questions 83-85 refer to the following excerpt from a meeting.

W: Thank you for joining today's meeting. As you all know, Balk Automotive has chosen our agency to create an ad series for their new line of sports cars. These vehicles will be out in March, so we'll need to finalize the designs soon. For the rest of the meeting today, I want to brainstorm some ideas. We'll split into groups of four. But before we do that, here's a brochure that provides some information about each of the cars that will come out.

Questions 86-88 refer to the following excerpt from a speech.

M: I am very pleased to see that such a large crowd has gathered here today for the retirement celebration of our dear colleague, Randy Milton. It's not really surprising that so many people want to honor Randy for his achievements with the company. Though he is multi-talented, what I appreciate most is Randy's ability to lead others. When he was promoted to Chief Marketing Officer, we were just a small agency advertising for local businesses. But thanks to his leadership, we are now one of the most renowned advertising agencies in the country. On behalf of everyone here, I would like to say thank you Randy, and best of luck in your retirement!

Questions 89-91 refer to the following excerpt from a meeting.

W: I'd like to thank all the executives for joining me today. As Vice President of Operations, it is my job to make sure that everything here runs smoothly and efficiently. As you recall, several departments transferred to our headquarters to make communication easier. However, the engineering team is saying that there is too much noise in the office now. The facility manager offered to set up bigger partitions to help block out the sound, but I think it would be better to rent another small office in the building for them. It would cost more, but it's definitely worth considering. We can't afford for Engineering to lose focus. They would be much more efficient if they didn't have to worry about other people distracting them.

Questions 92-94 refer to the following excerpt from a meeting.

W: And now, for our last order of business: our unlimited vacation policy. As you know, under this program, you are allowed to take as many personal days away from the office as you'd like. We understand that a well-rested employee is happier in the workplace, and as a result, performs much better. So, to motivate our staff to get out of the office more, we're willing to pay for a round-trip ticket for two to a destination of your choice. Now, you might ask yourself, "How do I take advantage of this opportunity?" Well, I have here a brochure that outlines the rules and process. I'll pass it out after this meeting.

Questions 95-97 refer to the following telephone message and list.

M: Ms. Menks, this is Roger calling from Mecho Auto. I'd like to inform you that we've finished checking your van. You can pick it up any time tomorrow. But make sure you come before 5 P.M. because we are closing early tomorrow to remodel our shop. Also, while we were performing the maintenance, we found several issues that you may want to consider fixing. Since we can't make the repairs without your approval, we made a list of the problems and sent it to your email address that you gave us yesterday. Please look it over and let us know if you'd like us to take care of any of the items on the list. And just so you know, for a limited time, we're offering a special reduced price on seat replacements.

Questions 98-100 refer to the following telephone message and map.

M: Hello, this is Hafiz from Allentown Realtors. I've got an excellent spot for your new hair salon. It's on the west side of town, directly across the street from Hooper's Supermarket. This area should give you a lot of visibility, especially now that the coffee shop is open 24 hours a day, and there are always people coming and going. I went ahead and called the owner, and he said that they've already gotten a few offers on the place. I know that this location is pricey, and it costs a bit more than what you initially had in mind. But it is an ideal spot, so I really think the higher price is worth it. Give me a call, and let's discuss it.

TEST 10   P. 150

PART 1

1. (A) She's carrying a basket.
    (B) She's washing some clothes.
    (C) She's folding a towel.
    (D) She's organizing some boxes.

2. (A) A server is standing by a table.
    (B) Some people are waiting to be seated.
    (C) Some customers are paying for their meal.
    (D) A woman is pouring a beverage into a glass.

3. (A) A fan is being installed in a room.
    (B) A photo is being removed from a frame.
    (C) Some furniture is being delivered to a home.
    (D) Some artwork has been hung on the walls.

4. (A) Some construction tools are being unloaded from a truck.
    (B) Some shelves are being disassembled.
    (C) A worker is taking measurements of a wooden board.
    (D) A man is operating machinery.

5. (A) Some books are being shelved by the door.
    (B) Some cords have been extended on the desk.
    (C) A man is connecting a keyboard to a computer.
    (D) A man is sliding a cart under a workstation.

6. (A) People are getting on a boat from a pier.
    (B) There's a parking area near the beach.
    (C) Yachts are floating under a bridge.
    (D) Some tables are being set up outside a restaurant.

PART 2

7. Who's the event coordinator for the car trade show?
   (A) In the display booth.
   (B) That'd be Brian Johnson.
   (C) Check the back of the truck.

8. Mr. Keith has completed the management training course, hasn't he?
   (A) No, the accounting manager.
   (B) Yes, last month.
   (C) Fifty people per session.

9. Pardon me. Why hasn't the performance started yet?
   (A) Two tickets for the 7 P.M. show.
   (B) At the Silverton Auditorium.
   (C) One of the musicians is running late.

10. Where can I find information on upcoming local events?
    (A) At the community center.
    (B) Throughout the summer.
    (C) She's a local artist.

11. How can we complete the project before the deadline?
    (A) To be honest, I don't know either.
    (B) By 5 P.M. on Wednesday.
    (C) Yes, the report has already been finished.

12. When will the company directory be completed?
    (A) I'm on my last page.
    (B) On the 4th floor.
    (C) A list of names.

13. Is there a phone charger I can borrow?
    (A) My battery is full.
    (B) I paid back my loan.
    (C) There's one by that wall.

14. Didn't you buy a jacket here last week?
    (A) I brought a coat, too.
    (B) It's supposed to be cold today.
    (C) Yes, a leather one.

15. Could you help the diners at that table?
    (A) They won't attend the conference.
    (B) I reserved a table for two.
    (C) Sure, no problem.

16. I'll get coffee for everyone before this morning's meeting.
    (A) No, to discuss the budget.
    (B) That's very nice of you.
    (C) A very popular café.

17. Doesn't the restaurant stay open until 10 P.M.?
    (A) It just opened this week.
    (B) That sounds like a great idea.
    (C) Not on weeknights.

18. When will the job interview in the meeting room finish?
    (A) She's a qualified candidate.
    (B) It's almost over.
    (C) I'll see you there.

19. It's OK to contact him on the weekend, isn't it?
    (A) The number of employees.
    (B) Next Sunday at noon.
    (C) It shouldn't be a problem.

20. Would you mind printing a report for me?
    (A) Yes, put it next to the printer.
    (B) In color please.
    (C) No, I don't mind at all.

21. Why did you modify the settings on the camera?
    (A) Three camera operators.
    (B) A new software.
    (C) The studio was too dark.

22. The home appliance convention was held in Berlin last year, right?
    (A) Yes, we unveiled our new products there.
    (B) No, I bought a TV.
    (C) Which speakers?

23. Should we order new monitors for the design team or not?
(A) Their current ones are too old.
(B) The sign was purchased yesterday.
(C) They offer free installation.

24. How will we recruit five new employees?
(A) They're at an orientation.
(B) The date for the interviews.
(C) By listing the openings on our Web site.

25. Your new car will be ready to be picked up at noon tomorrow.
(A) Great. I'll come by then.
(B) Change the tires.
(C) I can give you a ride.

26. Didn't you put in a request for a vacation leave?
(A) Yes, but it got declined.
(B) A trip to New Zealand.
(C) I requested a window seat.

27. How long did the marketing presentation last?
(A) Yes, for the advertising campaign.
(B) It's on the 1st floor.
(C) There was only one slide.

28. Why were so many train tickets sold this month?
(A) There's a long holiday coming up.
(B) Our monthly meeting is this afternoon.
(C) I like traveling by plane.

29. Is it going to snow during our charity event on Tuesday?
(A) Preparations are going really slow.
(B) Raising money for the arts program.
(C) Yes, make sure to dress warm.

30. Remember to pick up your personal belongings from the security desk.
(A) Of course. I won't forget.
(B) A jacket and a bag.
(C) It belongs to my coworker.

31. When are we going to update the computer software?
(A) Probably on the Web site.
(B) Hiro already took care of it.
(C) Faster than the current one.

PART 3

Questions 32-34 refer to the following conversation.

W: Hi, Clark. I attended the workshop yesterday on our company's new accounting software, but I'm having a hard time entering my expense report with it. Have you tried using it yet?

M: No. I wasn't at the workshop, but I'm on my way to see Alice in the IT Department. She's going to teach me how the program works.

W: Oh, I didn't know you weren't there yesterday. Is it OK if I go with you and ask for Alice's help as well?

Questions 35-37 refer to the following conversation with three speakers.

W1: Welcome to Falcor Public Library.

M: Hello, I'm Jeremy Kim, and I want to pick up a book that I reserved in advance.

W1: Of course, Mr. Kim.

M: Also, I was wondering if I would be able to keep this book for one month instead of two weeks. I'll be going on a business trip next week and won't be returning until the end of the month.

W1: Hmm… I'm not sure if that's possible. I'll talk to the head librarian. Ms. Chin, what is our rule about allowing patrons to extend their rental period for another two weeks?

W2: We can allow it, Tammy. Mr. Kim just needs to fill out a form acknowledging he'll return the book at the end of the month.

Questions 38-40 refer to the following conversation.

W: Mike, do you know if the new family restaurant by the natural history museum is any good? I'm in charge of organizing the monthly department luncheon, and I'm looking for a new place to have it this month.

M: Well, I went there with a friend last week, and they had a lot of menu choices. But it took too long to get our food. And it looked like they were understaffed. They should hire more employees.

W: Oh, that's too bad. Well, all of the other restaurants I've called in the area are already fully booked. So I guess we have no choice but to have our gathering in our company's banquet hall again.

Questions 41-43 refer to the following conversation.

W: Hi, Ted. You work at Gerry's House Furniture, right? I heard on the radio that a new factory is going to be built in the city. Do you have any more information about it?

M: Well, the company is expanding, and the owner plans on generating more jobs in this area. We expect to start production on the new site next month, and we will need to hire a lot of workers.

W: That's great. This will really boost the local economy. Also, my son's been looking for a job, and he's a skilled furniture designer.

M: Oh, why don't you send his résumé to my company email address? I'll personally review it and see if there is a suitable position for him at Gerry's.

Questions 44-46 refer to the following conversation.

W: Hello, the executive card holders in your store look great. I'd like to purchase some, but I want to know if it's possible for you to put our company logo on them.

M: Sure, we can do that for you. But since customizing the card holders is a special order, you'd have to go to our store's Web site to order them.

W: Oh, I see. I'll need to order about 100 card holders for an upcoming seminar, so do you think you can give me a discount on my order?

M: I'm sorry, but we don't offer discounts on any special orders.

Questions 47-49 refer to the following conversation.

W: Hi, my name is Cambria Price. I'm glad to see Weiman Global Associates at this year's career fair. I'm looking for employment at a law firm.

M: Thank you for coming by, Ms. Price. We have several openings, but all candidates must have experience working with international clients.

W: Well, I interned at a law office that offered its services to many international clients, and I'm also fluent in Mandarin and Russian. More details are listed in my résumé. Let me give you a copy.

M: Thank you. We're going to be conducting interviews after lunch. Could you come back then? We'd like to hear more about your skills and experience.

Questions 50-52 refer to the following conversation with three speakers.

W1: Hey, Kathy. I've got a caller from a law firm on the line. He may be interested in our services.

W2: Thank you for calling Eco Recyclers, this is Kathy. How may I be of assistance?

M: Hello, I'm an attorney in this area, and I'd like to dispose of some old computers and printers in a safe manner. Would your company be able to get rid of these items?

W2: Of course, I'll explain the process. Once you schedule an appointment, one of our workers will come by to pick up your equipment.

M: How much do you charge for that?

W2: That depends. If you'd like, I can stop by your office any time next week to go over the exact details.

M: Sure, I'm free next Wednesday.

Questions 53-55 refer to the following conversation.

M: Suzie, I talked to Michael in HR this morning, and he said that our new intern, Burt, is going to start work on November 21.

W: Oh, that means we won't be here to train him.

M: Right. We'll be at the technology conference in Tokyo that week.

W: Well, why don't we just have him start in December instead? After all, there will only be about a week left in November.

M: Yeah. That's a good idea. I'll call Michael and see what he says about it.

Questions 56-58 refer to the following conversation.

M: Excuse me. I'm looking for a door knob for my house. The original one broke recently. A friend of mine suggested that I come to this hardware store when I told her I was doing some repair work in my house. Here. I brought the door knob to show you.

W: Well, we carry quite a lot of replacement parts for homes, and we have the same type of knob you need, just not in that color, though. But let me show you what we have anyways.

M: Hmm, I was really hoping that I could find one in the same color so that it will match the other ones in the house.

W: I can probably order one for you from the manufacturer. But it's going to take quite a while for the item to arrive. Five to seven weeks at least. Would that be OK with you?

Questions 59-61 refer to the following conversation.

M: You've reached Bruno's. What can I assist you with?

W: Hello. I accidentally dropped my smartphone in my swimming pool. And I wanted to bring it into your store today to get it repaired.

M: I'm afraid all of our technicians are busy today. You should open the phone up and let it dry for a few hours.

W: I've tried that. Is there really no way you can help me? I'm going on vacation tomorrow, and I really need this device.

M: Well, I have some time before my next consultation, but you'll have to come in within the next 30 minutes.

W: Great. I'll be there in 15 minutes.

Questions 62-64 refer to the following conversation and order form.

W: Rodney, the catering company just called me.

M: Oh, regarding the holiday party?

W: Yeah. We need to send them the finalized order by the end of the week. I'm going over the form, and I realized we'll need additional fruit bowls.

M: Ah, yes. We forgot to account for the two vegetarians in R&D. Can you get in touch with the caterer again to let them know about this? By the way, did you talk to Gary Burke about what he needs for his live guitar show?

W: I did. He actually emailed me a list earlier. I'll go ahead and forward that to you right now so that you can look over it.

Questions 65-67 refer to the following conversation and voucher.

W: Hello, I'd like to purchase tickets for *Marvelous Fiction* for this Friday at 8 P.M.

M: I'm afraid all of the show times for that day are sold out because it's the opening night of the movie.

W: Hmm… What about the next day? Are there any available times?

M: Yes, but only for in evening.

W: That's fine. OK, I'd like two middle row seats for the 9 P.M. show then. Here's my credit card. Oh! And I also have this voucher.

M: Thank you. Let's see… This voucher can only be applied to one ticket.

W: I understand.

M: OK. Here's your receipt. Also, if you're planning to have dinner around here that day, you should try the Organic Planter. It just opened last week.

Questions 68-70 refer to the following conversation and warranty information.

M: Darho Electronics. What can I help you with?

W: Hello, the sports watch I ordered from you last month broke. I have a one-year warranty, so I want to exchange the item.

M: I see. While we do offer warranties on all of our merchandise, there are some restrictions. Not all issues are covered, so depending on the situation, you might not be able to exchange your device.

W: Oh, well… I accidentally dropped something on it, which cracked the screen.

M: Hmm… Regrettably, our warranty does not offer coverage for that kind of case.

W: Really?

M: I'm afraid so. You should just look into replacing the screen.

W: OK. I'll call different stores to see which place offers the cheapest repair rate.

PART 4

Questions 71-73 refer to the following instructions.

M: On behalf of Blumenthal Associates, I'd like to welcome you all to our firm. Let's get started with some forms. Please look at the first one, as it is the most important. The accounting team must receive this to enter you into the payroll system. If you do not turn it in by this Wednesday, you may not be able to receive your first month's salary on time. Take some time to carefully go over the rest of the paperwork. If you have any inquiries regarding the forms, feel free to direct them to me.

Questions 74-76 refer to the following excerpt from a workshop.

M: OK, that's the end of this class on sales techniques here at Cooper Solutions. I saw significant progress from some of you during our role-play activities. Don't forget, this session was recorded and will be available on our Web site for free. We recommend that you have a look at it from home, so you can review the key points you've learned today. And for those of you looking for a more personalized session, Francine has more than 25 years of experience.

Questions 77-79 refer to the following broadcast.

W: Today, Baleville transportation officials announced that some changes will be implemented to the city's subway service. On the nights of baseball games, trains will run every five minutes so that people can get to the stadium and go back home more quickly. The changes were made in response to the constant complaints about the lack of subway trains when a major event is held in the city. In addition, more express trains will be operating for people who live far from the stadium. So if you decide to take the subway on game nights, be sure to check out the route map to locate the station closest to you.

Questions 80-82 refer to the following talk.

M: I'm happy to see everyone here this morning. Today is the first day of the technology expo, and we want to make sure everything goes as planned. It's sure to be an exciting event. Jackie, I've noticed that you've set out the information pamphlets on the desks. Thanks for doing that. Martin will be bringing in some boxes of water bottles soon. They have our company logo on them. Please hand them out to people who stop by our booth. Alright, I see some hands up. But before I answer your questions, let's go over our schedule one more time.

Questions 83-85 refer to the following instructions.

W: Pay attention, everyone. Your job is to make sure that the laboratory is ready to be used by the technicians before they arrive here every day. First of all, make sure all the supplies are in stock. You do this by looking at the list on this wall and checking to see if all of the items are on that shelf. If something from the list is not there, look in the large cabinet in the corner of the room, or talk to Heather. OK, now, I'll show you how to put on the safety equipment.

Questions 86-88 refer to the following introduction.

M: Hello, everyone. Welcome to a special dinner to benefit the senior citizens of our community. It is our hope that we will raise enough money tonight to renovate the local park in order that we can provide a safe outdoor public space for the elderly. Arnold Vans, a civil engineer, will be leading this project, and he will talk about the renovation plans tonight. Arnold is an active member of our city, and we are pleased to have him oversee this effort. Also, before I forget, Sawyer's Department Store has prepared a gift set for everyone attending tonight's event, so make sure to pick one up on your way out.

Questions 89-91 refer to the following announcement.

W: Good morning. As I'm sure you're all aware, we heard from a lot of clients yesterday who were unhappy about being unable to access our online banking site. The site is working just fine now, but we're still getting lots of calls. In response, we've decided to offer account holders free access to our Premium services. I just emailed you all a file containing the terms and conditions of this offer. So I'd like all of you to read it now, and then, I'll take any questions.

Questions 92-94 refer to the following talk.

M: Welcome to our booth here at the Global Manufacturers Convention. Do you need a better tool for tracking and managing inventory at your warehouses? If so, I'd like to introduce you to our inventory barcode scanner. Think back to the times when you physically counted your items, only to realize that the numbers don't match the ones in your system. Well, you won't have to worry about that anymore. With our barcode scanner, you'll always have the accurate figures. OK, now, let me teach you how to use the scanner. I'll begin by scanning this item.

Questions 95-97 refer to the following telephone message and schedule.

W: Hi, Eric. This is Rita from Kansai Productions. I wanted to confirm that I looked over your proposal for a new live television series in Osaka. I'd like you to come by our studio on Friday to talk about it in more detail. My 11 o'clock appointment got postponed, so it'd be good to meet at that time. Oh, by the way, it would be helpful if you could send me a list of expected costs for the project. Talk to you soon.

Questions 98-100 refer to the following excerpt from a meeting and sales chart.

M: Welcome to our quarterly sales meeting. Today, we'll be looking at our best-selling television model. Since its release in the summer, the Clarity Pro has been very popular with consumers. Unfortunately, after our biggest rival unveiled their new model, there was a sharp decrease in sales for the Clarity Pro. In response, we temporarily reduced the price of the Clarity Pro. During this promotional period, we broke our record for most units sold in a month. This was a great idea from our marketing team to help boost sales.

ANSWERS

TEST 1

1 (A)	11 (B)	21 (B)	31 (C)	41 (A)	51 (C)	61 (A)	71 (C)	81 (D)	91 (D)
2 (B)	12 (A)	22 (C)	32 (D)	42 (D)	52 (A)	62 (B)	72 (A)	82 (B)	92 (A)
3 (A)	13 (B)	23 (C)	33 (C)	43 (A)	53 (A)	63 (D)	73 (D)	83 (B)	93 (A)
4 (D)	14 (A)	24 (B)	34 (B)	44 (B)	54 (C)	64 (C)	74 (D)	84 (B)	94 (D)
5 (A)	15 (C)	25 (A)	35 (D)	45 (C)	55 (B)	65 (A)	75 (B)	85 (D)	95 (C)
6 (D)	16 (A)	26 (C)	36 (A)	46 (A)	56 (D)	66 (D)	76 (C)	86 (C)	96 (D)
7 (A)	17 (A)	27 (A)	37 (A)	47 (A)	57 (C)	67 (D)	77 (B)	87 (A)	97 (A)
8 (C)	18 (C)	28 (B)	38 (C)	48 (D)	58 (B)	68 (B)	78 (D)	88 (A)	98 (A)
9 (A)	19 (A)	29 (C)	39 (A)	49 (B)	59 (B)	69 (A)	79 (C)	89 (C)	99 (C)
10 (C)	20 (C)	30 (A)	40 (D)	50 (D)	60 (D)	70 (D)	80 (D)	90 (C)	100 (D)

TEST 2

1 (C)	11 (B)	21 (B)	31 (B)	41 (D)	51 (C)	61 (C)	71 (B)	81 (A)	91 (D)
2 (B)	12 (C)	22 (A)	32 (B)	42 (B)	52 (C)	62 (A)	72 (D)	82 (C)	92 (B)
3 (C)	13 (C)	23 (A)	33 (A)	43 (D)	53 (A)	63 (B)	73 (A)	83 (A)	93 (A)
4 (D)	14 (A)	24 (C)	34 (D)	44 (B)	54 (D)	64 (D)	74 (D)	84 (D)	94 (B)
5 (B)	15 (A)	25 (A)	35 (A)	45 (D)	55 (B)	65 (A)	75 (A)	85 (A)	95 (C)
6 (B)	16 (C)	26 (A)	36 (D)	46 (A)	56 (D)	66 (B)	76 (D)	86 (C)	96 (A)
7 (A)	17 (B)	27 (B)	37 (C)	47 (B)	57 (B)	67 (D)	77 (D)	87 (D)	97 (A)
8 (A)	18 (B)	28 (C)	38 (B)	48 (D)	58 (A)	68 (A)	78 (C)	88 (A)	98 (B)
9 (B)	19 (B)	29 (C)	39 (D)	49 (B)	59 (C)	69 (D)	79 (B)	89 (B)	99 (B)
10 (C)	20 (C)	30 (A)	40 (C)	50 (B)	60 (B)	70 (D)	80 (D)	90 (A)	100 (A)

TEST 3

1 (D)	11 (A)	21 (A)	31 (A)	41 (D)	51 (B)	61 (D)	71 (B)	81 (B)	91 (C)
2 (A)	12 (A)	22 (A)	32 (D)	42 (B)	52 (A)	62 (B)	72 (D)	82 (A)	92 (D)
3 (B)	13 (C)	23 (A)	33 (B)	43 (A)	53 (B)	63 (A)	73 (C)	83 (A)	93 (D)
4 (A)	14 (A)	24 (B)	34 (A)	44 (C)	54 (C)	64 (B)	74 (A)	84 (C)	94 (B)
5 (D)	15 (A)	25 (A)	35 (A)	45 (D)	55 (D)	65 (A)	75 (A)	85 (C)	95 (C)
6 (A)	16 (A)	26 (A)	36 (A)	46 (C)	56 (B)	66 (C)	76 (A)	86 (A)	96 (D)
7 (C)	17 (C)	27 (B)	37 (D)	47 (D)	57 (A)	67 (C)	77 (C)	87 (B)	97 (A)
8 (B)	18 (C)	28 (C)	38 (D)	48 (B)	58 (B)	68 (B)	78 (D)	88 (D)	98 (A)
9 (A)	19 (A)	29 (A)	39 (C)	49 (A)	59 (A)	69 (A)	79 (D)	89 (B)	99 (C)
10 (A)	20 (A)	30 (B)	40 (A)	50 (D)	60 (B)	70 (A)	80 (B)	90 (A)	100 (A)

TEST 4

1 (D)	11 (C)	21 (C)	31 (C)	41 (D)	51 (B)	61 (A)	71 (C)	81 (C)	91 (A)
2 (C)	12 (C)	22 (B)	32 (A)	42 (A)	52 (D)	62 (B)	72 (C)	82 (D)	92 (B)
3 (C)	13 (A)	23 (A)	33 (A)	43 (D)	53 (B)	63 (A)	73 (A)	83 (A)	93 (D)
4 (B)	14 (A)	24 (A)	34 (D)	44 (D)	54 (A)	64 (C)	74 (B)	84 (C)	94 (D)
5 (B)	15 (A)	25 (C)	35 (C)	45 (D)	55 (D)	65 (C)	75 (C)	85 (A)	95 (C)
6 (D)	16 (A)	26 (C)	36 (D)	46 (C)	56 (A)	66 (A)	76 (D)	86 (D)	96 (B)
7 (B)	17 (C)	27 (A)	37 (C)	47 (C)	57 (D)	67 (C)	77 (D)	87 (C)	97 (C)
8 (B)	18 (C)	28 (A)	38 (C)	48 (D)	58 (B)	68 (A)	78 (D)	88 (C)	98 (A)
9 (A)	19 (A)	29 (B)	39 (D)	49 (A)	59 (B)	69 (C)	79 (A)	89 (D)	99 (C)
10 (B)	20 (A)	30 (B)	40 (A)	50 (D)	60 (C)	70 (C)	80 (A)	90 (D)	100 (A)

TEST 5

1 (C)	11 (C)	21 (B)	31 (A)	41 (C)	51 (A)	61 (A)	71 (C)	81 (D)	91 (C)
2 (C)	12 (C)	22 (A)	32 (A)	42 (B)	52 (C)	62 (D)	72 (D)	82 (C)	92 (C)
3 (A)	13 (A)	23 (A)	33 (D)	43 (A)	53 (A)	63 (C)	73 (C)	83 (B)	93 (A)
4 (B)	14 (B)	24 (B)	34 (C)	44 (A)	54 (B)	64 (B)	74 (A)	84 (A)	94 (C)
5 (C)	15 (C)	25 (C)	35 (C)	45 (A)	55 (C)	65 (D)	75 (A)	85 (A)	95 (B)
6 (C)	16 (C)	26 (A)	36 (B)	46 (D)	56 (C)	66 (B)	76 (A)	86 (A)	96 (C)
7 (C)	17 (C)	27 (C)	37 (D)	47 (D)	57 (B)	67 (C)	77 (B)	87 (C)	97 (A)
8 (B)	18 (B)	28 (A)	38 (B)	48 (B)	58 (C)	68 (A)	78 (C)	88 (B)	98 (C)
9 (C)	19 (C)	29 (B)	39 (D)	49 (C)	59 (D)	69 (B)	79 (D)	89 (B)	99 (A)
10 (B)	20 (A)	30 (B)	40 (B)	50 (B)	60 (B)	70 (D)	80 (D)	90 (A)	100 (A)

TEST 6

1 (A)	11 (C)	21 (B)	31 (B)	41 (B)	51 (D)	61 (B)	71 (C)	81 (C)	91 (B)
2 (B)	12 (B)	22 (B)	32 (D)	42 (A)	52 (B)	62 (C)	72 (D)	82 (D)	92 (A)
3 (C)	13 (A)	23 (B)	33 (B)	43 (C)	53 (C)	63 (C)	73 (C)	83 (B)	93 (B)
4 (B)	14 (C)	24 (C)	34 (D)	44 (D)	54 (D)	64 (D)	74 (B)	84 (B)	94 (D)
5 (B)	15 (A)	25 (C)	35 (D)	45 (B)	55 (D)	65 (D)	75 (D)	85 (C)	95 (C)
6 (D)	16 (C)	26 (A)	36 (B)	46 (C)	56 (D)	66 (A)	76 (A)	86 (A)	96 (A)
7 (C)	17 (A)	27 (A)	37 (D)	47 (C)	57 (C)	67 (C)	77 (C)	87 (D)	97 (A)
8 (B)	18 (A)	28 (C)	38 (C)	48 (D)	58 (A)	68 (D)	78 (B)	88 (B)	98 (B)
9 (A)	19 (B)	29 (B)	39 (D)	49 (A)	59 (D)	69 (A)	79 (A)	89 (D)	99 (A)
10 (B)	20 (A)	30 (C)	40 (B)	50 (B)	60 (C)	70 (D)	80 (A)	90 (C)	100 (A)

TEST 7

1 (C)	11 (B)	21 (B)	31 (C)	41 (C)	51 (C)	61 (A)	71 (D)	81 (A)	91 (A)
2 (D)	12 (A)	22 (A)	32 (C)	42 (A)	52 (B)	62 (D)	72 (B)	82 (C)	92 (D)
3 (C)	13 (C)	23 (C)	33 (B)	43 (D)	53 (D)	63 (B)	73 (C)	83 (B)	93 (A)
4 (C)	14 (A)	24 (B)	34 (B)	44 (B)	54 (B)	64 (A)	74 (B)	84 (C)	94 (C)
5 (B)	15 (B)	25 (A)	35 (D)	45 (C)	55 (C)	65 (B)	75 (C)	85 (A)	95 (C)
6 (D)	16 (C)	26 (C)	36 (A)	46 (A)	56 (A)	66 (C)	76 (C)	86 (B)	96 (B)
7 (B)	17 (B)	27 (A)	37 (D)	47 (B)	57 (D)	67 (C)	77 (C)	87 (A)	97 (D)
8 (B)	18 (A)	28 (A)	38 (C)	48 (A)	58 (B)	68 (B)	78 (B)	88 (B)	98 (D)
9 (A)	19 (B)	29 (A)	39 (B)	49 (B)	59 (B)	69 (A)	79 (D)	89 (B)	99 (A)
10 (C)	20 (A)	30 (A)	40 (C)	50 (A)	60 (A)	70 (B)	80 (C)	90 (D)	100 (B)

TEST 8

1 (A)	11 (B)	21 (B)	31 (C)	41 (A)	51 (A)	61 (C)	71 (C)	81 (C)	91 (D)
2 (D)	12 (C)	22 (C)	32 (D)	42 (A)	52 (B)	62 (D)	72 (A)	82 (B)	92 (C)
3 (A)	13 (A)	23 (A)	33 (C)	43 (D)	53 (B)	63 (A)	73 (A)	83 (C)	93 (D)
4 (B)	14 (B)	24 (C)	34 (B)	44 (D)	54 (A)	64 (C)	74 (C)	84 (B)	94 (B)
5 (B)	15 (B)	25 (A)	35 (C)	45 (B)	55 (D)	65 (C)	75 (A)	85 (A)	95 (A)
6 (B)	16 (A)	26 (C)	36 (B)	46 (C)	56 (D)	66 (B)	76 (D)	86 (A)	96 (B)
7 (A)	17 (A)	27 (B)	37 (A)	47 (A)	57 (B)	67 (C)	77 (D)	87 (C)	97 (C)
8 (A)	18 (A)	28 (C)	38 (B)	48 (C)	58 (D)	68 (C)	78 (A)	88 (B)	98 (A)
9 (A)	19 (A)	29 (C)	39 (D)	49 (B)	59 (D)	69 (C)	79 (B)	89 (C)	99 (D)
10 (B)	20 (C)	30 (A)	40 (A)	50 (D)	60 (A)	70 (D)	80 (A)	90 (B)	100 (C)

TEST 9

1 (D)	11 (C)	21 (C)	31 (B)	41 (B)	51 (A)	61 (D)	71 (A)	81 (C)	91 (C)
2 (D)	12 (B)	22 (A)	32 (A)	42 (D)	52 (B)	62 (B)	72 (D)	82 (C)	92 (A)
3 (B)	13 (C)	23 (B)	33 (D)	43 (D)	53 (D)	63 (D)	73 (A)	83 (D)	93 (C)
4 (C)	14 (C)	24 (A)	34 (D)	44 (C)	54 (A)	64 (B)	74 (A)	84 (C)	94 (A)
5 (B)	15 (B)	25 (B)	35 (B)	45 (B)	55 (D)	65 (B)	75 (A)	85 (B)	95 (C)
6 (A)	16 (C)	26 (B)	36 (D)	46 (D)	56 (A)	66 (D)	76 (A)	86 (B)	96 (A)
7 (B)	17 (A)	27 (B)	37 (A)	47 (A)	57 (D)	67 (C)	77 (C)	87 (A)	97 (A)
8 (A)	18 (A)	28 (C)	38 (B)	48 (C)	58 (B)	68 (C)	78 (B)	88 (C)	98 (D)
9 (C)	19 (C)	29 (A)	39 (D)	49 (B)	59 (A)	69 (B)	79 (C)	89 (C)	99 (C)
10 (B)	20 (C)	30 (B)	40 (C)	50 (C)	60 (D)	70 (D)	80 (A)	90 (B)	100 (B)

TEST 10

1 (A)	11 (A)	21 (C)	31 (B)	41 (C)	51 (D)	61 (B)	71 (B)	81 (D)	91 (A)
2 (A)	12 (A)	22 (A)	32 (B)	42 (B)	52 (D)	62 (B)	72 (C)	82 (A)	92 (D)
3 (D)	13 (C)	23 (A)	33 (C)	43 (B)	53 (C)	63 (D)	73 (A)	83 (B)	93 (A)
4 (C)	14 (C)	24 (C)	34 (A)	44 (B)	54 (B)	64 (B)	74 (D)	84 (A)	94 (D)
5 (B)	15 (C)	25 (A)	35 (C)	45 (A)	55 (A)	65 (C)	75 (B)	85 (D)	95 (B)
6 (B)	16 (B)	26 (A)	36 (D)	46 (C)	56 (C)	66 (A)	76 (A)	86 (B)	96 (B)
7 (B)	17 (C)	27 (C)	37 (C)	47 (B)	57 (A)	67 (B)	77 (D)	87 (A)	97 (D)
8 (B)	18 (B)	28 (A)	38 (B)	48 (D)	58 (D)	68 (D)	78 (C)	88 (D)	98 (B)
9 (C)	19 (C)	29 (C)	39 (D)	49 (C)	59 (A)	69 (B)	79 (B)	89 (A)	99 (D)
10 (A)	20 (C)	30 (A)	40 (C)	50 (A)	60 (D)	70 (D)	80 (A)	90 (B)	100 (C)

토익 점수 환산표

<table>
<tr><td colspan="2">

Section I Listening Comprehension
</td><td colspan="2">

Section II Reading Comprehension
</td></tr>
<tr><td>정답 수</td><td>환산 점수대</td><td>정답 수</td><td>환산 점수대</td></tr>
<tr><td>96 ~ 100</td><td>480 ~ 495</td><td>96 ~ 100</td><td>450 ~ 495</td></tr>
<tr><td>91 ~ 95</td><td>470 ~ 495</td><td>91 ~ 95</td><td>420 ~ 465</td></tr>
<tr><td>86 ~ 90</td><td>440 ~ 490</td><td>86 ~ 90</td><td>400 ~ 435</td></tr>
<tr><td>81 ~ 85</td><td>410 ~ 460</td><td>81 ~ 85</td><td>370 ~ 410</td></tr>
<tr><td>76 ~ 80</td><td>390 ~ 430</td><td>76 ~ 80</td><td>340 ~ 380</td></tr>
<tr><td>71 ~ 75</td><td>360 ~ 400</td><td>71 ~ 75</td><td>310 ~ 355</td></tr>
<tr><td>66 ~ 70</td><td>330 ~ 370</td><td>66 ~ 70</td><td>280 ~ 325</td></tr>
<tr><td>61 ~ 65</td><td>300 ~ 345</td><td>61 ~ 65</td><td>260 ~ 300</td></tr>
<tr><td>56 ~ 60</td><td>270 ~ 315</td><td>56 ~ 60</td><td>230 ~ 270</td></tr>
<tr><td>51 ~ 55</td><td>240 ~ 285</td><td>51 ~ 55</td><td>200 ~ 245</td></tr>
<tr><td>46 ~ 50</td><td>210 ~ 255</td><td>46 ~ 50</td><td>170 ~ 215</td></tr>
<tr><td>41 ~ 45</td><td>180 ~ 225</td><td>41 ~ 45</td><td>140 ~ 185</td></tr>
<tr><td>36 ~ 40</td><td>150 ~ 195</td><td>36 ~ 40</td><td>120 ~ 160</td></tr>
<tr><td>31 ~ 35</td><td>120 ~ 165</td><td>31 ~ 35</td><td>90 ~ 130</td></tr>
<tr><td>26 ~ 30</td><td>90 ~ 135</td><td>26 ~ 30</td><td>60 ~ 105</td></tr>
<tr><td>21 ~ 25</td><td>60 ~ 105</td><td>21 ~ 25</td><td>30 ~ 75</td></tr>
<tr><td>16 ~ 20</td><td>40 ~ 75</td><td>16 ~ 20</td><td>10 ~ 50</td></tr>
<tr><td>11 ~ 15</td><td>10 ~ 45</td><td>11 ~ 15</td><td>5 ~ 20</td></tr>
<tr><td>6 ~ 10</td><td>5 ~ 20</td><td>6 ~ 10</td><td>5</td></tr>
<tr><td>1 ~ 5</td><td>5</td><td>1 ~ 5</td><td>5</td></tr>
<tr><td>0</td><td>0</td><td>0</td><td>0</td></tr>
</table>

ANSWER SHEET

파고다 토익 적중 실전 LC - TEST 1

LISTENING (Part I-IV)

NO.	ANSWER A B C D	NO.	ANSWER A B C D	NO.	ANSWER A B C D	NO.	ANSWER A B C D	NO.	ANSWER A B C D
1	Ⓐ Ⓑ Ⓒ Ⓓ	21	Ⓐ Ⓑ Ⓒ	41	Ⓐ Ⓑ Ⓒ Ⓓ	61	Ⓐ Ⓑ Ⓒ Ⓓ	81	Ⓐ Ⓑ Ⓒ Ⓓ
2	Ⓐ Ⓑ Ⓒ Ⓓ	22	Ⓐ Ⓑ Ⓒ	42	Ⓐ Ⓑ Ⓒ Ⓓ	62	Ⓐ Ⓑ Ⓒ Ⓓ	82	Ⓐ Ⓑ Ⓒ Ⓓ
3	Ⓐ Ⓑ Ⓒ Ⓓ	23	Ⓐ Ⓑ Ⓒ	43	Ⓐ Ⓑ Ⓒ Ⓓ	63	Ⓐ Ⓑ Ⓒ Ⓓ	83	Ⓐ Ⓑ Ⓒ Ⓓ
4	Ⓐ Ⓑ Ⓒ Ⓓ	24	Ⓐ Ⓑ Ⓒ	44	Ⓐ Ⓑ Ⓒ Ⓓ	64	Ⓐ Ⓑ Ⓒ Ⓓ	84	Ⓐ Ⓑ Ⓒ Ⓓ
5	Ⓐ Ⓑ Ⓒ Ⓓ	25	Ⓐ Ⓑ Ⓒ	45	Ⓐ Ⓑ Ⓒ Ⓓ	65	Ⓐ Ⓑ Ⓒ Ⓓ	85	Ⓐ Ⓑ Ⓒ Ⓓ
6	Ⓐ Ⓑ Ⓒ Ⓓ	26	Ⓐ Ⓑ Ⓒ	46	Ⓐ Ⓑ Ⓒ Ⓓ	66	Ⓐ Ⓑ Ⓒ Ⓓ	86	Ⓐ Ⓑ Ⓒ Ⓓ
7	Ⓐ Ⓑ Ⓒ	27	Ⓐ Ⓑ Ⓒ	47	Ⓐ Ⓑ Ⓒ Ⓓ	67	Ⓐ Ⓑ Ⓒ Ⓓ	87	Ⓐ Ⓑ Ⓒ Ⓓ
8	Ⓐ Ⓑ Ⓒ	28	Ⓐ Ⓑ Ⓒ	48	Ⓐ Ⓑ Ⓒ Ⓓ	68	Ⓐ Ⓑ Ⓒ Ⓓ	88	Ⓐ Ⓑ Ⓒ Ⓓ
9	Ⓐ Ⓑ Ⓒ	29	Ⓐ Ⓑ Ⓒ	49	Ⓐ Ⓑ Ⓒ Ⓓ	69	Ⓐ Ⓑ Ⓒ Ⓓ	89	Ⓐ Ⓑ Ⓒ Ⓓ
10	Ⓐ Ⓑ Ⓒ	30	Ⓐ Ⓑ Ⓒ	50	Ⓐ Ⓑ Ⓒ Ⓓ	70	Ⓐ Ⓑ Ⓒ Ⓓ	90	Ⓐ Ⓑ Ⓒ Ⓓ
11	Ⓐ Ⓑ Ⓒ	31	Ⓐ Ⓑ Ⓒ	51	Ⓐ Ⓑ Ⓒ Ⓓ	71	Ⓐ Ⓑ Ⓒ Ⓓ	91	Ⓐ Ⓑ Ⓒ Ⓓ
12	Ⓐ Ⓑ Ⓒ	32	Ⓐ Ⓑ Ⓒ Ⓓ	52	Ⓐ Ⓑ Ⓒ Ⓓ	72	Ⓐ Ⓑ Ⓒ Ⓓ	92	Ⓐ Ⓑ Ⓒ Ⓓ
13	Ⓐ Ⓑ Ⓒ	33	Ⓐ Ⓑ Ⓒ Ⓓ	53	Ⓐ Ⓑ Ⓒ Ⓓ	73	Ⓐ Ⓑ Ⓒ Ⓓ	93	Ⓐ Ⓑ Ⓒ Ⓓ
14	Ⓐ Ⓑ Ⓒ	34	Ⓐ Ⓑ Ⓒ Ⓓ	54	Ⓐ Ⓑ Ⓒ Ⓓ	74	Ⓐ Ⓑ Ⓒ Ⓓ	94	Ⓐ Ⓑ Ⓒ Ⓓ
15	Ⓐ Ⓑ Ⓒ	35	Ⓐ Ⓑ Ⓒ Ⓓ	55	Ⓐ Ⓑ Ⓒ Ⓓ	75	Ⓐ Ⓑ Ⓒ Ⓓ	95	Ⓐ Ⓑ Ⓒ Ⓓ
16	Ⓐ Ⓑ Ⓒ	36	Ⓐ Ⓑ Ⓒ Ⓓ	56	Ⓐ Ⓑ Ⓒ Ⓓ	76	Ⓐ Ⓑ Ⓒ Ⓓ	96	Ⓐ Ⓑ Ⓒ Ⓓ
17	Ⓐ Ⓑ Ⓒ	37	Ⓐ Ⓑ Ⓒ Ⓓ	57	Ⓐ Ⓑ Ⓒ Ⓓ	77	Ⓐ Ⓑ Ⓒ Ⓓ	97	Ⓐ Ⓑ Ⓒ Ⓓ
18	Ⓐ Ⓑ Ⓒ	38	Ⓐ Ⓑ Ⓒ Ⓓ	58	Ⓐ Ⓑ Ⓒ Ⓓ	78	Ⓐ Ⓑ Ⓒ Ⓓ	98	Ⓐ Ⓑ Ⓒ Ⓓ
19	Ⓐ Ⓑ Ⓒ	39	Ⓐ Ⓑ Ⓒ Ⓓ	59	Ⓐ Ⓑ Ⓒ Ⓓ	79	Ⓐ Ⓑ Ⓒ Ⓓ	99	Ⓐ Ⓑ Ⓒ Ⓓ
20	Ⓐ Ⓑ Ⓒ	40	Ⓐ Ⓑ Ⓒ Ⓓ	60	Ⓐ Ⓑ Ⓒ Ⓓ	80	Ⓐ Ⓑ Ⓒ Ⓓ	100	Ⓐ Ⓑ Ⓒ Ⓓ

ANSWER SHEET

ANSWER SHEET

파고다 토익 적중 실전 LC - TEST 2

LISTENING (Part I-IV)

NO.	ANSWER A B C D	NO.	ANSWER A B C D	NO.	ANSWER A B C D	NO.	ANSWER A B C D	NO.	ANSWER A B C D
1	Ⓐ Ⓑ Ⓒ Ⓓ	21	Ⓐ Ⓑ Ⓒ	41	Ⓐ Ⓑ Ⓒ Ⓓ	61	Ⓐ Ⓑ Ⓒ Ⓓ	81	Ⓐ Ⓑ Ⓒ Ⓓ
2	Ⓐ Ⓑ Ⓒ Ⓓ	22	Ⓐ Ⓑ Ⓒ	42	Ⓐ Ⓑ Ⓒ Ⓓ	62	Ⓐ Ⓑ Ⓒ Ⓓ	82	Ⓐ Ⓑ Ⓒ Ⓓ
3	Ⓐ Ⓑ Ⓒ Ⓓ	23	Ⓐ Ⓑ Ⓒ	43	Ⓐ Ⓑ Ⓒ Ⓓ	63	Ⓐ Ⓑ Ⓒ Ⓓ	83	Ⓐ Ⓑ Ⓒ Ⓓ
4	Ⓐ Ⓑ Ⓒ Ⓓ	24	Ⓐ Ⓑ Ⓒ	44	Ⓐ Ⓑ Ⓒ Ⓓ	64	Ⓐ Ⓑ Ⓒ Ⓓ	84	Ⓐ Ⓑ Ⓒ Ⓓ
5	Ⓐ Ⓑ Ⓒ Ⓓ	25	Ⓐ Ⓑ Ⓒ	45	Ⓐ Ⓑ Ⓒ Ⓓ	65	Ⓐ Ⓑ Ⓒ Ⓓ	85	Ⓐ Ⓑ Ⓒ Ⓓ
6	Ⓐ Ⓑ Ⓒ Ⓓ	26	Ⓐ Ⓑ Ⓒ	46	Ⓐ Ⓑ Ⓒ Ⓓ	66	Ⓐ Ⓑ Ⓒ Ⓓ	86	Ⓐ Ⓑ Ⓒ Ⓓ
7	Ⓐ Ⓑ Ⓒ	27	Ⓐ Ⓑ Ⓒ	47	Ⓐ Ⓑ Ⓒ Ⓓ	67	Ⓐ Ⓑ Ⓒ Ⓓ	87	Ⓐ Ⓑ Ⓒ Ⓓ
8	Ⓐ Ⓑ Ⓒ	28	Ⓐ Ⓑ Ⓒ	48	Ⓐ Ⓑ Ⓒ Ⓓ	68	Ⓐ Ⓑ Ⓒ Ⓓ	88	Ⓐ Ⓑ Ⓒ Ⓓ
9	Ⓐ Ⓑ Ⓒ	29	Ⓐ Ⓑ Ⓒ	49	Ⓐ Ⓑ Ⓒ Ⓓ	69	Ⓐ Ⓑ Ⓒ Ⓓ	89	Ⓐ Ⓑ Ⓒ Ⓓ
10	Ⓐ Ⓑ Ⓒ	30	Ⓐ Ⓑ Ⓒ	50	Ⓐ Ⓑ Ⓒ Ⓓ	70	Ⓐ Ⓑ Ⓒ Ⓓ	90	Ⓐ Ⓑ Ⓒ Ⓓ
11	Ⓐ Ⓑ Ⓒ	31	Ⓐ Ⓑ Ⓒ	51	Ⓐ Ⓑ Ⓒ Ⓓ	71	Ⓐ Ⓑ Ⓒ Ⓓ	91	Ⓐ Ⓑ Ⓒ Ⓓ
12	Ⓐ Ⓑ Ⓒ	32	Ⓐ Ⓑ Ⓒ Ⓓ	52	Ⓐ Ⓑ Ⓒ Ⓓ	72	Ⓐ Ⓑ Ⓒ Ⓓ	92	Ⓐ Ⓑ Ⓒ Ⓓ
13	Ⓐ Ⓑ Ⓒ	33	Ⓐ Ⓑ Ⓒ Ⓓ	53	Ⓐ Ⓑ Ⓒ Ⓓ	73	Ⓐ Ⓑ Ⓒ Ⓓ	93	Ⓐ Ⓑ Ⓒ Ⓓ
14	Ⓐ Ⓑ Ⓒ	34	Ⓐ Ⓑ Ⓒ Ⓓ	54	Ⓐ Ⓑ Ⓒ Ⓓ	74	Ⓐ Ⓑ Ⓒ Ⓓ	94	Ⓐ Ⓑ Ⓒ Ⓓ
15	Ⓐ Ⓑ Ⓒ	35	Ⓐ Ⓑ Ⓒ Ⓓ	55	Ⓐ Ⓑ Ⓒ Ⓓ	75	Ⓐ Ⓑ Ⓒ Ⓓ	95	Ⓐ Ⓑ Ⓒ Ⓓ
16	Ⓐ Ⓑ Ⓒ	36	Ⓐ Ⓑ Ⓒ Ⓓ	56	Ⓐ Ⓑ Ⓒ Ⓓ	76	Ⓐ Ⓑ Ⓒ Ⓓ	96	Ⓐ Ⓑ Ⓒ Ⓓ
17	Ⓐ Ⓑ Ⓒ	37	Ⓐ Ⓑ Ⓒ Ⓓ	57	Ⓐ Ⓑ Ⓒ Ⓓ	77	Ⓐ Ⓑ Ⓒ Ⓓ	97	Ⓐ Ⓑ Ⓒ Ⓓ
18	Ⓐ Ⓑ Ⓒ	38	Ⓐ Ⓑ Ⓒ Ⓓ	58	Ⓐ Ⓑ Ⓒ Ⓓ	78	Ⓐ Ⓑ Ⓒ Ⓓ	98	Ⓐ Ⓑ Ⓒ Ⓓ
19	Ⓐ Ⓑ Ⓒ	39	Ⓐ Ⓑ Ⓒ Ⓓ	59	Ⓐ Ⓑ Ⓒ Ⓓ	79	Ⓐ Ⓑ Ⓒ Ⓓ	99	Ⓐ Ⓑ Ⓒ Ⓓ
20	Ⓐ Ⓑ Ⓒ	40	Ⓐ Ⓑ Ⓒ Ⓓ	60	Ⓐ Ⓑ Ⓒ Ⓓ	80	Ⓐ Ⓑ Ⓒ Ⓓ	100	Ⓐ Ⓑ Ⓒ Ⓓ

ANSWER SHEET

ANSWER SHEET

파고다 토익 적중 실전 LC - TEST 3

LISTENING (Part I-IV)

NO.	ANSWER A B C D	NO.	ANSWER A B C D	NO.	ANSWER A B C D	NO.	ANSWER A B C D	NO.	ANSWER A B C D
1	Ⓐ Ⓑ Ⓒ Ⓓ	21	Ⓐ Ⓑ Ⓒ	41	Ⓐ Ⓑ Ⓒ Ⓓ	61	Ⓐ Ⓑ Ⓒ Ⓓ	81	Ⓐ Ⓑ Ⓒ Ⓓ
2	Ⓐ Ⓑ Ⓒ Ⓓ	22	Ⓐ Ⓑ Ⓒ	42	Ⓐ Ⓑ Ⓒ Ⓓ	62	Ⓐ Ⓑ Ⓒ Ⓓ	82	Ⓐ Ⓑ Ⓒ Ⓓ
3	Ⓐ Ⓑ Ⓒ Ⓓ	23	Ⓐ Ⓑ Ⓒ	43	Ⓐ Ⓑ Ⓒ Ⓓ	63	Ⓐ Ⓑ Ⓒ Ⓓ	83	Ⓐ Ⓑ Ⓒ Ⓓ
4	Ⓐ Ⓑ Ⓒ Ⓓ	24	Ⓐ Ⓑ Ⓒ	44	Ⓐ Ⓑ Ⓒ Ⓓ	64	Ⓐ Ⓑ Ⓒ Ⓓ	84	Ⓐ Ⓑ Ⓒ Ⓓ
5	Ⓐ Ⓑ Ⓒ Ⓓ	25	Ⓐ Ⓑ Ⓒ	45	Ⓐ Ⓑ Ⓒ Ⓓ	65	Ⓐ Ⓑ Ⓒ Ⓓ	85	Ⓐ Ⓑ Ⓒ Ⓓ
6	Ⓐ Ⓑ Ⓒ Ⓓ	26	Ⓐ Ⓑ Ⓒ	46	Ⓐ Ⓑ Ⓒ Ⓓ	66	Ⓐ Ⓑ Ⓒ Ⓓ	86	Ⓐ Ⓑ Ⓒ Ⓓ
7	Ⓐ Ⓑ Ⓒ	27	Ⓐ Ⓑ Ⓒ	47	Ⓐ Ⓑ Ⓒ Ⓓ	67	Ⓐ Ⓑ Ⓒ Ⓓ	87	Ⓐ Ⓑ Ⓒ Ⓓ
8	Ⓐ Ⓑ Ⓒ	28	Ⓐ Ⓑ Ⓒ	48	Ⓐ Ⓑ Ⓒ Ⓓ	68	Ⓐ Ⓑ Ⓒ Ⓓ	88	Ⓐ Ⓑ Ⓒ Ⓓ
9	Ⓐ Ⓑ Ⓒ	29	Ⓐ Ⓑ Ⓒ	49	Ⓐ Ⓑ Ⓒ Ⓓ	69	Ⓐ Ⓑ Ⓒ Ⓓ	89	Ⓐ Ⓑ Ⓒ Ⓓ
10	Ⓐ Ⓑ Ⓒ	30	Ⓐ Ⓑ Ⓒ	50	Ⓐ Ⓑ Ⓒ Ⓓ	70	Ⓐ Ⓑ Ⓒ Ⓓ	90	Ⓐ Ⓑ Ⓒ Ⓓ
11	Ⓐ Ⓑ Ⓒ	31	Ⓐ Ⓑ Ⓒ	51	Ⓐ Ⓑ Ⓒ Ⓓ	71	Ⓐ Ⓑ Ⓒ Ⓓ	91	Ⓐ Ⓑ Ⓒ Ⓓ
12	Ⓐ Ⓑ Ⓒ	32	Ⓐ Ⓑ Ⓒ Ⓓ	52	Ⓐ Ⓑ Ⓒ Ⓓ	72	Ⓐ Ⓑ Ⓒ Ⓓ	92	Ⓐ Ⓑ Ⓒ Ⓓ
13	Ⓐ Ⓑ Ⓒ	33	Ⓐ Ⓑ Ⓒ Ⓓ	53	Ⓐ Ⓑ Ⓒ Ⓓ	73	Ⓐ Ⓑ Ⓒ Ⓓ	93	Ⓐ Ⓑ Ⓒ Ⓓ
14	Ⓐ Ⓑ Ⓒ	34	Ⓐ Ⓑ Ⓒ Ⓓ	54	Ⓐ Ⓑ Ⓒ Ⓓ	74	Ⓐ Ⓑ Ⓒ Ⓓ	94	Ⓐ Ⓑ Ⓒ Ⓓ
15	Ⓐ Ⓑ Ⓒ	35	Ⓐ Ⓑ Ⓒ Ⓓ	55	Ⓐ Ⓑ Ⓒ Ⓓ	75	Ⓐ Ⓑ Ⓒ Ⓓ	95	Ⓐ Ⓑ Ⓒ Ⓓ
16	Ⓐ Ⓑ Ⓒ	36	Ⓐ Ⓑ Ⓒ Ⓓ	56	Ⓐ Ⓑ Ⓒ Ⓓ	76	Ⓐ Ⓑ Ⓒ Ⓓ	96	Ⓐ Ⓑ Ⓒ Ⓓ
17	Ⓐ Ⓑ Ⓒ	37	Ⓐ Ⓑ Ⓒ Ⓓ	57	Ⓐ Ⓑ Ⓒ Ⓓ	77	Ⓐ Ⓑ Ⓒ Ⓓ	97	Ⓐ Ⓑ Ⓒ Ⓓ
18	Ⓐ Ⓑ Ⓒ	38	Ⓐ Ⓑ Ⓒ Ⓓ	58	Ⓐ Ⓑ Ⓒ Ⓓ	78	Ⓐ Ⓑ Ⓒ Ⓓ	98	Ⓐ Ⓑ Ⓒ Ⓓ
19	Ⓐ Ⓑ Ⓒ	39	Ⓐ Ⓑ Ⓒ Ⓓ	59	Ⓐ Ⓑ Ⓒ Ⓓ	79	Ⓐ Ⓑ Ⓒ Ⓓ	99	Ⓐ Ⓑ Ⓒ Ⓓ
20	Ⓐ Ⓑ Ⓒ	40	Ⓐ Ⓑ Ⓒ Ⓓ	60	Ⓐ Ⓑ Ⓒ Ⓓ	80	Ⓐ Ⓑ Ⓒ Ⓓ	100	Ⓐ Ⓑ Ⓒ Ⓓ

ANSWER SHEET

ANSWER SHEET

파고다 토익 적중 실전 LC - TEST 4

LISTENING (Part I-IV)

NO.	ANSWER A B C D	NO.	ANSWER A B C D	NO.	ANSWER A B C D	NO.	ANSWER A B C D	NO.	ANSWER A B C D
1	Ⓐ Ⓑ Ⓒ Ⓓ	21	Ⓐ Ⓑ Ⓒ	41	Ⓐ Ⓑ Ⓒ Ⓓ	61	Ⓐ Ⓑ Ⓒ Ⓓ	81	Ⓐ Ⓑ Ⓒ Ⓓ
2	Ⓐ Ⓑ Ⓒ Ⓓ	22	Ⓐ Ⓑ Ⓒ	42	Ⓐ Ⓑ Ⓒ Ⓓ	62	Ⓐ Ⓑ Ⓒ Ⓓ	82	Ⓐ Ⓑ Ⓒ Ⓓ
3	Ⓐ Ⓑ Ⓒ Ⓓ	23	Ⓐ Ⓑ Ⓒ	43	Ⓐ Ⓑ Ⓒ Ⓓ	63	Ⓐ Ⓑ Ⓒ Ⓓ	83	Ⓐ Ⓑ Ⓒ Ⓓ
4	Ⓐ Ⓑ Ⓒ Ⓓ	24	Ⓐ Ⓑ Ⓒ	44	Ⓐ Ⓑ Ⓒ Ⓓ	64	Ⓐ Ⓑ Ⓒ Ⓓ	84	Ⓐ Ⓑ Ⓒ Ⓓ
5	Ⓐ Ⓑ Ⓒ Ⓓ	25	Ⓐ Ⓑ Ⓒ	45	Ⓐ Ⓑ Ⓒ Ⓓ	65	Ⓐ Ⓑ Ⓒ Ⓓ	85	Ⓐ Ⓑ Ⓒ Ⓓ
6	Ⓐ Ⓑ Ⓒ Ⓓ	26	Ⓐ Ⓑ Ⓒ	46	Ⓐ Ⓑ Ⓒ Ⓓ	66	Ⓐ Ⓑ Ⓒ Ⓓ	86	Ⓐ Ⓑ Ⓒ Ⓓ
7	Ⓐ Ⓑ Ⓒ	27	Ⓐ Ⓑ Ⓒ	47	Ⓐ Ⓑ Ⓒ Ⓓ	67	Ⓐ Ⓑ Ⓒ Ⓓ	87	Ⓐ Ⓑ Ⓒ Ⓓ
8	Ⓐ Ⓑ Ⓒ	28	Ⓐ Ⓑ Ⓒ	48	Ⓐ Ⓑ Ⓒ Ⓓ	68	Ⓐ Ⓑ Ⓒ Ⓓ	88	Ⓐ Ⓑ Ⓒ Ⓓ
9	Ⓐ Ⓑ Ⓒ	29	Ⓐ Ⓑ Ⓒ	49	Ⓐ Ⓑ Ⓒ Ⓓ	69	Ⓐ Ⓑ Ⓒ Ⓓ	89	Ⓐ Ⓑ Ⓒ Ⓓ
10	Ⓐ Ⓑ Ⓒ	30	Ⓐ Ⓑ Ⓒ	50	Ⓐ Ⓑ Ⓒ Ⓓ	70	Ⓐ Ⓑ Ⓒ Ⓓ	90	Ⓐ Ⓑ Ⓒ Ⓓ
11	Ⓐ Ⓑ Ⓒ	31	Ⓐ Ⓑ Ⓒ	51	Ⓐ Ⓑ Ⓒ Ⓓ	71	Ⓐ Ⓑ Ⓒ Ⓓ	91	Ⓐ Ⓑ Ⓒ Ⓓ
12	Ⓐ Ⓑ Ⓒ	32	Ⓐ Ⓑ Ⓒ Ⓓ	52	Ⓐ Ⓑ Ⓒ Ⓓ	72	Ⓐ Ⓑ Ⓒ Ⓓ	92	Ⓐ Ⓑ Ⓒ Ⓓ
13	Ⓐ Ⓑ Ⓒ	33	Ⓐ Ⓑ Ⓒ Ⓓ	53	Ⓐ Ⓑ Ⓒ Ⓓ	73	Ⓐ Ⓑ Ⓒ Ⓓ	93	Ⓐ Ⓑ Ⓒ Ⓓ
14	Ⓐ Ⓑ Ⓒ	34	Ⓐ Ⓑ Ⓒ Ⓓ	54	Ⓐ Ⓑ Ⓒ Ⓓ	74	Ⓐ Ⓑ Ⓒ Ⓓ	94	Ⓐ Ⓑ Ⓒ Ⓓ
15	Ⓐ Ⓑ Ⓒ	35	Ⓐ Ⓑ Ⓒ Ⓓ	55	Ⓐ Ⓑ Ⓒ Ⓓ	75	Ⓐ Ⓑ Ⓒ Ⓓ	95	Ⓐ Ⓑ Ⓒ Ⓓ
16	Ⓐ Ⓑ Ⓒ	36	Ⓐ Ⓑ Ⓒ Ⓓ	56	Ⓐ Ⓑ Ⓒ Ⓓ	76	Ⓐ Ⓑ Ⓒ Ⓓ	96	Ⓐ Ⓑ Ⓒ Ⓓ
17	Ⓐ Ⓑ Ⓒ	37	Ⓐ Ⓑ Ⓒ Ⓓ	57	Ⓐ Ⓑ Ⓒ Ⓓ	77	Ⓐ Ⓑ Ⓒ Ⓓ	97	Ⓐ Ⓑ Ⓒ Ⓓ
18	Ⓐ Ⓑ Ⓒ	38	Ⓐ Ⓑ Ⓒ Ⓓ	58	Ⓐ Ⓑ Ⓒ Ⓓ	78	Ⓐ Ⓑ Ⓒ Ⓓ	98	Ⓐ Ⓑ Ⓒ Ⓓ
19	Ⓐ Ⓑ Ⓒ	39	Ⓐ Ⓑ Ⓒ Ⓓ	59	Ⓐ Ⓑ Ⓒ Ⓓ	79	Ⓐ Ⓑ Ⓒ Ⓓ	99	Ⓐ Ⓑ Ⓒ Ⓓ
20	Ⓐ Ⓑ Ⓒ	40	Ⓐ Ⓑ Ⓒ Ⓓ	60	Ⓐ Ⓑ Ⓒ Ⓓ	80	Ⓐ Ⓑ Ⓒ Ⓓ	100	Ⓐ Ⓑ Ⓒ Ⓓ

ANSWER SHEET

ANSWER SHEET

파고다 토익 적중 실전 LC - TEST 5

LISTENING (Part I-IV)

NO.	ANSWER A B C D	NO.	ANSWER A B C D	NO.	ANSWER A B C D	NO.	ANSWER A B C D	NO.	ANSWER A B C D
1	Ⓐ Ⓑ Ⓒ Ⓓ	21	Ⓐ Ⓑ Ⓒ	41	Ⓐ Ⓑ Ⓒ Ⓓ	61	Ⓐ Ⓑ Ⓒ Ⓓ	81	Ⓐ Ⓑ Ⓒ Ⓓ
2	Ⓐ Ⓑ Ⓒ Ⓓ	22	Ⓐ Ⓑ Ⓒ	42	Ⓐ Ⓑ Ⓒ Ⓓ	62	Ⓐ Ⓑ Ⓒ Ⓓ	82	Ⓐ Ⓑ Ⓒ Ⓓ
3	Ⓐ Ⓑ Ⓒ Ⓓ	23	Ⓐ Ⓑ Ⓒ	43	Ⓐ Ⓑ Ⓒ Ⓓ	63	Ⓐ Ⓑ Ⓒ Ⓓ	83	Ⓐ Ⓑ Ⓒ Ⓓ
4	Ⓐ Ⓑ Ⓒ Ⓓ	24	Ⓐ Ⓑ Ⓒ	44	Ⓐ Ⓑ Ⓒ Ⓓ	64	Ⓐ Ⓑ Ⓒ Ⓓ	84	Ⓐ Ⓑ Ⓒ Ⓓ
5	Ⓐ Ⓑ Ⓒ Ⓓ	25	Ⓐ Ⓑ Ⓒ	45	Ⓐ Ⓑ Ⓒ Ⓓ	65	Ⓐ Ⓑ Ⓒ Ⓓ	85	Ⓐ Ⓑ Ⓒ Ⓓ
6	Ⓐ Ⓑ Ⓒ Ⓓ	26	Ⓐ Ⓑ Ⓒ	46	Ⓐ Ⓑ Ⓒ Ⓓ	66	Ⓐ Ⓑ Ⓒ Ⓓ	86	Ⓐ Ⓑ Ⓒ Ⓓ
7	Ⓐ Ⓑ Ⓒ	27	Ⓐ Ⓑ Ⓒ	47	Ⓐ Ⓑ Ⓒ Ⓓ	67	Ⓐ Ⓑ Ⓒ Ⓓ	87	Ⓐ Ⓑ Ⓒ Ⓓ
8	Ⓐ Ⓑ Ⓒ	28	Ⓐ Ⓑ Ⓒ	48	Ⓐ Ⓑ Ⓒ Ⓓ	68	Ⓐ Ⓑ Ⓒ Ⓓ	88	Ⓐ Ⓑ Ⓒ Ⓓ
9	Ⓐ Ⓑ Ⓒ	29	Ⓐ Ⓑ Ⓒ	49	Ⓐ Ⓑ Ⓒ Ⓓ	69	Ⓐ Ⓑ Ⓒ Ⓓ	89	Ⓐ Ⓑ Ⓒ Ⓓ
10	Ⓐ Ⓑ Ⓒ	30	Ⓐ Ⓑ Ⓒ	50	Ⓐ Ⓑ Ⓒ Ⓓ	70	Ⓐ Ⓑ Ⓒ Ⓓ	90	Ⓐ Ⓑ Ⓒ Ⓓ
11	Ⓐ Ⓑ Ⓒ	31	Ⓐ Ⓑ Ⓒ	51	Ⓐ Ⓑ Ⓒ Ⓓ	71	Ⓐ Ⓑ Ⓒ Ⓓ	91	Ⓐ Ⓑ Ⓒ Ⓓ
12	Ⓐ Ⓑ Ⓒ	32	Ⓐ Ⓑ Ⓒ Ⓓ	52	Ⓐ Ⓑ Ⓒ Ⓓ	72	Ⓐ Ⓑ Ⓒ Ⓓ	92	Ⓐ Ⓑ Ⓒ Ⓓ
13	Ⓐ Ⓑ Ⓒ	33	Ⓐ Ⓑ Ⓒ Ⓓ	53	Ⓐ Ⓑ Ⓒ Ⓓ	73	Ⓐ Ⓑ Ⓒ Ⓓ	93	Ⓐ Ⓑ Ⓒ Ⓓ
14	Ⓐ Ⓑ Ⓒ	34	Ⓐ Ⓑ Ⓒ Ⓓ	54	Ⓐ Ⓑ Ⓒ Ⓓ	74	Ⓐ Ⓑ Ⓒ Ⓓ	94	Ⓐ Ⓑ Ⓒ Ⓓ
15	Ⓐ Ⓑ Ⓒ	35	Ⓐ Ⓑ Ⓒ Ⓓ	55	Ⓐ Ⓑ Ⓒ Ⓓ	75	Ⓐ Ⓑ Ⓒ Ⓓ	95	Ⓐ Ⓑ Ⓒ Ⓓ
16	Ⓐ Ⓑ Ⓒ	36	Ⓐ Ⓑ Ⓒ Ⓓ	56	Ⓐ Ⓑ Ⓒ Ⓓ	76	Ⓐ Ⓑ Ⓒ Ⓓ	96	Ⓐ Ⓑ Ⓒ Ⓓ
17	Ⓐ Ⓑ Ⓒ	37	Ⓐ Ⓑ Ⓒ Ⓓ	57	Ⓐ Ⓑ Ⓒ Ⓓ	77	Ⓐ Ⓑ Ⓒ Ⓓ	97	Ⓐ Ⓑ Ⓒ Ⓓ
18	Ⓐ Ⓑ Ⓒ	38	Ⓐ Ⓑ Ⓒ Ⓓ	58	Ⓐ Ⓑ Ⓒ Ⓓ	78	Ⓐ Ⓑ Ⓒ Ⓓ	98	Ⓐ Ⓑ Ⓒ Ⓓ
19	Ⓐ Ⓑ Ⓒ	39	Ⓐ Ⓑ Ⓒ Ⓓ	59	Ⓐ Ⓑ Ⓒ Ⓓ	79	Ⓐ Ⓑ Ⓒ Ⓓ	99	Ⓐ Ⓑ Ⓒ Ⓓ
20	Ⓐ Ⓑ Ⓒ	40	Ⓐ Ⓑ Ⓒ Ⓓ	60	Ⓐ Ⓑ Ⓒ Ⓓ	80	Ⓐ Ⓑ Ⓒ Ⓓ	100	Ⓐ Ⓑ Ⓒ Ⓓ

ANSWER SHEET

ANSWER SHEET

파고다 토익 적중 실전 LC - TEST 6

LISTENING (Part I-IV)

NO.	ANSWER A B C D	NO.	ANSWER A B C D	NO.	ANSWER A B C D	NO.	ANSWER A B C D	NO.	ANSWER A B C D
1	Ⓐ Ⓑ Ⓒ Ⓓ	21	Ⓐ Ⓑ Ⓒ	41	Ⓐ Ⓑ Ⓒ Ⓓ	61	Ⓐ Ⓑ Ⓒ Ⓓ	81	Ⓐ Ⓑ Ⓒ Ⓓ
2	Ⓐ Ⓑ Ⓒ Ⓓ	22	Ⓐ Ⓑ Ⓒ	42	Ⓐ Ⓑ Ⓒ Ⓓ	62	Ⓐ Ⓑ Ⓒ Ⓓ	82	Ⓐ Ⓑ Ⓒ Ⓓ
3	Ⓐ Ⓑ Ⓒ Ⓓ	23	Ⓐ Ⓑ Ⓒ	43	Ⓐ Ⓑ Ⓒ Ⓓ	63	Ⓐ Ⓑ Ⓒ Ⓓ	83	Ⓐ Ⓑ Ⓒ Ⓓ
4	Ⓐ Ⓑ Ⓒ Ⓓ	24	Ⓐ Ⓑ Ⓒ	44	Ⓐ Ⓑ Ⓒ Ⓓ	64	Ⓐ Ⓑ Ⓒ Ⓓ	84	Ⓐ Ⓑ Ⓒ Ⓓ
5	Ⓐ Ⓑ Ⓒ Ⓓ	25	Ⓐ Ⓑ Ⓒ	45	Ⓐ Ⓑ Ⓒ Ⓓ	65	Ⓐ Ⓑ Ⓒ Ⓓ	85	Ⓐ Ⓑ Ⓒ Ⓓ
6	Ⓐ Ⓑ Ⓒ Ⓓ	26	Ⓐ Ⓑ Ⓒ	46	Ⓐ Ⓑ Ⓒ Ⓓ	66	Ⓐ Ⓑ Ⓒ Ⓓ	86	Ⓐ Ⓑ Ⓒ Ⓓ
7	Ⓐ Ⓑ Ⓒ	27	Ⓐ Ⓑ Ⓒ	47	Ⓐ Ⓑ Ⓒ Ⓓ	67	Ⓐ Ⓑ Ⓒ Ⓓ	87	Ⓐ Ⓑ Ⓒ Ⓓ
8	Ⓐ Ⓑ Ⓒ	28	Ⓐ Ⓑ Ⓒ	48	Ⓐ Ⓑ Ⓒ Ⓓ	68	Ⓐ Ⓑ Ⓒ Ⓓ	88	Ⓐ Ⓑ Ⓒ Ⓓ
9	Ⓐ Ⓑ Ⓒ	29	Ⓐ Ⓑ Ⓒ	49	Ⓐ Ⓑ Ⓒ Ⓓ	69	Ⓐ Ⓑ Ⓒ Ⓓ	89	Ⓐ Ⓑ Ⓒ Ⓓ
10	Ⓐ Ⓑ Ⓒ	30	Ⓐ Ⓑ Ⓒ	50	Ⓐ Ⓑ Ⓒ Ⓓ	70	Ⓐ Ⓑ Ⓒ Ⓓ	90	Ⓐ Ⓑ Ⓒ Ⓓ
11	Ⓐ Ⓑ Ⓒ	31	Ⓐ Ⓑ Ⓒ	51	Ⓐ Ⓑ Ⓒ Ⓓ	71	Ⓐ Ⓑ Ⓒ Ⓓ	91	Ⓐ Ⓑ Ⓒ Ⓓ
12	Ⓐ Ⓑ Ⓒ	32	Ⓐ Ⓑ Ⓒ Ⓓ	52	Ⓐ Ⓑ Ⓒ Ⓓ	72	Ⓐ Ⓑ Ⓒ Ⓓ	92	Ⓐ Ⓑ Ⓒ Ⓓ
13	Ⓐ Ⓑ Ⓒ	33	Ⓐ Ⓑ Ⓒ Ⓓ	53	Ⓐ Ⓑ Ⓒ Ⓓ	73	Ⓐ Ⓑ Ⓒ Ⓓ	93	Ⓐ Ⓑ Ⓒ Ⓓ
14	Ⓐ Ⓑ Ⓒ	34	Ⓐ Ⓑ Ⓒ Ⓓ	54	Ⓐ Ⓑ Ⓒ Ⓓ	74	Ⓐ Ⓑ Ⓒ Ⓓ	94	Ⓐ Ⓑ Ⓒ Ⓓ
15	Ⓐ Ⓑ Ⓒ	35	Ⓐ Ⓑ Ⓒ Ⓓ	55	Ⓐ Ⓑ Ⓒ Ⓓ	75	Ⓐ Ⓑ Ⓒ Ⓓ	95	Ⓐ Ⓑ Ⓒ Ⓓ
16	Ⓐ Ⓑ Ⓒ	36	Ⓐ Ⓑ Ⓒ Ⓓ	56	Ⓐ Ⓑ Ⓒ Ⓓ	76	Ⓐ Ⓑ Ⓒ Ⓓ	96	Ⓐ Ⓑ Ⓒ Ⓓ
17	Ⓐ Ⓑ Ⓒ	37	Ⓐ Ⓑ Ⓒ Ⓓ	57	Ⓐ Ⓑ Ⓒ Ⓓ	77	Ⓐ Ⓑ Ⓒ Ⓓ	97	Ⓐ Ⓑ Ⓒ Ⓓ
18	Ⓐ Ⓑ Ⓒ	38	Ⓐ Ⓑ Ⓒ Ⓓ	58	Ⓐ Ⓑ Ⓒ Ⓓ	78	Ⓐ Ⓑ Ⓒ Ⓓ	98	Ⓐ Ⓑ Ⓒ Ⓓ
19	Ⓐ Ⓑ Ⓒ	39	Ⓐ Ⓑ Ⓒ Ⓓ	59	Ⓐ Ⓑ Ⓒ Ⓓ	79	Ⓐ Ⓑ Ⓒ Ⓓ	99	Ⓐ Ⓑ Ⓒ Ⓓ
20	Ⓐ Ⓑ Ⓒ	40	Ⓐ Ⓑ Ⓒ Ⓓ	60	Ⓐ Ⓑ Ⓒ Ⓓ	80	Ⓐ Ⓑ Ⓒ Ⓓ	100	Ⓐ Ⓑ Ⓒ Ⓓ

ANSWER SHEET

ANSWER SHEET

파고다 토익 적중 실전 LC – TEST 7

LISTENING (Part I-IV)

NO.	ANSWER A B C D	NO.	ANSWER A B C D	NO.	ANSWER A B C D	NO.	ANSWER A B C D	NO.	ANSWER A B C D
1	Ⓐ Ⓑ Ⓒ Ⓓ	21	Ⓐ Ⓑ Ⓒ	41	Ⓐ Ⓑ Ⓒ Ⓓ	61	Ⓐ Ⓑ Ⓒ Ⓓ	81	Ⓐ Ⓑ Ⓒ Ⓓ
2	Ⓐ Ⓑ Ⓒ Ⓓ	22	Ⓐ Ⓑ Ⓒ	42	Ⓐ Ⓑ Ⓒ Ⓓ	62	Ⓐ Ⓑ Ⓒ Ⓓ	82	Ⓐ Ⓑ Ⓒ Ⓓ
3	Ⓐ Ⓑ Ⓒ Ⓓ	23	Ⓐ Ⓑ Ⓒ	43	Ⓐ Ⓑ Ⓒ Ⓓ	63	Ⓐ Ⓑ Ⓒ Ⓓ	83	Ⓐ Ⓑ Ⓒ Ⓓ
4	Ⓐ Ⓑ Ⓒ Ⓓ	24	Ⓐ Ⓑ Ⓒ	44	Ⓐ Ⓑ Ⓒ Ⓓ	64	Ⓐ Ⓑ Ⓒ Ⓓ	84	Ⓐ Ⓑ Ⓒ Ⓓ
5	Ⓐ Ⓑ Ⓒ Ⓓ	25	Ⓐ Ⓑ Ⓒ	45	Ⓐ Ⓑ Ⓒ Ⓓ	65	Ⓐ Ⓑ Ⓒ Ⓓ	85	Ⓐ Ⓑ Ⓒ Ⓓ
6	Ⓐ Ⓑ Ⓒ Ⓓ	26	Ⓐ Ⓑ Ⓒ	46	Ⓐ Ⓑ Ⓒ Ⓓ	66	Ⓐ Ⓑ Ⓒ Ⓓ	86	Ⓐ Ⓑ Ⓒ Ⓓ
7	Ⓐ Ⓑ Ⓒ	27	Ⓐ Ⓑ Ⓒ	47	Ⓐ Ⓑ Ⓒ Ⓓ	67	Ⓐ Ⓑ Ⓒ Ⓓ	87	Ⓐ Ⓑ Ⓒ Ⓓ
8	Ⓐ Ⓑ Ⓒ	28	Ⓐ Ⓑ Ⓒ	48	Ⓐ Ⓑ Ⓒ Ⓓ	68	Ⓐ Ⓑ Ⓒ Ⓓ	88	Ⓐ Ⓑ Ⓒ Ⓓ
9	Ⓐ Ⓑ Ⓒ	29	Ⓐ Ⓑ Ⓒ	49	Ⓐ Ⓑ Ⓒ Ⓓ	69	Ⓐ Ⓑ Ⓒ Ⓓ	89	Ⓐ Ⓑ Ⓒ Ⓓ
10	Ⓐ Ⓑ Ⓒ	30	Ⓐ Ⓑ Ⓒ	50	Ⓐ Ⓑ Ⓒ Ⓓ	70	Ⓐ Ⓑ Ⓒ Ⓓ	90	Ⓐ Ⓑ Ⓒ Ⓓ
11	Ⓐ Ⓑ Ⓒ	31	Ⓐ Ⓑ Ⓒ	51	Ⓐ Ⓑ Ⓒ Ⓓ	71	Ⓐ Ⓑ Ⓒ Ⓓ	91	Ⓐ Ⓑ Ⓒ Ⓓ
12	Ⓐ Ⓑ Ⓒ	32	Ⓐ Ⓑ Ⓒ Ⓓ	52	Ⓐ Ⓑ Ⓒ Ⓓ	72	Ⓐ Ⓑ Ⓒ Ⓓ	92	Ⓐ Ⓑ Ⓒ Ⓓ
13	Ⓐ Ⓑ Ⓒ	33	Ⓐ Ⓑ Ⓒ Ⓓ	53	Ⓐ Ⓑ Ⓒ Ⓓ	73	Ⓐ Ⓑ Ⓒ Ⓓ	93	Ⓐ Ⓑ Ⓒ Ⓓ
14	Ⓐ Ⓑ Ⓒ	34	Ⓐ Ⓑ Ⓒ Ⓓ	54	Ⓐ Ⓑ Ⓒ Ⓓ	74	Ⓐ Ⓑ Ⓒ Ⓓ	94	Ⓐ Ⓑ Ⓒ Ⓓ
15	Ⓐ Ⓑ Ⓒ	35	Ⓐ Ⓑ Ⓒ Ⓓ	55	Ⓐ Ⓑ Ⓒ Ⓓ	75	Ⓐ Ⓑ Ⓒ Ⓓ	95	Ⓐ Ⓑ Ⓒ Ⓓ
16	Ⓐ Ⓑ Ⓒ	36	Ⓐ Ⓑ Ⓒ Ⓓ	56	Ⓐ Ⓑ Ⓒ Ⓓ	76	Ⓐ Ⓑ Ⓒ Ⓓ	96	Ⓐ Ⓑ Ⓒ Ⓓ
17	Ⓐ Ⓑ Ⓒ	37	Ⓐ Ⓑ Ⓒ Ⓓ	57	Ⓐ Ⓑ Ⓒ Ⓓ	77	Ⓐ Ⓑ Ⓒ Ⓓ	97	Ⓐ Ⓑ Ⓒ Ⓓ
18	Ⓐ Ⓑ Ⓒ	38	Ⓐ Ⓑ Ⓒ Ⓓ	58	Ⓐ Ⓑ Ⓒ Ⓓ	78	Ⓐ Ⓑ Ⓒ Ⓓ	98	Ⓐ Ⓑ Ⓒ Ⓓ
19	Ⓐ Ⓑ Ⓒ	39	Ⓐ Ⓑ Ⓒ Ⓓ	59	Ⓐ Ⓑ Ⓒ Ⓓ	79	Ⓐ Ⓑ Ⓒ Ⓓ	99	Ⓐ Ⓑ Ⓒ Ⓓ
20	Ⓐ Ⓑ Ⓒ	40	Ⓐ Ⓑ Ⓒ Ⓓ	60	Ⓐ Ⓑ Ⓒ Ⓓ	80	Ⓐ Ⓑ Ⓒ Ⓓ	100	Ⓐ Ⓑ Ⓒ Ⓓ

ANSWER SHEET

ANSWER SHEET

파고다 토익 적중 실전 LC - TEST 8

LISTENING (Part I-IV)

NO.	ANSWER A B C D	NO.	ANSWER A B C D	NO.	ANSWER A B C D	NO.	ANSWER A B C D	NO.	ANSWER A B C D
1	Ⓐ Ⓑ Ⓒ Ⓓ	21	Ⓐ Ⓑ Ⓒ	41	Ⓐ Ⓑ Ⓒ Ⓓ	61	Ⓐ Ⓑ Ⓒ Ⓓ	81	Ⓐ Ⓑ Ⓒ Ⓓ
2	Ⓐ Ⓑ Ⓒ Ⓓ	22	Ⓐ Ⓑ Ⓒ	42	Ⓐ Ⓑ Ⓒ Ⓓ	62	Ⓐ Ⓑ Ⓒ Ⓓ	82	Ⓐ Ⓑ Ⓒ Ⓓ
3	Ⓐ Ⓑ Ⓒ Ⓓ	23	Ⓐ Ⓑ Ⓒ	43	Ⓐ Ⓑ Ⓒ Ⓓ	63	Ⓐ Ⓑ Ⓒ Ⓓ	83	Ⓐ Ⓑ Ⓒ Ⓓ
4	Ⓐ Ⓑ Ⓒ Ⓓ	24	Ⓐ Ⓑ Ⓒ	44	Ⓐ Ⓑ Ⓒ Ⓓ	64	Ⓐ Ⓑ Ⓒ Ⓓ	84	Ⓐ Ⓑ Ⓒ Ⓓ
5	Ⓐ Ⓑ Ⓒ Ⓓ	25	Ⓐ Ⓑ Ⓒ	45	Ⓐ Ⓑ Ⓒ Ⓓ	65	Ⓐ Ⓑ Ⓒ Ⓓ	85	Ⓐ Ⓑ Ⓒ Ⓓ
6	Ⓐ Ⓑ Ⓒ Ⓓ	26	Ⓐ Ⓑ Ⓒ	46	Ⓐ Ⓑ Ⓒ Ⓓ	66	Ⓐ Ⓑ Ⓒ Ⓓ	86	Ⓐ Ⓑ Ⓒ Ⓓ
7	Ⓐ Ⓑ Ⓒ	27	Ⓐ Ⓑ Ⓒ	47	Ⓐ Ⓑ Ⓒ Ⓓ	67	Ⓐ Ⓑ Ⓒ Ⓓ	87	Ⓐ Ⓑ Ⓒ Ⓓ
8	Ⓐ Ⓑ Ⓒ	28	Ⓐ Ⓑ Ⓒ	48	Ⓐ Ⓑ Ⓒ Ⓓ	68	Ⓐ Ⓑ Ⓒ Ⓓ	88	Ⓐ Ⓑ Ⓒ Ⓓ
9	Ⓐ Ⓑ Ⓒ	29	Ⓐ Ⓑ Ⓒ	49	Ⓐ Ⓑ Ⓒ Ⓓ	69	Ⓐ Ⓑ Ⓒ Ⓓ	89	Ⓐ Ⓑ Ⓒ Ⓓ
10	Ⓐ Ⓑ Ⓒ	30	Ⓐ Ⓑ Ⓒ	50	Ⓐ Ⓑ Ⓒ Ⓓ	70	Ⓐ Ⓑ Ⓒ Ⓓ	90	Ⓐ Ⓑ Ⓒ Ⓓ
11	Ⓐ Ⓑ Ⓒ	31	Ⓐ Ⓑ Ⓒ	51	Ⓐ Ⓑ Ⓒ Ⓓ	71	Ⓐ Ⓑ Ⓒ Ⓓ	91	Ⓐ Ⓑ Ⓒ Ⓓ
12	Ⓐ Ⓑ Ⓒ	32	Ⓐ Ⓑ Ⓒ Ⓓ	52	Ⓐ Ⓑ Ⓒ Ⓓ	72	Ⓐ Ⓑ Ⓒ Ⓓ	92	Ⓐ Ⓑ Ⓒ Ⓓ
13	Ⓐ Ⓑ Ⓒ	33	Ⓐ Ⓑ Ⓒ Ⓓ	53	Ⓐ Ⓑ Ⓒ Ⓓ	73	Ⓐ Ⓑ Ⓒ Ⓓ	93	Ⓐ Ⓑ Ⓒ Ⓓ
14	Ⓐ Ⓑ Ⓒ	34	Ⓐ Ⓑ Ⓒ Ⓓ	54	Ⓐ Ⓑ Ⓒ Ⓓ	74	Ⓐ Ⓑ Ⓒ Ⓓ	94	Ⓐ Ⓑ Ⓒ Ⓓ
15	Ⓐ Ⓑ Ⓒ	35	Ⓐ Ⓑ Ⓒ Ⓓ	55	Ⓐ Ⓑ Ⓒ Ⓓ	75	Ⓐ Ⓑ Ⓒ Ⓓ	95	Ⓐ Ⓑ Ⓒ Ⓓ
16	Ⓐ Ⓑ Ⓒ	36	Ⓐ Ⓑ Ⓒ Ⓓ	56	Ⓐ Ⓑ Ⓒ Ⓓ	76	Ⓐ Ⓑ Ⓒ Ⓓ	96	Ⓐ Ⓑ Ⓒ Ⓓ
17	Ⓐ Ⓑ Ⓒ	37	Ⓐ Ⓑ Ⓒ Ⓓ	57	Ⓐ Ⓑ Ⓒ Ⓓ	77	Ⓐ Ⓑ Ⓒ Ⓓ	97	Ⓐ Ⓑ Ⓒ Ⓓ
18	Ⓐ Ⓑ Ⓒ	38	Ⓐ Ⓑ Ⓒ Ⓓ	58	Ⓐ Ⓑ Ⓒ Ⓓ	78	Ⓐ Ⓑ Ⓒ Ⓓ	98	Ⓐ Ⓑ Ⓒ Ⓓ
19	Ⓐ Ⓑ Ⓒ	39	Ⓐ Ⓑ Ⓒ Ⓓ	59	Ⓐ Ⓑ Ⓒ Ⓓ	79	Ⓐ Ⓑ Ⓒ Ⓓ	99	Ⓐ Ⓑ Ⓒ Ⓓ
20	Ⓐ Ⓑ Ⓒ	40	Ⓐ Ⓑ Ⓒ Ⓓ	60	Ⓐ Ⓑ Ⓒ Ⓓ	80	Ⓐ Ⓑ Ⓒ Ⓓ	100	Ⓐ Ⓑ Ⓒ Ⓓ

ANSWER SHEET

ANSWER SHEET

파고다 토익 적중 실전 LC - TEST 9

LISTENING (Part I-IV)

NO.	ANSWER A B C D	NO.	ANSWER A B C D	NO.	ANSWER A B C D	NO.	ANSWER A B C D	NO.	ANSWER A B C D
1	Ⓐ Ⓑ Ⓒ Ⓓ	21	Ⓐ Ⓑ Ⓒ	41	Ⓐ Ⓑ Ⓒ Ⓓ	61	Ⓐ Ⓑ Ⓒ Ⓓ	81	Ⓐ Ⓑ Ⓒ Ⓓ
2	Ⓐ Ⓑ Ⓒ Ⓓ	22	Ⓐ Ⓑ Ⓒ	42	Ⓐ Ⓑ Ⓒ Ⓓ	62	Ⓐ Ⓑ Ⓒ Ⓓ	82	Ⓐ Ⓑ Ⓒ Ⓓ
3	Ⓐ Ⓑ Ⓒ Ⓓ	23	Ⓐ Ⓑ Ⓒ	43	Ⓐ Ⓑ Ⓒ Ⓓ	63	Ⓐ Ⓑ Ⓒ Ⓓ	83	Ⓐ Ⓑ Ⓒ Ⓓ
4	Ⓐ Ⓑ Ⓒ Ⓓ	24	Ⓐ Ⓑ Ⓒ	44	Ⓐ Ⓑ Ⓒ Ⓓ	64	Ⓐ Ⓑ Ⓒ Ⓓ	84	Ⓐ Ⓑ Ⓒ Ⓓ
5	Ⓐ Ⓑ Ⓒ Ⓓ	25	Ⓐ Ⓑ Ⓒ	45	Ⓐ Ⓑ Ⓒ Ⓓ	65	Ⓐ Ⓑ Ⓒ Ⓓ	85	Ⓐ Ⓑ Ⓒ Ⓓ
6	Ⓐ Ⓑ Ⓒ Ⓓ	26	Ⓐ Ⓑ Ⓒ	46	Ⓐ Ⓑ Ⓒ Ⓓ	66	Ⓐ Ⓑ Ⓒ Ⓓ	86	Ⓐ Ⓑ Ⓒ Ⓓ
7	Ⓐ Ⓑ Ⓒ	27	Ⓐ Ⓑ Ⓒ	47	Ⓐ Ⓑ Ⓒ Ⓓ	67	Ⓐ Ⓑ Ⓒ Ⓓ	87	Ⓐ Ⓑ Ⓒ Ⓓ
8	Ⓐ Ⓑ Ⓒ	28	Ⓐ Ⓑ Ⓒ	48	Ⓐ Ⓑ Ⓒ Ⓓ	68	Ⓐ Ⓑ Ⓒ Ⓓ	88	Ⓐ Ⓑ Ⓒ Ⓓ
9	Ⓐ Ⓑ Ⓒ	29	Ⓐ Ⓑ Ⓒ	49	Ⓐ Ⓑ Ⓒ Ⓓ	69	Ⓐ Ⓑ Ⓒ Ⓓ	89	Ⓐ Ⓑ Ⓒ Ⓓ
10	Ⓐ Ⓑ Ⓒ	30	Ⓐ Ⓑ Ⓒ	50	Ⓐ Ⓑ Ⓒ Ⓓ	70	Ⓐ Ⓑ Ⓒ Ⓓ	90	Ⓐ Ⓑ Ⓒ Ⓓ
11	Ⓐ Ⓑ Ⓒ	31	Ⓐ Ⓑ Ⓒ	51	Ⓐ Ⓑ Ⓒ Ⓓ	71	Ⓐ Ⓑ Ⓒ Ⓓ	91	Ⓐ Ⓑ Ⓒ Ⓓ
12	Ⓐ Ⓑ Ⓒ	32	Ⓐ Ⓑ Ⓒ Ⓓ	52	Ⓐ Ⓑ Ⓒ Ⓓ	72	Ⓐ Ⓑ Ⓒ Ⓓ	92	Ⓐ Ⓑ Ⓒ Ⓓ
13	Ⓐ Ⓑ Ⓒ	33	Ⓐ Ⓑ Ⓒ Ⓓ	53	Ⓐ Ⓑ Ⓒ Ⓓ	73	Ⓐ Ⓑ Ⓒ Ⓓ	93	Ⓐ Ⓑ Ⓒ Ⓓ
14	Ⓐ Ⓑ Ⓒ	34	Ⓐ Ⓑ Ⓒ Ⓓ	54	Ⓐ Ⓑ Ⓒ Ⓓ	74	Ⓐ Ⓑ Ⓒ Ⓓ	94	Ⓐ Ⓑ Ⓒ Ⓓ
15	Ⓐ Ⓑ Ⓒ	35	Ⓐ Ⓑ Ⓒ Ⓓ	55	Ⓐ Ⓑ Ⓒ Ⓓ	75	Ⓐ Ⓑ Ⓒ Ⓓ	95	Ⓐ Ⓑ Ⓒ Ⓓ
16	Ⓐ Ⓑ Ⓒ	36	Ⓐ Ⓑ Ⓒ Ⓓ	56	Ⓐ Ⓑ Ⓒ Ⓓ	76	Ⓐ Ⓑ Ⓒ Ⓓ	96	Ⓐ Ⓑ Ⓒ Ⓓ
17	Ⓐ Ⓑ Ⓒ	37	Ⓐ Ⓑ Ⓒ Ⓓ	57	Ⓐ Ⓑ Ⓒ Ⓓ	77	Ⓐ Ⓑ Ⓒ Ⓓ	97	Ⓐ Ⓑ Ⓒ Ⓓ
18	Ⓐ Ⓑ Ⓒ	38	Ⓐ Ⓑ Ⓒ Ⓓ	58	Ⓐ Ⓑ Ⓒ Ⓓ	78	Ⓐ Ⓑ Ⓒ Ⓓ	98	Ⓐ Ⓑ Ⓒ Ⓓ
19	Ⓐ Ⓑ Ⓒ	39	Ⓐ Ⓑ Ⓒ Ⓓ	59	Ⓐ Ⓑ Ⓒ Ⓓ	79	Ⓐ Ⓑ Ⓒ Ⓓ	99	Ⓐ Ⓑ Ⓒ Ⓓ
20	Ⓐ Ⓑ Ⓒ	40	Ⓐ Ⓑ Ⓒ Ⓓ	60	Ⓐ Ⓑ Ⓒ Ⓓ	80	Ⓐ Ⓑ Ⓒ Ⓓ	100	Ⓐ Ⓑ Ⓒ Ⓓ

ANSWER SHEET

ANSWER SHEET

파고다 토익 적중 실전 LC - TEST 10

LISTENING (Part I-IV)

NO.	ANSWER A B C D	NO.	ANSWER A B C D	NO.	ANSWER A B C D	NO.	ANSWER A B C D	NO.	ANSWER A B C D
1	Ⓐ Ⓑ Ⓒ Ⓓ	21	Ⓐ Ⓑ Ⓒ	41	Ⓐ Ⓑ Ⓒ Ⓓ	61	Ⓐ Ⓑ Ⓒ Ⓓ	81	Ⓐ Ⓑ Ⓒ Ⓓ
2	Ⓐ Ⓑ Ⓒ Ⓓ	22	Ⓐ Ⓑ Ⓒ	42	Ⓐ Ⓑ Ⓒ Ⓓ	62	Ⓐ Ⓑ Ⓒ Ⓓ	82	Ⓐ Ⓑ Ⓒ Ⓓ
3	Ⓐ Ⓑ Ⓒ Ⓓ	23	Ⓐ Ⓑ Ⓒ	43	Ⓐ Ⓑ Ⓒ Ⓓ	63	Ⓐ Ⓑ Ⓒ Ⓓ	83	Ⓐ Ⓑ Ⓒ Ⓓ
4	Ⓐ Ⓑ Ⓒ Ⓓ	24	Ⓐ Ⓑ Ⓒ	44	Ⓐ Ⓑ Ⓒ Ⓓ	64	Ⓐ Ⓑ Ⓒ Ⓓ	84	Ⓐ Ⓑ Ⓒ Ⓓ
5	Ⓐ Ⓑ Ⓒ Ⓓ	25	Ⓐ Ⓑ Ⓒ	45	Ⓐ Ⓑ Ⓒ Ⓓ	65	Ⓐ Ⓑ Ⓒ Ⓓ	85	Ⓐ Ⓑ Ⓒ Ⓓ
6	Ⓐ Ⓑ Ⓒ Ⓓ	26	Ⓐ Ⓑ Ⓒ	46	Ⓐ Ⓑ Ⓒ Ⓓ	66	Ⓐ Ⓑ Ⓒ Ⓓ	86	Ⓐ Ⓑ Ⓒ Ⓓ
7	Ⓐ Ⓑ Ⓒ	27	Ⓐ Ⓑ Ⓒ	47	Ⓐ Ⓑ Ⓒ Ⓓ	67	Ⓐ Ⓑ Ⓒ Ⓓ	87	Ⓐ Ⓑ Ⓒ Ⓓ
8	Ⓐ Ⓑ Ⓒ	28	Ⓐ Ⓑ Ⓒ	48	Ⓐ Ⓑ Ⓒ Ⓓ	68	Ⓐ Ⓑ Ⓒ Ⓓ	88	Ⓐ Ⓑ Ⓒ Ⓓ
9	Ⓐ Ⓑ Ⓒ	29	Ⓐ Ⓑ Ⓒ	49	Ⓐ Ⓑ Ⓒ Ⓓ	69	Ⓐ Ⓑ Ⓒ Ⓓ	89	Ⓐ Ⓑ Ⓒ Ⓓ
10	Ⓐ Ⓑ Ⓒ	30	Ⓐ Ⓑ Ⓒ	50	Ⓐ Ⓑ Ⓒ Ⓓ	70	Ⓐ Ⓑ Ⓒ Ⓓ	90	Ⓐ Ⓑ Ⓒ Ⓓ
11	Ⓐ Ⓑ Ⓒ	31	Ⓐ Ⓑ Ⓒ	51	Ⓐ Ⓑ Ⓒ Ⓓ	71	Ⓐ Ⓑ Ⓒ Ⓓ	91	Ⓐ Ⓑ Ⓒ Ⓓ
12	Ⓐ Ⓑ Ⓒ	32	Ⓐ Ⓑ Ⓒ Ⓓ	52	Ⓐ Ⓑ Ⓒ Ⓓ	72	Ⓐ Ⓑ Ⓒ Ⓓ	92	Ⓐ Ⓑ Ⓒ Ⓓ
13	Ⓐ Ⓑ Ⓒ	33	Ⓐ Ⓑ Ⓒ Ⓓ	53	Ⓐ Ⓑ Ⓒ Ⓓ	73	Ⓐ Ⓑ Ⓒ Ⓓ	93	Ⓐ Ⓑ Ⓒ Ⓓ
14	Ⓐ Ⓑ Ⓒ	34	Ⓐ Ⓑ Ⓒ Ⓓ	54	Ⓐ Ⓑ Ⓒ Ⓓ	74	Ⓐ Ⓑ Ⓒ Ⓓ	94	Ⓐ Ⓑ Ⓒ Ⓓ
15	Ⓐ Ⓑ Ⓒ	35	Ⓐ Ⓑ Ⓒ Ⓓ	55	Ⓐ Ⓑ Ⓒ Ⓓ	75	Ⓐ Ⓑ Ⓒ Ⓓ	95	Ⓐ Ⓑ Ⓒ Ⓓ
16	Ⓐ Ⓑ Ⓒ	36	Ⓐ Ⓑ Ⓒ Ⓓ	56	Ⓐ Ⓑ Ⓒ Ⓓ	76	Ⓐ Ⓑ Ⓒ Ⓓ	96	Ⓐ Ⓑ Ⓒ Ⓓ
17	Ⓐ Ⓑ Ⓒ	37	Ⓐ Ⓑ Ⓒ Ⓓ	57	Ⓐ Ⓑ Ⓒ Ⓓ	77	Ⓐ Ⓑ Ⓒ Ⓓ	97	Ⓐ Ⓑ Ⓒ Ⓓ
18	Ⓐ Ⓑ Ⓒ	38	Ⓐ Ⓑ Ⓒ Ⓓ	58	Ⓐ Ⓑ Ⓒ Ⓓ	78	Ⓐ Ⓑ Ⓒ Ⓓ	98	Ⓐ Ⓑ Ⓒ Ⓓ
19	Ⓐ Ⓑ Ⓒ	39	Ⓐ Ⓑ Ⓒ Ⓓ	59	Ⓐ Ⓑ Ⓒ Ⓓ	79	Ⓐ Ⓑ Ⓒ Ⓓ	99	Ⓐ Ⓑ Ⓒ Ⓓ
20	Ⓐ Ⓑ Ⓒ	40	Ⓐ Ⓑ Ⓒ Ⓓ	60	Ⓐ Ⓑ Ⓒ Ⓓ	80	Ⓐ Ⓑ Ⓒ Ⓓ	100	Ⓐ Ⓑ Ⓒ Ⓓ

ANSWER SHEET